Personal Insurance: Property and Liability

Personal Insurance: Property and Liability

Karen L. Hamilton, Ph.D., CPCU
Director of Curriculum
American Institute for CPCU

Donald S. Malecki, CPCU
President
Donald S. Malecki & Associates, Inc.

First Edition • 1994

American Institute for CPCU
720 Providence Road, Malvern, Pennsylvania 19355-0770

First Edition • July 1994

Library of Congress Catalog Number 94-71922
International Standard Book Number 0-89463-067-9

Printed in the United States of America

Foreword

The American Institute for Chartered Property Casualty Underwriters and the Insurance Institute of America are independent, nonprofit, educational organizations serving the needs of the property and liability insurance business. The Institutes develop a wide range of programs—curricula, study materials, and examinations—in response to the educational requirements of various elements of the business.

The American Institute confers the Chartered Property Casualty Underwriter (CPCU®) professional designation on those who meet the Institute's experience, ethics, and examination requirements.

The Insurance Institute of America offers associate designations and certificate programs in the following technical and managerial disciplines:

Accredited Adviser in Insurance (AAI®)
Associate in Claims (AIC)
Associate in Underwriting (AU)
Associate in Risk Management (ARM)
Associate in Loss Control Management (ALCM®)
Associate in Premium Auditing (APA®)
Associate in Management (AIM)
Associate in Research and Planning (ARP®)
Associate in Insurance Accounting and Finance (AIAF)
Associate in Automation Management (AAM®)
Associate in Marine Insurance Management (AMIM®)
Associate in Reinsurance (ARe)
Associate in Fidelity and Surety Bonding (AFSB)
Associate in Insurance Services (AIS)
Certificate in General Insurance
Certificate in Supervisory Management

Certificate in Introduction to Claims
Certificate in Introduction to Property and Liability Insurance
Certificate in Business Writing

The Institutes began publishing textbooks in 1976 to help students meet the national examination standards. Since that time, we have produced more than eighty individual textbook volumes. Despite the vast differences in the subjects and purposes of these volumes, they all have much in common. First, each book is specifically designed to increase knowledge and develop skills that can improve job performance and help students achieve the educational objectives of the course for which it is assigned. Second, all of the manuscripts of our texts are widely reviewed before publication, by both insurance business practitioners and members of the academic community. In addition, all of our texts and course guides reflect the work of Institute staff members. These writing or editing duties are seen as an integral part of their professional responsibilities, and no one earns a royalty based on the sale of our texts. We have proceeded in this way to avoid even the appearance of any conflict of interests. Finally, the revisions of our texts often incorporate improvements suggested by students and course leaders.

We welcome criticisms of and suggestions for improving our publications. It is only with such constructive comments that we can hope to improve the quality of our study materials. Please direct any comments you may have on this text to the Curriculum Department of the Institutes.

Norman A. Baglini, Ph.D., CPCU, CLU
President and Chief Executive Officer

Preface

CPCU 2 provides information and fosters learning that is valuable to CPCU candidates on both a professional level and a personal level. Many insurance professionals deal with personal insurance and help their clients to better insure and more appropriately manage their personal loss exposures. Information in this textbook will prepare CPCU candidates for these current professional demands. In addition, CPCU candidates must manage and insure their own personal loss exposures, and the CPCU 2 text can be of great aid in that area as well.

Personal Insurance: Property and Liability is one of the texts used for the CPCU 2 curriculum because it focuses on the treatment and coverage of property and liability loss exposures. It covers the use of personal risk management to treat personal loss exposures and concentrates on the types of personal insurance available to cover personal property and liability loss exposures. Specific attention is given to the Insurance Services Office (ISO) homeowners policies and the ISO personal auto policy (PAP).

Many reviewers contributed a substantial amount of time and effort to develop a text that is accurate, up to date, and readable. The following reviewers' constructive comments and suggestions are greatly appreciated:

James E. Brennan, CPCU, CLU, CIC
Academic Advisor for the Professional Insurance Program
Lecturer, Finance and Insurance
University of Connecticut

Linda Hoffman, CPCU

Roland J. Jones, CPCU
Gaspar-Jones & Associates, Inc.

James Kane
Operations Manager
Sigel Insurance Group

Gerald J. Krol, CPCU
Territorial Agency Manager
Allstate Insurance

Claude C. Lilly III, Ph.D., CLU, CPCU
Professor of Risk Management and Insurance
Florida State University

Charles Morgan, JD, CPCU, ARM, CLU
Zurich-American Insurance Group

Elaine O'Rourke, CPCU, AIM, ARP, AIAF
Transamerica Insurance Company

William A. Quinn, CPCU
Assistant Vice President—Mid-Atlantic Regional Office
USAA Property & Casualty Insurance

Richard M. Spiers, Jr., CPCU, CIC
Marketing Rep—Virginia
Utica National Insurance Group

David S. Tubolino
Assistant Vice President—Sales Management
Amerisure Co.

William C. Wilson, Jr., CPCU
Director of Education
Insurers of Tennessee

Special thanks go also to Michael W. Elliott, Assistant Vice President, American Institute for CPCU, and to Karen K. Porter, Assistant Director of Curriculum, American Institute for CPCU, for their useful suggestions and assistance.

Our goal is to help develop an understanding of this material that will sufficiently prepare CPCU candidates for the future. In order to reach this goal, we must pay close attention to reader responses. Your comments regarding this text are welcome and extremely valuable. In preparation for the next edition, we need any suggestions or advice you might offer. Please call or write to us, at the American Institute for CPCU, and give your input.

Karen L. Hamilton
Donald S. Malecki

Contributing Authors

The authors acknowledge, with deep appreciation, the help of the following contributing authors:

Arthur L. Flitner, CPCU, ARM
Director of Curriculum
American Institute for CPCU

Eric A. Wiening, CPCU, ARM, AU
Assistant Vice President
American Institute for CPCU

Contents

Chapter 1

Personal Loss Exposures and Personal Risk Management

This text deals with risk management and insurance for individuals and families, specifically with *personal risk management* and the use of *personal insurance* and other financial planning tools for meeting the risk management objectives of an individual or family. The word **personal** in these phrases refers to individuals and families as opposed to *commercial* enterprises, *public* entities, and *nonprofit* organizations.

Chapter 1 introduces these topics by discussing various loss exposures and financial needs and examining the nature of risk management. The first section outlines loss exposures faced by individuals and families. The second section describes the personal risk management process.

Personal Loss Exposures

A **loss exposure** is any condition or situation that presents a *possibility* of loss, whether or not an actual loss ever occurs. In other words, there is only a chance that something undesirable and unexpected may occur, and that an individual may experience a personal loss. For example, whenever a person drives down a street, it is possible, but not inevitable, that he or she may be involved in an automobile accident. The person does not think it will happen, nor does he or she want to have a car accident. In most cases, a car accident will not occur, but the chance is there all the same. This is a loss exposure most individuals face daily.

The term "risk" is commonly used as a synonym for "loss exposure." However, because "risk" has several shades of meaning, "loss exposure" will be used in this text in order to avoid confusion.

A loss exposure can be present even if an individual has not noticed or identified it. Even if a person is aware of a loss exposure, it can be more likely or less likely to occur than an individual perceives. For instance, when asbestos was first developed, no one realized its potential to contribute to lung cancer and respiratory ailments; the risk had not yet been identified even though it did exist. Many people underestimate the possibility of harm coming their way; they believe it can't happen to me. Other people exaggerate the risks they face. A hypochondriac fears the worst each time he or she coughs or sneezes. Everyone faces loss exposures. Some are obvious; others are not.

The most important aspect of loss exposures is the potential for harm to an individual or family. This possibility of loss affects people in two ways: it causes individuals to worry about a potential loss and, if a loss occurs, they must accept and deal with its consequences.

Loss exposures faced by individuals and families can be grouped into six categories: property, liability, illness and injury, death, retirement, and unemployment. The remainder of this chapter further introduces these categories of loss exposures. Later chapters explore each of these loss exposures in greater detail.

Property Loss Exposures

Individuals and families suffer losses when property they own or use is damaged or destroyed. If a property loss does occur, two consequences are possible: the individual or family faces the loss of the property, which might have to be repaired or replaced; and the individual or family might not be able to use the property, either temporarily or permanently.

Types of Property

Property is commonly classified as either real property or personal property. **Real property** applies to land and items attached to land such as a house or a tree. **Personal property** comprises all other property.

Real Property

Real property is the term applied to (1) unimproved land and (2) improved land. **Unimproved land** is real property that does not include permanent improvements. Unimproved land may contain valuable resources such as water, mineral resources, tillable soil, growing timber, or wildlife. The owner of unimproved land is still exposed to a reduction in land value through such perils as contamination, pollution, erosion, flood, earthquake, or fire (which may damage vegetation). **Improved land** is real property that contains something of additional permanent value, such as structures, affixed to it. Structures include not only buildings, but also such tangible property as in-ground swimming pools and equipment, underground lawn sprinkler systems, other underground piping or wiring, septic tanks, wells, and paved driveways and walks.

Houses and dwelling buildings are real property, because they are structures affixed to improved land. Dwellings include not only the living space, but also excavations, foundations, pipes or other supports, underground flues and pipes, and plumbing and heating systems. Dwellings can take a variety of forms besides that of a single-family house, including condominiums, townhouses, apartments, and mobile homes. These dwellings may be occupied by their owners or by tenants.

Fixtures are personal property that become part of the land or the dwelling when installed or attached to it. In general, if the personal property cannot be removed from land or a building without substantial damage to the land or building or was specifically designed for use on the land or in the building, it is a fixture. For example, custom-ordered drapes and wall lamps may be considered fixtures attached to a dwelling, but standard curtains and floor lamps are not fixtures. A flagpole cemented into the ground may be considered a fixture attached to the land because removing it may damage the surrounding turf.

Personal Property

Personal property encompasses all property that is not realty. This property can be tangible or intangible, and it can be owned or merely in one's possession.

Personal property is **tangible** if it may be physically touched. Examples are furniture, clothing, pets, money, securities, automobiles, motorcycles, snowmobiles, boats, aircraft, jewelry, and furs.

Personal property is **intangible** if it is not physical in nature. Examples of intangible personal property include an insurer's promise under an insurance policy, a copyright, and a bank deposit.

Ownership of personal property establishes an exclusive right by the owner to use and enjoy the property. The owner also has the right to transfer title by sale and the obligation to pay outstanding debt on the property, such as a municipal tax or a mortgage on the property. Ownership, or legal title, is the highest property right a person can possess.

In many cases, legal possession of personal property without owning it is a **bailment**. The individual lending the property to another is the **bailor**, and the person receiving possession without ownership is the **bailee**. For example, when John lends his lawnmower to his neighbor Mike, John is the bailor and Mike is the bailee. A bailment consists of three elements:

1. Transfer of personal property possession without transfer of title
2. Acceptance of possession by the bailee
3. Express or implied agreement of the bailee to return the property to the bailor or to a person the bailor designates

Personal property can also be associated with an individual's or family's business. Losses can occur (1) to a person's property kept at a business location, such as a painting in one's office, or (2) to business property located at one's home, such as a file or sample that one brings home from work.

Causes of Property Loss

Both real and personal property are exposed to loss by many perils. In many cases one cause of loss can easily be identified, but sometimes more than one cause of loss is involved in a single loss situation. At other times, the cause of loss cannot be identified. Under circumstances in which more than one cause leads to a single loss, each cause of loss is referred to as a **concurrent cause**.

Several causes of loss to real property and tangible personal property receive more attention than others, including fire, vandalism, flood, windstorm, earthquake, theft, and collision. The type of tangible property tends to influence the major causes of loss. For example, loss by fire, flood, or earthquake is commonly associated with buildings, whereas theft is commonly associated with valuable personal property like money, jewelry, and automobiles.

Intangible personal property does not physically exist and cannot experience the physical causes of loss identified, but it is still subject to loss. Loss to intangible personal property generally involves interference with the use and enjoyment of, or with the right to use and enjoy, the property. For example, Damian owns the copyright to a song he wrote. A person copying Damian's song without permission diminishes the value of Damian's copyright. Thus, Damian has suffered an intangible personal property loss.

Loss Consequences

Property is exposed to loss by many causes, with a variety of loss consequences. These loss consequences fall into two broad categories: (1) direct loss that reduces the value of the property and (2) consequences associated with the loss of use of the property.

Reduction in Value

Real property and personal property can sustain reductions in value when property is directly damaged or destroyed. For example, when flood damages a dwelling and ruins the personal property within the dwelling, the owner sustains a reduction in value of both the dwelling and its contents. Generally, flood-soiled carpets must be replaced, and water-damaged wood furniture must at least be refinished.

Consequences Associated With Loss of Use

When property is damaged, it may not be fit for use. In some cases, damage to nearby property or general environmental hazards (such as an impending flood, hurricane, or tornado) may interfere with use of one's property. When property cannot be used, loss can result. For example, a fire may damage a family's dwelling and make it uninhabitable, or damage to an adjacent building may make occupying the undamaged dwelling dangerous. In either situation, family members must now find another place to stay until they can return home. This may lead to additional living expenses, and it may cause emotional distress, both of which are loss consequences of the family's inability to use the dwelling.

For personal property in the possession of the owner, loss consequences associated with loss of use are principally additional expenses. As with residential property, an owner who is no longer able to use the property may have to find some other means of filling the void until the property is replaced or restored, and this may result in expenses that would not otherwise have arisen. For example, if Sue normally drives to work but her car cannot be driven due to collision damage, she must find another means of transportation. Sue might rent a car or take a train. Both of these alternatives require payment, and if the cost of these choices exceeds the normal costs of maintaining and using the owned auto, Sue sustains a loss. In another case, consider Bob, a student whose backpack containing his class notes has been stolen. He has an exam at the end of the week and, in order to study for the test, Bob may have to photocopy or spend time hand-copying the notes of a fellow-student or a teacher. Both of these alternatives entail expenditures that he would not otherwise have experienced.

If personal property is in the possession of someone other than its owner at the time of loss, the loss consequences associated with the loss of use depend on the amount of care owed by the person in possession of the property. For example, if Don borrows Renee's bicycle and breaks the chain while riding it, neither he nor Renee can ride the bike. Because Don borrowed the bicycle, he may have to replace the chain. If Renee had rented her bike to Don, she would most likely be responsible for replacing the chain unless Don had deliberately caused the damage.

Liability Loss Exposures

The basis of all liability is that an individual, family, or organization may be held financially responsible—**liable**—for harm caused to another individual, family, or organization. The harm may involve bodily injury, property damage, financial harm, emotional injury, ruin to reputation, or invasion of privacy as well as many other forms of injury. In addition to liability for their own acts, individuals may be held liable for harm caused by the action(s) of some other person or organization. Furthermore, an individual or family may suffer a liability loss—in the form of defense costs—even when found ultimately not liable.

Legal Sources of Liability

To better understand the liability loss exposure, individuals and families should be aware that the legal system establishes various legal sources of liability. Exhibit 1-1 shows the general framework for establishing liability in the legal system.

Criminal Versus Civil Law

The body of law that governs society can be divided into two broad categories: criminal law and civil law. **Criminal law** defines certain activities deemed by society to be harmful to public welfare (a **crime**) and the punishment that may be inflicted upon the perpetrator of such an activity. **Civil law** is concerned with all other legal matters and the remedies available when wrongs are committed.

The government prosecutes those people who have allegedly committed a crime. If an individual is found guilty, beyond a reasonable doubt, of a crime, **criminal liability** results and the individual may be required to pay a fine, serve time in jail, participate in community service, or all three. The severity of the crime determines the relative severity of the punishment. If a person commits murder, he or she may be sentenced to life in prison, while a thief may be imprisoned for two years.

Exhibit 1-1
Framework for Legal Liability

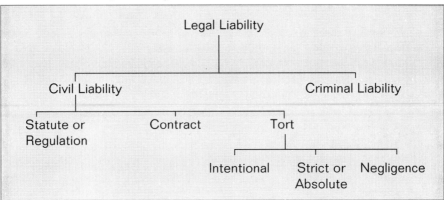

Civil liability may result when a person interferes, or allegedly interferes, with the rights of another individual, family, or organization. The rights may be set out in a statute or a regulation, or in a contract, or they may be established through the law of torts. The party who suffers the violation brings a claim or suit against the alleged wrongdoer. To prove civil liability, a preponderance of the evidence must show that an individual did interfere with the rights of another person, family, or organization. If found liable, the individual is generally required to pay damages to the injured party.

One act may constitute both a crime and a violation of another's rights and may result in both criminal and civil liability. For example, when Chad punches Hank (both are adults), Chad has committed the crime of battery and has also violated Hank's right to be free from bodily harm. Thus, Chad may be found liable under criminal *and* civil law.

An individual or family is exposed to both criminal and civil liability loss. A loss may occur even if the individual or family is innocent of the allegations or is not found liable. If a claim is falsely made against a person, he or she may still have to expend resources to fight the claim and maintain his or her innocence.

In some civil litigation, an individual may be found liable for the actions of another person. This is referred to as **vicarious liability**, and it is allowed only in certain situations—most notably employer-employee, principal-agent, partnerships, and, in some states, families. For example, if an employee accidentally damages the property of a customer, the customer may claim that both the employee and the employer are liable. Either or both may be found financially responsible for the harm caused to the customer, even though it was only the employee's actions that caused the damage.

The Law of Torts

As shown in Exhibit 1-1, civil law establishes the rights of individuals through statutes or regulations, contracts, and the law of torts. Basically, a **tort** is any civil wrong other than the breach of a contract. It may be intentional or unintentional, and it may or may not result in civil liability against the **tortfeasor** (the party responsible for committing the wrong).

Unintentional torts generally result in liability against the tortfeasor if **negligence**—the failure to exercise the degree of care that a reasonably prudent person in a similar situation would exercise—is proven. To prove negligence, the party harmed by the tortfeasor's actions must show he or she has suffered actual harm as a result of the tortfeasor's failure to act in a prudent manner.

In some cases, a person or organization is determined to be liable in specific circumstances, regardless of whether that person or organization has been negligent. This is referred to as **absolute liability**. For example, an employer is generally responsible for paying workers compensation benefits for injuries an employee sustains while working for the employer, regardless of how the injuries were caused and whose negligence caused the injuries.

Situational Sources of Liability

Given the above legal framework, any activity or relationship that an individual or family takes part in, or any property that individual or family owns or uses, may create a liability loss exposure for the individual or family. The events that may lead to payment for injuries or damages are as unpredictable as the dollar amounts involved. Some of the more common situations in which individuals and families may incur liability exposures are discussed below.

Premises Liability

Occupying real property carries with it the responsibility for many events that can occur on the property. The following are some of the **hazards** (characteristics of a situation that increase the possibility of loss) associated with the ownership or control of premises:

- Accumulation of ice and snow on sidewalks and steps
- Unrepaired sidewalks and steps or torn rugs
- Unprotected swimming pools or unfenced vacant land
- Careless smoking
- Landscaping that causes water to drain onto neighboring property

Libel, Slander, and Other Intentional Torts

At times, individuals may, with or without malice, intentionally infringe on the rights of others—such as the right of security of reputation, the right of privacy, and the right of enjoyment of property. Examples involving intentional acts include the following:

- Injuring a person's reputation either through **slander** (untrue oral communications that cause harm to a person's reputation) or **libel** (untrue written, printed, or otherwise recorded communication that causes harm to a person's reputation)
- The landlord's entering the leased part of a building without the tenant's permission
- Causing loud noise at night, thereby creating a nuisance that invades a neighbor's peace and quiet

Employment of Domestics

Many people hire domestic employees to do household chores and care for dependents. Although domestic employees relieve their employers of many of the burdens that go with caring for the home, for the children, or for the elderly or the handicapped, domestic employees also create liability exposures.

Individuals and families may be accountable for injuries sustained by domestic employees in the course of their employment. They also may be held vicariously liable for the actions of their domestic employees who harm others.

Autos and Recreational Vehicles

The widespread use of and dependence on automobiles has created a complex legal environment for auto ownership and operation. Although dependence on *recreational vehicles*—motorized land vehicles such as snowmobiles, motor homes, and dirt bikes, that are used for personal recreation—is not as great as on autos, recreational vehicles create a liability loss exposure similar to that of autos. Auto and recreational vehicle liability loss exposures can arise out of ownership and out of the maintenance, operation, and use of owned and nonowned autos and recreational vehicles.

Personal liability for damages to pedestrians, other motorists, and property may arise when individuals carelessly operate any auto or recreational vehicle. Examples of accident-causing factors include the following:

- Backing an auto or recreational vehicle without first determining whether the way is clear
- Driving at an unreasonable speed
- Disregarding a traffic signal
- Driving under the influence of alcohol or drugs

In most states, mere ownership of an auto or a recreational vehicle generally does not make the owner liable for the negligent operation or use of the vehicle by others. However, some common law and statutory exceptions to this rule exist, whereby liability may be imputed to the owner because of certain circumstances.

One of these exceptions is the law in some states holding the parent who signs a minor child's application for an operator's license legally responsible for the minor's operation or use of any auto. In some states, merely furnishing an auto to a minor may make the parent or owner liable for resulting damages. Owners of autos may also be vicariously liable for operators who are acting as legal representatives (agents) for the owners.

Another important exception that makes an owner liable for the actions of an operator is negligent entrustment. **Negligent entrustment** occurs when the owner or other person in control of the auto entrusts the vehicle to one who is unskilled or otherwise incompetent to operate it, such as a child. Generally, liability is imposed only when the entruster knows, or should have known, of the other person's incompetence, and an injury results from it. Liability may exist for injury to the user as well as to others.

Exposures to loss can also arise when individuals are transferring ownership of autos. In some states, the seller of an auto may remain liable for any consequences stemming from the vehicle's use until the purchaser has the certificate of title.

Watercraft Liability

Watercraft present liability exposures for owners and operators regardless of location or use. For instance, a boat towed to a launch area poses a liability exposure just as it does while navigated in water or parked in a driveway. A person who operates a boat can cause serious harm if any of the following acts occur:

- Colliding with another watercraft
- Striking docks, boat sheds, and other property
- Striking swimmers or water-skiers

Almost anyone may operate a boat without meeting age, experience, or licensing qualifications. Individuals and families who are not well trained in boat operation or who entrust their watercraft to inexperienced operators are likely to incur serious liability losses.

Business-Related Liability

Some individual and family activities on or off the residence premises may be more of a business nature than a personal nature. The distinction between commercial and personal activities can be important in the context of insurance, because personal liability insurance may not cover business-related activities. The sources of business-related liability for individuals and families include professional activities, volunteer work, ownership in closely-held corporations, service as directors or officers, fellow-employee suits, and use of personal property, especially autos, for business purposes.

Other Incidental Situations

The situations in which individuals and families may be exposed to liability loss are limitless. Aside from the major categories discussed above, some other situations deserve mention.

Host Liquor Liability   Hosts who entertain and serve alcoholic beverages to their social guests may be held accountable for damage caused by intoxicated guests. This type of liability is commonly referred to as **host liquor liability**.

Personal Activities   The personal activities that can create liability are limitless. In addition to host liquor liability, other such activities that create liability include the following:

- Borrowing, abusing, and damaging the property of another person, such as a camera or an electric saw
- Injuring another person or others' property in a sporting or hunting accident
- Permitting the family dog to run loose in the neighborhood
- Baby-sitting a neighbor's children

Loss Consequences

Liability loss exposures may lead to at least one of three general types of financial loss for an individual or family: damages, legal costs, and court costs.

Damages

Damages represent the amount of restitution or fines a liable party must make to the injured party or the government. With respect to civil liability, damages compensate the injured party for the harm caused by another party. With respect to criminal liability, damages represent the punishment inflicted by the government on the party responsible for the crime committed.

Damages in Civil Liability   For civil liability cases, damages may be compensation for bodily injury, property damage, financial loss, emotional injury, and so on. The amount of damages may be determined by a settlement process that allows the party responsible for causing the harm (the wrongdoer) and the injured party to negotiate, in some way, the amount of restitution the wrongdoer should provide to the injured party. In the most simple scenario, the two parties and their legal representatives negotiate with each other to determine the amount of damages. However, in many cases, damages are determined through a court trial and its resulting judgment. Yet, even when a court becomes involved, the parties still may settle during the process of court proceedings prior to trial or to a judgment.

When determination of damages involves court proceedings, the injured party (the **plaintiff**) sues the wrongdoer (the **defendant**) alleging the defendant's responsibility for the plaintiff's injuries. Damages are determined by the court's judgment, and the defendant may be required to pay nominal, compensatory, or punitive damages or to provide equitable relief other than damages, such as specific performance or an injunction. Each of these forms of relief is discussed below.

Nominal damages indicate that the plaintiff sustained some harm, but the injury is not one warranting substantial monetary relief. For example, Isabel sues for slander. A jury decides that, although the defendant slandered her, the harm was trivial. The court may award nominal damages of only one dollar. This decision confirms that the defendant was wrong but acknowledges that, even so, Isabel's harm was minuscule.

Compensatory damages are those amounts determined to be reasonable compensation to the plaintiff for harm done and nothing more. They include the following:

- *Special damages.* **Special damages** cover specific, identifiable expenses associated with the injured person's loss, such as medical expenses actually incurred or wages lost by the injured person and costs to replace or repair damaged property.
- *General damages.* **General damages** are amounts awarded by a court for injuries that are not readily quantified, such as pain and suffering and emotional distress.

Punitive damages serve as punishment for intentional, malicious, or outrageous conduct. Also called **exemplary**, punitive damages make an example of the defendant to keep others from acting in a similar manner.

In many cases, damages are an inadequate or inappropriate form of relief, and the court can make the plaintiff whole by requiring **equitable relief**—ordering the defendant to do something. Two forms of equitable relief are specific performance and an injunction.

- *Specific performance.* In contract cases, a court may require the party in breach (not fulfilling its part of the agreement) to perform a certain action or service. This is referred to as **specific performance**.[1] For example, suppose that Rita agrees to sell her land to Joe, but later refuses. A court may order Rita to sell her land to Joe, which is specific performance of the contract, with no damages involved.

- *Injunction.* Under an **injunction**, the court orders the defendant to stop the activity that is causing injury to the other party. For example, a court might issue an injunction ordering an individual not to build a fence until the court can determine that the fence is on that person's property and not on a neighbor's land.

When settlement is achieved without court proceedings, damages generally include only compensatory damages. However, in cases involving a breach of contract, a new contract may be negotiated that requires specific performance or includes an agreement to stop certain activities.

In some cases, individuals and families may choose to settle even if they are not responsible for the harm caused to the other parties. Court judgments do not always accurately determine innocence or guilt, and settlements can be less expensive than defending an individual's innocence.

Damages in Criminal Liability Damages for criminal liability are the fines, community service, and jail time assessed against the party committing the crime. The guidelines used to set damages for specific crimes are determined at the time the crime is defined. For example, murder is a felony offense that can lead to life in prison or the death penalty. For minor crimes, such as traffic citations, a ticket is given to the wrongdoer, who usually must pay a fine. Major crimes, such as murder, may involve court proceedings that determine the damages—such as the time to be spent in jail. Criminal liability cases can also be settled out of court through a plea bargaining process or simply by the admission of guilt by the wrongdoer.

Legal Costs

Because many liability claims require representation by a lawyer, liability losses include the cost of legal representation for both the person suing and the person defending the claim. In addition, there are the costs of any investigation and of fact-finding procedures as well as the time spent in court.

Individuals and families may be required to pay legal costs even if they are not responsible for the harm caused to another party. When suits are brought against innocent parties, these parties may choose to prove their innocence. This choice involves the same types of legal costs as discussed above.

Court Costs

Aside from legal costs, other court fees exist. A plaintiff, for example, may have to file a bond to protect property claimed by both the plaintiff and the defendant in a dispute involving property. Courts also require filing fees at various stages of litigation, which represent another cost one party may ultimately recover from the other party.

Illness and Injury Loss Exposures

Every human being is exposed to the chance of illness or injury. Illness and injury can arise from a variety of sources. A vast number of infectious agents make people sick. An individual can be injured in an infinite number of ways. When illness or injury occurs, the financial consequences may involve medical care expenses and loss of income during the period in which the sick or injured person is unable to work. These consequences can be catastrophic to individuals and families.

Relation to Employment

Determining whether an illness or injury is employment-related is important in establishing who is responsible for paying for the financial consequences of the illness or injury. As the term suggests, an employment-related illness or injury is caused by conditions at the employer's premises or while an individual is working whether on or off premises; otherwise illness or injury is non-employment-related.

This distinction may not be as clear as the definition makes it out to be. In many situations, it is difficult to determine whether an illness or injury is employment related. For example, a heart attack may occur at work but may be unrelated to the working environment. The distinction is often an issue in coverage disagreements between workers compensation insurers and health insurers and may need to be resolved through litigation.

Loss Consequences

Illness and injury usually decrease the income available to the individual or family. This decrease can result from expenses associated with the purchase of medical treatment, the inability to earn income, expenses to replace loss of services, and the need for long-term care.

Medical Care Expenses

Medical care expenses reflect the costs of restoring the sick or injured person to health. As many people realize, medical care can be quite expensive. In

1992, total spending on health care was conservatively estimated at over $860 billion, and this amount is expected to rise to $1,679 billion by the year 2000. In 1992, at least 14.2 percent of the United States Gross Domestic Product (GDP) was spent on health care, and health-care costs are expected to rise to above 18 percent of GDP by the year 2000.[2] These figures represent the big picture and include the cost of program administration, the net cost of insurance, and the cost of government public health activities.

Many people think of medical care expenses as the costs of physician care and hospital stays. Hospital and physician expenses are by no means the only medical care expenses that may be incurred. Other expenses include those for nursing home care, dentists' services, counseling and other professional services, prescription drugs, and eyeglasses.

Estimating the severity of a family's medical care expenses is difficult. Even if it can be determined that annual medical care expenses average $2,000 per person, this does not mean that the typical family of four will have annual medical expenses in the neighborhood of $8,000. Some families may be very healthy, while others may run up medical bills totaling hundreds of thousands of dollars.

Family medical care expenses fall into three categories:

- **Ordinary** medical care expenses are those that are more or less routine—treatment of small illnesses (such as colds or flu), or injuries (for example, cuts and sprains), routine dental care (including checkups and fillings), routine medical checkups (for instance, physicals), and routine medication (such as aspirin and blood pressure medicine).

- **Extraordinary** medical care expenses are those that go beyond what is routinely expected—for example, expenses associated with an appendectomy, a broken wrist, or hepatitis.

- **Catastrophic** medical expenses are extremely large and generally unexpected—for example, expenses associated with organ transplant or open heart surgery, or conditions that require extended medical care in a hospital or nursing home.

Inability To Earn Income

The inability to earn income due to illness or injury is referred to as **disability**. Unless or until health is restored, the person is partially or totally disabled and may be unable to earn income. This loss of income can dramatically affect an individual or family.

The person who is disabled may not be the only individual involved who cannot earn income. In some cases, one family member's disability also keeps other family members from earning incomes, because one or more family members must stay home to care for the disabled individual.

Disability can be divided into two categories—acute and chronic. An **acute** condition typically is one that lasts less than three months and involves either medical attention or restricted work activity. A **chronic** condition is more severe, since it generally involves either a long-term inability to perform an occupation or a lengthy period during which the kind or duration of activity is limited.

Extra Expenses and Loss of Services

Illness or injury can lead to increased expenses that must be borne to care for and to replace the services once provided by the sick or injured individual. For example, Edna has her right leg in a cast and is unable to drive. She must find another way to get to work or to go to the store. This alternative may be by taxi, bus, or train, which involves costs generally not present in driving her auto. Furthermore, Edna cares for a house and her children when she is not at work. A maid and a babysitter may need to be hired to take over these duties while Edna recuperates.

Long-Term Care

Long-term care may be defined as diagnostic, preventive, therapeutic, rehabilitative, maintenance, or personal care services for a period of at least one year, provided in a setting other than an acute care unit of a hospital. This is differentiated from chronic disability, because a chronically disabled person may not need long-term care. The costs of long-term care are differentiated from medical care costs because long-term care services are provided for an extended period of time, are provided outside of the hospital, and may only apply to maintenance or personal care.

Long-term care is generally associated with older individuals who are no longer able to take care of themselves, but long-term care may be necessary for someone of any age, such as a comatose child or a young adult suffering from AIDS.

The Death Exposure

Everyone is going to die at some point; the loss exposure due to death arises because the time and cause of death usually are not known.

Chances of Death

Statistics that deal with the characteristics of death, such as the age at which a person dies and the cause of an individual's death, are constantly collected by insurance companies and others. From some of this data, a mortality table can be constructed. **Mortality tables** provide the probability of death at a certain age with a high degree of accuracy. This probability of death is referred to as the **mortality rate** and equals the number of deaths at a given age divided by the number of observed lives at that age.

It is important to remember that mortality tables report conservative, smoothed averages. While these tables are invaluable to life insurers because they show the experience of a large number of people, the tables are not useful to one individual attempting to determine his or her age of death.

Loss Consequences

Death financially affects the survivors of the **decedent** (the person who has died). Death-related financial losses may be categorized as (1) costs associated with death and (2) loss of income.

Costs Associated With Death

Expenses, including last illness and burial expenses, may be incurred when a person dies. Moreover, a variety of expenses—such as taxes; estate administration fees and other cash outlays; and decreased values resulting from forced sale of assets—reduce the value of the decedent's assets.

Costs associated with death depend on the wealth of the decedent. At one extreme, if a person has virtually no property, then burial expenses might be the only cost incurred at that person's death. For wealthy individuals, however, the costs associated with death can be enormous. For example, an estate valued at $1 million may be subject to the federal estate tax, a state death tax, and estate settlement fees, such as the cost of an executor, the cost of a trustee, and costs associated with delivering property to heirs. Indeed, those with large estates often concentrate on minimizing these costs.

Loss of Income

The most valuable asset of most individuals is their ability to earn income. Except for income that does not depend on the continued life of an individual—such as interest earnings from a savings account, dividends, rents, and royalties—this asset is lost when an individual dies.

During their life cycles, most people go through a period when others (usually spouses and children) depend on them for financial support. If a person dies while financially supporting others, the dependent survivors suffer the loss of their financial support. This loss is generally catastrophic to the surviving dependents.

It is difficult to determine the amount of income that will be lost because of death. An individual's income changes periodically with work experience, years employed, and training. Income is affected by economic conditions and factors such as inflation and demand for products and services. Retirement age is often uncertain. These issues are compounded by the fact that financial dependents usually do not receive 100 percent of the breadwinner's income. Individuals have personal living expenses such as clothing, hobbies, and meals that are financed with their incomes but do not continue beyond their deaths.

The Retirement Loss Exposure

People who die before reaching retirement age are said to die prematurely. As a result, they do not actively earn income as long as might normally be expected. Those who live past the age of retirement face the opposite problem. This problem is sometimes referred to as **superannuation**, which means that a person may outlive his or her income and financial resources.

The loss consequence of retirement is that the retiree does not actively earn a living. The retiree's needs for income do not go away, but his or her earning power is diminished. Thus, the retiree and his or her dependents are faced with a shortage of funds with which to meet their living needs.

The Unemployment Loss Exposure

In many cases, an individual wants to work or is able to work but is not employed. This is a general definition of **unemployment**. Several sources of unemployment exist, but the result is that an individual is unable to actively earn an income.

Government Definition of Unemployment

It is important to recognize that federal and state governments regard an unemployed person as one who wants to work *and* is able to work. If an individual is willing to work but is unable to, he or she is not considered unemployed. On the other hand, if a person is able to work but does not want to, he or she is not considered unemployed. Both criteria must be met in order for someone to count as an unemployed individual according to the government.

Loss Consequences

The loss exposure of unemployment results in loss of income to individuals and their dependents. Unemployment may also give rise to an increase in costs associated with searching for a new job, going back to school for retraining or higher education, and job and psychological counseling. Thus individuals and families can incur increased expenses at the same time a major source of income is not available.

Personal Risk Management

Personal risk management may be defined as the process for making and carrying out decisions that will minimize the adverse effects of an individual's or family's loss exposures. Risk management can minimize worry and can ease the harmful impact of an actual loss because it helps people to identify loss exposures and decide how to deal with the possible losses before they happen.

Setting Personal Objectives

Personal objectives are the goals an individual or family wishes to achieve. For example, an individual may want to be a senior vice president in a Fortune 500 company by age thirty-eight, or a couple may plan to own a house within two years of their marriage and have two children within four more years. These are specific goals that these people want to meet. Other objectives may be more general. Many people simply desire to be happy and successful.

The setting of personal objectives focuses the risk management process by helping in the identification and evaluation of loss exposures and in the decision concerning the techniques for dealing with these loss exposures. By establishing the objectives they wish to meet, families and individuals may recognize loss exposures that they otherwise would not have identified. These people can then determine which loss exposures could keep them from achieving or could drastically increase the time necessary to attain specific objectives. Loss exposures that keep goals from being obtained are generally more serious than those exposures that delay attainment. Once the effects of the loss exposures are ascertained, the appropriate methods for dealing with them can be determined. These treatments will take into account the seriousness of the loss exposure and the impact of the treatment upon the objectives. If a method for dealing with an exposure does not correct the adverse impact on the personal objective, that method is not appropriate for the situation.

Consider the following example. Chris is a young man who wants to play on a top-ten college basketball team as a college freshman. One loss exposure he faces is that he might be injured while playing for his high school team. To keep this loss from occurring, Chris could quit the team and wait to play when he starts college. This treatment is generally not appropriate because in order to get on such a college team he must prove, and improve, his abilities while playing in high school. An alternative method of dealing with this exposure is for Chris to take time to condition himself by running and practicing during the off-season and doing stretching exercises before and after games and practices during the season. This method allows him to prove himself fit for a top-ten college team and helps to prevent injuries while playing in high school.

The Risk Management Process

Risk management is carried out through a five-step process appropriately referred to as the **risk management process**. Before beginning the process, an individual or family should have established some specific goals or objectives as discussed above. The risk management process can then proceed according to the following steps:

1. Identify and analyze the loss exposures that could keep an individual or family from, or interfere with, their achieving their objectives.
2. Examine alternative risk management techniques.
3. Select the best risk management techniques.
4. Implement the risk management plan.
5. Monitor and revise the plan as necessary.

Identifying and Analyzing Loss Exposures

Individuals and families face a multitude of loss exposures. These exposures can be sorted into the six general areas discussed in the first half of this chapter: property, liability, illness and injury, death, retirement, and unemployment. Considering these categories can help individuals and families identify their particular loss exposures. Once the exposures have been identified, the impact of the losses, should they occur, can be determined. It is especially important that serious loss exposures do not go unnoticed.

Information Sources for Identifying Personal Loss Exposures

The identification of loss exposures faced by an individual or family requires information on the individual's or family's obligations, possessions, and general goals including the following:

*   Spouse, dependents, and other family commitments
*   Age, condition of health, and related factors
*   Property owned and used
*   Other tangible and intangible assets
*   Debts and other liabilities

- Activities or behaviors that can cause injury to others or the property of others
- Status under Social Security program
- Current employee benefits and available options
- Participation in past and current retirement plans, and available options
- Provisions of current will, other estate plans

Various approaches can be used to gather this information. A relatively simplistic and unsystematic approach is to "think through" the preceding list. This list can lead one to think about various loss exposures. However, a more systematic approach is usually in order.

A questionnaire that focuses on an individual's or family's loss exposures may be useful for evaluating in detail an individual's or family's situation. Part of a typical risk management questionnaire is shown in Exhibit 1-2. This part of the questionnaire concentrates on real property loss exposures. Question-naires also generally cover exposures associated with personal property, per-sonal liability, death, illness and injury, retirement, and professional dealings.

Questionnaires often contain a number of items that go beyond the level of information needed for risk management planning but that provide informa-tion needed to complete an insurance application. For example, the name and address of the mortgagee (item 15 in Exhibit 1-2) is seldom necessary in establishing personal objectives or in determining means for meeting those objectives. However, this information must appear on a homeowners insur-ance application, and the mortgagee must be named on a homeowners insurance policy.

Questionnaires may also not ask enough questions. For example, the excerpt in Exhibit 1-2 does not ask about past loss experience. The answer to this question might identify certain loss exposures that are more likely to occur than others.

A variety of questionnaires and checklists exists, many of which are oriented toward particular loss exposures and risk management measures. Insurance agents often have insurance policy checklists available. Loss control special-ists such as alarm system vendors have their own checklists and question-naires. Because questionnaires may not ask about each loss exposure an individual or family faces, questionnaires should be used only as a guide to loss exposure identification.

Analyzing Loss Exposures

Each loss exposure has a cause of loss and at least one consequence of loss. It is

Exhibit 1-2
Excerpt From Exposure Questionnaire

Real Property Data

1. Address of principal residence:_____

   _____

2. Additional buildings (e.g., barns, greenhouses, docks, or outbuildings): ___

   _____

   _____

3. Is your property owned or rented? _____

4. Type of construction of the principal residence: _____

   _____

5. Number of rooms in principal residence: _____

6. Is the principal residence a private dwelling?_____

7. Does the principal dwelling contain any unusual glass (e.g., picture windows or expensive chandeliers)?_____

   _____

8. Type of heating system utilized in the principal dwelling: _____

   _____

9. Is there a garage? ___ If the answer is yes, answer the following questions:

   a. Type of construction used in garage: _____

   _____

   b. Attached or detached to the principal dwelling: _____

   _____

   c. Living quarters connected with the garage:_____

   _____

10. Value of standard alterations in progress or contemplated for principal residence or garages: _____

    _____

11. Date principal residence was built:_____

12. Original (purchase) price of the principal dwelling: _____
    Original price of any additional building: _____
    Cost of any improvements that have been made:_____

13. Current appraisal value of the:
    a. principal dwelling: _____
    b. additional buildings:_____

14. Current replacement cost of the:
    a. principal dwelling: _____
    b. additional buildings:_____

15. Name and address of mortgagee, if any: _____

    _____

16. Current value of trees and shrubs:_____

17. Additional living expenses needed if principal residence cannot be occupied:

    _____

18. Are there any secondary residences? If so, provide necessary information.

important to consider each of these factors when determining the impact a loss exposure could have on an individual or family and how to deal with the loss exposure.

The Cause of Loss   The **cause of loss**, also referred to as the **peril**, is the actual means by which damage, injury, destruction, or death has been inflicted upon the item subject to loss. The causes of loss to property include, among other perils, fire, flood, theft, and collision. Persons can be injured or prematurely killed by a bullet, an accident at work, or fire, among other things. Measles and pneumonia can make people ill or cause premature death. Furthermore, illness, injury, or death can lead to medical expenses and lost income. Liability losses can arise when a person causes injury to another individual or damages the property of other people. For both retirement and unemployment loss exposures, the cause of loss is the retirement or unemployment that keeps the individual from actively earning income.

The Consequences of Loss   If a loss occurs, it can have a variety of consequences. Some results may be more serious than others. Consequences of loss are commonly classified as critical, severe, or bearable.

- **Critical consequences** result when an individual or family is no longer able to meet a personal objective because of the outcome of a loss. A person's death is probably the most critical consequence an individual or family can experience. Besides keeping an individual from attaining personal goals, death can affect whole families in the same manner. Severe disability can also hold a person or family back from personal objectives. For example, reconsider Chris, the young man who desires to play on a top-ten college basketball team. If he loses a leg in an auto accident, he will not be able to achieve his objective. This loss would be critical for Chris. He can set new goals, but he will not play basketball as he had planned.

- **Severe consequences** result in a substantial delay in achieving a personal goal. While the objective may still be attainable, the successful completion of the goal will take longer than originally expected. Returning to the basketball scenario, Chris would experience a severe loss consequence from the auto accident if he suffered a compound break of his pelvis and thigh. He may recover to play basketball at his pre-injury caliber and eventually play for a top-ten college team, but he may first have to take a year or two off to recuperate.

- **Bearable consequences** have little effect on personal objectives. The consequence occurs and it is adverse, but it does not keep the individual or family from achieving its goals, nor does it delay the attainment of these goals. For Chris, a bearable loss consequence of an auto accident might be a slight concussion. He may have to take a few days or a couple of weeks off from high school play, but he can still meet his objective without delay.

Examining Alternative Risk Management Techniques

Personal risk management involves risk control and risk financing. **Risk control** deals with modifying the loss exposure prior to loss to prevent loss or modifying the conditions after loss to reduce the harmful effects of loss. **Risk financing** identifies who will pay for a loss should it occur. Exhibit 1-3 shows the various risk management techniques that fall in each of these categories.

Exhibit 1-3
Personal Risk Management Techniques

Risk Control	Risk Financing
Avoidance	Personal Insurance
Loss Control	Noninsurance Transfer for
Loss Prevention	Risk Financing
Loss Reduction	Retention
Noninsurance Transfer	
for Risk Control	

Risk Control

Avoidance, loss prevention and loss reduction, and noninsurance transfer are risk control techniques available to individuals and families.

Avoidance   The **avoidance** technique is used when a loss exposure is not assumed or when an existing exposure is eliminated. For example, a family can avoid many, but not all, auto liability loss exposures by not owning a car. In practice, the avoidance technique may not be feasible for many personal loss exposures. No one can eliminate the possibility of sickness or injury, and death is a certainty.

Loss Control   **Loss control** techniques change, or control, the loss exposure, and include loss prevention and loss reduction. **Loss prevention** focuses on lowering the likelihood, or the **frequency**, of a loss, while **loss reduction** deals with reducing the adverse impact, or the **severity**, of a loss. Many loss control measures involve both loss prevention and loss reduction. Consider a smoke detector. It sounds an alarm if it senses smoke or heat. It can help lower the probability that people will be harmed by fire, and it can help to reduce the spread of fire.

Prevention and reduction are highly appropriate personal risk management tools. For example, an individual can prevent injuries in auto accidents by lowering the probability of having an accident. Among other things, the individual can periodically check his or her car's brakes and have them repaired whenever necessary. In addition, wearing seat belts can prevent injury and can also reduce the severity of injury.

Loss control measures are not limited to property and liability exposures. Measures such as participating in physical fitness programs, having medical checkups, and consulting a medical professional at the first sign of a problem can prevent illness or reduce its impact.

Because lives and property may be saved as a result of loss control, safety efforts deserve serious consideration; even if funding is available to pay for the financial consequences of a loss. For instance, even when funds are available to replace wages lost because of disability, most people prefer to prevent disability. Yet, safety efforts do not always pay off in success, and potential benefits do not always justify the cost of the loss control measure.

Noninsurance Transfer for Risk Control **Noninsurance transfer for risk control** involves shifting an entire loss exposure and its consequences to another person, family, or organization (the *transferee*) in exchange for performance of some activity that the *transferor* (the person or family transferring the loss exposure) cannot or will not perform. The shift is generally achieved by a contract between the transferor and the transferee. The following examples illustrate noninsurance transfers for loss control:

- A family sells its summer cottage to another family. Loss exposures are transferred along with the ownership. This is transfer, not avoidance, because the cottage is not destroyed; it continues to exist, but any related losses now fall to the new owners.

- In some leases, a tenant is responsible for certain types of property damage. For example, if Joan rents a furnished garage apartment, she may be required to replace any damaged furniture with furniture of similar quality. Thus, the landlord shifts the furniture damage loss exposure to Joan.

Risk Financing

Personal insurance, noninsurance transfer, and retention are risk financing techniques available to individuals and families to deal with the possibility of loss.

Personal Insurance **Personal insurance** is the risk management technique that permits individuals and families to transfer the financial consequences of loss exposures to a commercial insurance company or to a government agency.

As illustrated in Exhibit 1-4, personal insurance is comprised of three layers:

- Social programs of insurance
- Group benefits
- Individual insurance

Exhibit 1-4
Three Layers of Personal Insurance

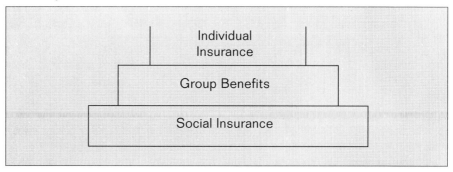

Social programs of insurance, commonly referred to as **social insurance**, often provide the base layer of protection for some losses arising out of injury and illness, premature death, retirement, and unemployment. Since most people are covered by some form of social insurance, it is the foundation for insurance planning upon which other insurance coverages build. Examples of social insurance include Social Security, workers compensation, and unemployment insurance programs.

The second layer of protection, **group benefits**, is available to many individuals as a result of their employment. Most commonly offered on a group basis are (1) retirement plans and (2) life and health insurance. Auto and homeowners coverages are also available to a few groups.

Individual insurance covers the smallest number of insureds as far as health-related coverages are concerned. In 1991, group health insurance accounted for 72.9 percent of health insurance premiums written. However, individual life insurance is somewhat more significant than group life insurance, both in terms of the number of people insured and the amount of insurance in force. In 1991, group life insurance premiums accounted for 22.8 percent of life insurance premiums written, and 40.6 percent of life insurance in force was group life. Most property and liability insurance is provided on an individual basis.

Individual insurance generally allows individuals and families the most flexibility in choosing the amount of insurance (indicated by the lack of a line at the top of Exhibit 1-4). When individual insurance is purchased, the policyowner is the one who decides what coverages to purchase, from whom to purchase the insurance, and when to change insurers. Individual insurance can remain in force regardless of unemployment, change of employer, or termination of group insurance plans. However, to qualify for individual insurance, an individual must meet the underwriting requirements of the insurer.

Noninsurance Transfer for Risk Financing Noninsurance transfers can be used to transfer the cost of losses to a party that is not a commercial insurance company or a government agency that provides insurance. With a **noninsurance transfer for risk financing**, only the financial consequences of the loss are shifted to another person, family, or organization. The transferor still faces the loss exposure and its nonfinancial consequences, such as mental anguish. However, if the transferee is unable or unwilling to honor its promise, the financial consequences will also fall on the transferee, despite the attempted transfer. Noninsurance transfers are not very useful or dependable for handling personal loss exposures.

For example, Greg signs a lease in which he agrees to assume liability for all accidents on the leased premises. The lease transfers the financial impact of Wilson's (the landlord's) liability losses to Greg. Suppose Tiffany, Greg's guest, is injured on the leased premises by a falling chandelier. Greg, under the lease, is liable for Tiffany's injuries. However, Greg has neither the resources nor the insurance to cover Tiffany's injuries. Wilson may be held liable for Tiffany's injuries, despite his lease with Greg.

An individual is more likely to experience a noninsurance transfer as the transferee than as a transferor. The following list provides examples of noninsurance transfers to which individuals may be subjected:

- Tool rental agreements often include a provision that makes the renter responsible for *all* losses to the rented tool, including those for which the renter is not liable under common law. For example, if the rented tool is stolen, the renter is liable for the loss.
- Car rental contracts may also include a provision that makes the customer responsible for *all* loss to the rented auto. For example, if the auto is not properly maintained by the rental company and an accident results, the customer may be held liable.
- "Swim at Your Own Risk" signs posted near swimming pools indicate that the owner transfers to the swimmer risk for any loss or accident.

In each of these examples, organizations and property owners are attempting to transfer the financial consequences of their loss exposures to an individual.

Retention   Unless a person or a family has avoided a given loss exposure, a loss may occur. Some losses are transferred through insurance or noninsurance transfers. Unless the financial consequences of losses have been transferred, they will fall directly on that person or family who has not avoided or transferred the losses. If they are not transferred, they are kept, or **retained**.

Retention may be partial or total. **Partial retention** occurs when a portion of the loss is retained and the rest is transferred. An insurance policy with a deductible is a common example of partial retention. The insured retains that part of the loss that falls within the deductible, and the remainder of the covered loss is paid by the insurer. With **total retention**, the person or family bears the entire cost of the loss.

Although it may be inappropriate to retain loss exposures for which an individual or family does not have the resources to cover the loss, retention is not inherently bad. In fact, retention is a part of many carefully conceived risk management plans. In the long run, it may be more economical to pay some losses directly out-of-pocket than to pay an insurance company a premium large enough to cover the same losses at the insurer's expense. Many factors must be considered when deciding the extent to which insurance should be used.

Selecting the Best Risk Management Techniques

Because many states require auto insurance and because mortgage holders require homeowners insurance, many people consider insurance to be the only practical personal risk management technique. This attitude can lead to the unwise use of insurance merely because it is available, rather than using other risk management techniques, alone or in combination with insurance. Many complex and interrelated factors must be considered in designing a personal risk management program. The best solution is usually *not* to purchase all the insurance that is available, but rather to treat all identified exposures with *appropriate* control and financing techniques, including insurance. In many cases, a number of measures may be considered appropriate.

Frequency and Severity

To select the appropriate risk management tool for handling a loss exposure, the potential frequency and severity of the exposure must be considered. Loss exposures with very low frequency may be so insignificant that they can be disregarded without any great concern. On the other hand, exposures with high potential severity should be carefully considered. For example, a home-owner in Tampa, Florida, might decide to disregard the earthquake exposure since severe earthquakes hardly ever occur in that area. Such an evaluation might lead to a decision to retain the exposure. On the other hand, given the destruction south of Miami due to, and Tampa's close call with, Hurricane Andrew in 1992, a Tampa homeowner would be unlikely to retain windstorm losses.

Handling Loss Exposures

Exhibit 1-5 depicts the **frequency-severity matrix**, a tool that can be used to identify the appropriate risk management technique for a given loss frequency and loss severity. It serves only as a *preliminary guide* in the selection process. More detailed analysis is required beyond the use of the matrix. The techniques shown in each frequency-severity block are listed from most to least appropriate. For example, it is best to avoid a loss exposure with high frequency and high severity. Windstorm damage occurs often along the Gulf Coast of Florida and, when it occurs, can severely damage or destroy homes. Many people avoid this exposure by not owning a home on the Gulf Coast.

Exhibit 1-5
The Frequency-Severity Matrix*

		SEVERITY	
		HIGH	LOW
F R E Q U E N C Y	H I G H	Avoid Prevent and Reduce Transfer Retain	Prevent Retain
	L O W	Prevent and Reduce Transfer	Retain Prevent

*Treatment alternatives are listed in order of importance (most successful to least successful).

If a high frequency-high severity loss exposure cannot be avoided, then it must be prevented and reduced before it can be transferred. Many homes along the Gulf Coast are made of cinder blocks with specially designed roofs that will not easily blow off during a windstorm. This helps to keep windstorm damage from occurring and reduces the risk of damage to a point at which some insurers may be willing to sell windstorm coverage to homeowners. In other words, at this point the homeowners can transfer the risk. If the loss exposure cannot be avoided or transferred, it must be retained.

In general, unless a loss exposure is avoided, it should be treated. Often this requires considering both risk control measures and risk financing methods. Proper risk management involves the consideration of at least one risk control technique and one risk financing technique. As noted earlier, noninsurance transfers have limited application in personal risk management. Most personal risk management is concerned with loss control, insurance, and retention.

Many personal loss control measures are obvious. For example, placing a four-foot-high fence around a swimming pool is a loss prevention measure. The fence tends to keep neighborhood children and pets, as well as nondomesticated animals, from entering the pool and drowning. The fence does not completely eliminate the possibility that somebody or something might drown in the pool, but it does reduce the frequency of drowning.

Smoke detectors and fire extinguishers are commonly used loss reduction devices. Neither of these measures prevents a fire from starting, but both can help to minimize property damage from a fire that has started. Smoke detectors can also prevent loss of life.

Conducting periodic home and car inspections can be both prevention and reduction measures. Conditions that could cause damage can be repaired and corrected before damage occurs. For example, a worn hose might be discovered and replaced before the auto breaks down on a limited access highway. Minor losses can be discovered before they become major. For instance, a minor home plumbing leak might be discovered and corrected before major damage is done to the ceilings and walls.

Exposures that have not been avoided must also be financed. The most difficult decision for many individuals and families is not whether to buy any insurance, but which exposures to insure and which to retain.

When individuals and families purchase unnecessary insurance, they may forgo additional necessary insurance. Many individuals and families rely upon insurance as the only recognized method of financing loss exposures whether the potential size of the loss is significant or not. In many cases, insureds are only "exchanging dollars" with insurers—paying a premium that is equal to the severity of the exposure being transferred. This can be both expensive and wasteful.

General Guidelines for Financing Personal Loss Exposures

Three general guidelines have been established for determining how to finance personal loss exposures:

1. Consider the severity of the loss exposure that the individual or family is capable of retaining.
2. Compare the severity of the loss exposure to the cost of treating it.
3. Consider the effect of frequency on the severity of the loss exposure.

The Severity That Can Be Retained   Individuals and families must determine at what point they can no longer pay for a loss. In other words, they must determine how much of a loss they can retain. When the possible maximum loss for a given exposure exceeds what individuals or families could bear without seriously impairing their financial resources, insurance makes sense. Assuming that the cost of insurance bears a reasonable relationship to the exposure, and that the exposure involves a peril that is not extremely remote, insurance is virtually essential. The following example illustrates this point.

Carol is a television newscaster who rents an apartment. She purchased insurance on her possessions several years ago for the minimum limit of $6,000. At that time she had no need of a higher policy limit. She has renewed her policy every year, but she has never increased the limit. Over the years Carol has acquired new furniture valued at over $6,000 alone. She has also established an extensive wardrobe and jewelry collection that are essential to her career. If Carol were to sustain a total loss to her apartment and personal possessions, she would certainly not be able to replace all of her belongings with her $6,000 insurance coverage. Carol might be retaining more of a loss than she can afford.

The Exposure's Severity Versus the Cost of Treatment   It is important to compare the possible severity of the loss to the cost of the available risk control or risk financing measures. It is not in an individual's or family's best interests to use a treatment if the severity of the loss is less than the cost of the treatment. On the other hand, if the cost of the treatment is much less than the severity of the loss, the individual or family should seriously consider taking advantage of a risk management measure.

For example, in many cases insurance that is not essential is available at a relatively low cost. Term life insurance costs a minimal amount for a twenty-year-old, but if that twenty-year-old has no dependents, no debt outstanding, and his or her parents have a policy that will cover his or her death expenses if necessary, he or she has little financial need for term life insurance, even if it is inexpensive. However, the twenty-year-old may purchase term life insurance now to preserve his or her ability to qualify for life insurance protection later.[3]

In other cases, the added security is worth a small premium. For example, a $1 million personal umbrella policy with a $250 deductible might cost as little as $125 per year. For many people, it is good risk management to pay $125 to transfer a possible loss of many thousands of dollars to an insurer.

The Effect of Frequency on the Severity   While considering the severity of a loss exposure, it is also important to determine how often the loss could occur. If a loss with a small severity takes place several times, the severity may become unbearable. For example, suppose an individual has decided to retain a loss exposure that could result in a $400 loss. This person has enough money saved to pay for this loss if it should occur. But, the loss exposure has the chance of occurring six times this year, leading to a potential severity for the year of $2,400. The individual may not have enough funds to cover all of these losses should they take place. If the individual had considered the frequency as well as the severity, he or she might have arrived at a different or additional risk treatment.

Methods Commonly Selected for Specific Exposures

Common risk treatment plans exist for each of the six categories of loss exposures discussed at the beginning of this chapter. These are described in the following paragraphs.

Property Loss Exposures   Property loss exposures can be controlled and financed. Most personal risk control is achieved through loss prevention and loss reduction. Personal risk financing primarily involves insurance and relatively small retentions.

Property loss exposures may be avoided, for the most part, by not possessing, owning, or using a type of property. For example, an individual can avoid the direct and consequential losses associated with a snowmobile by not owning, renting, borrowing, or otherwise using one. However, in some cases, it is impossible to avoid a property loss exposure. For instance, everyone needs cash and, thus, faces the possibility of losing cash.

Many property loss exposures can be prevented or reduced. Personal safety experts recommend that all homes have at least one smoke detector and a fire extinguisher on each floor. Detectors and extinguishers help to reduce the severity of a fire once it occurs. Many homes are also protected by a security system. Security systems can prevent theft by deterring the criminal from trying to enter the home and can reduce the loss by encouraging the thief to flee once the home has been entered. Intangible personal property loss exposures can also be reduced and prevented. For example, a person may try to protect his or her credit record by always paying bills on time and never overcharging credit cards or overdrafting checking accounts.

Most property loss exposures are retained or insured. Property loss exposures should be retained only if the individual or family is able to bear the costs of the exposure without financial hardship. Loss exposures that cannot be avoided or transferred must be retained, but these exposures should be reduced and prevented if the potential costs of the loss are severe.

Dwellings are usually insured, although a small portion of the exposure may be retained through a deductible. The potential loss of a dwelling is too severe for most individuals and families to bear without transferring much of the cost to an insurance company. Personal property that is of relatively large value is generally also insured. For example, autos that are fewer than five years old usually are of enough value that most individuals and families could not replace them without the aid of an insurance policy. However, for many people, a car valued at less than $1,000 is not worth insuring for physical damage. The contents of one's home are often insured, because an individual or family might be financially unable to replace all of this property at once, without suffering financial hardship, in the event of major or total loss to the residence. Relatively small property exposures cannot be efficiently insured and are usually within one's ability to retain, and thus are not transferred to an insurance company.

Liability Loss Exposures   The liability loss exposures of individuals and families can be severe. People can lose their savings, have their personal and real property attached, and have their wages garnished to pay for liability losses. Upon carefully identifying their liability loss exposures, individuals and families should ensure that these exposures are adequately controlled and financed.

Exposure to liability loss cannot be completely avoided, although people can try to avoid certain sources of liability. For example, an individual who does not want liability arising from recreational vehicles must not own or use any such vehicles. To completely avoid this exposure, that individual must also make sure that any other individual for which he or she is responsible, such as a child or an employee, does not own or use a recreational vehicle. An individual may also try to avoid criminal liability. However, it is extremely difficult to completely avoid most liability loss exposures.

Because liability loss exposures can rarely be avoided, they must be prevented or reduced. Furthermore, some liability loss exposures cannot be insured and must also be controlled. Criminal liability and intentional injury (apart from actions taken in self-defense and some forms of injury to a person's reputation) are generally not covered by insurance, so it is particularly important to control these types of liability loss exposures. Individuals can prevent many liability exposures simply by acting as prudent and reasonable persons and by obeying laws and customs. Examples of techniques for preventing liability include the following:

- Obey all traffic laws.
- Keep one's driveway and sidewalks in safe condition.
- Restrain one's pets.

Individuals and families can also try to reduce liability loss exposures once an injury has occurred for which the individual or family might be held responsible. Reducing liability loss exposures often requires an effort by the individual or family to comfort and deal with the injured party directly and in a courteous or pleasant manner even under circumstances in which the fault of the individual or family is not clear.

For example, Jill visits her neighbor, Amy. While walking in Amy's garden, Jill trips on a hose and falls, breaking her arm. Because the incident happened on Amy's property, Jill may sue Amy for damages. Amy can try to reduce her liability exposure by immediately soothing Jill, taking her to the hospital, and keeping in touch with her while she is recuperating. Jill may be less likely to take Amy to court if she feels that Amy cares about what has happened. On the other hand, Amy could tell Jill how stupid she was for not seeing the hose and let Jill take care of her injury alone. Under these circumstances, Jill is more likely to respond by suing Amy.

Because it is difficult to avoid liability loss exposures and because they can be quite severe, individuals and families should arrange to transfer these loss exposures. Usually this involves personal liability insurance.

Personal liability insurance generally targets specific situational sources of personal liability. For example, the personal liability insurance provided by homeowners policies covers most sources of personal liability. However, it excludes coverage for certain significant liability exposures, such as personal auto liability, personal recreational vehicle liability, personal watercraft liability, and most business-related liability. Personal auto liability can be insured under personal auto policies, and other sources of personal liability can be covered by other specific policies, such as recreational vehicle policies, watercraft liability policies, or business or professional liability policies.

However, personal liability insurance does not cover all forms of liability. For example, criminal liability and liability for intentional injury (apart from actions taken in self-defense and some forms of injury to a person's reputation) are not covered by any personal liability policies. These liability loss exposures must often be retained.

Illness and Injury Exposures The costs of treating illness and injury can be staggering to many individuals and families. Many people are concerned about controlling their health loss exposures and actively plan for the financial consequences of this loss exposure.

Some accidental injuries can be avoided by forgoing the exposure. For example, a person who never enters a mine is unlikely to be injured in a mine collapse. However, the avoidance technique is not practical for most health-related loss exposures. Nobody can eliminate all possibility of sickness or injury.

Since many health loss exposures cannot be avoided, loss control is a must. Attempting to prevent and reduce illness and injury is becoming increasingly important to many individuals. Measures such as "wellness" programs, mental relaxation seminars, and health fairs are common. Many people are much more diet-conscious—cutting down on fat-laden foods and increasing consumption of fresh vegetables and fruits. Smoking and overeating are increasingly considered socially unacceptable, and exercise is often considered necessary. Taking each of these actions helps to prevent illness and injury or to reduce their impact.

The cost of dealing with illness and injury losses can be severe. Since these loss exposures cannot be avoided and are too severe for most people to retain, most individuals and families depend on health insurance. Many people receive group health insurance as an employee benefit, and some individuals and families are insured by individual health policies. Social Security and Medicare provide health insurance for many individuals who are disabled or retired. Medicaid programs offer health coverage for poor individuals and families. Workers compensation is also available for injuries and illnesses that are employment related. But many individuals and families still have no health insurance, and many do not have adequate amounts for reasons usually related to the cost or availability of insurance and to unemployment.

The Death Exposure Death is inevitable, but its financial consequences can be treated. The death exposure can be controlled to some extent and financed.

Death cannot be avoided, but one can prevent specific causes of death. A person who does not want to die in a plane crash can refuse to fly and choose not to live near an airport or under a flight path. For the most part, doing so would postpone the exposure to death and reduce its financial consequences.

People can attempt to postpone death by taking care of themselves—by (1) not smoking, (2) not consuming too much alcohol or using other drugs, (3) eating right, and (4) exercising. Measures such as blood pressure screening and mammograms can help postpone death by identifying health problems early enough to treat them.

Some measures can reduce the financial impact of death on survivors. **Living wills**—in which people, while in good health, express their desire to die naturally and without the use of life support and other technological means if the only possible outcome is death—try to keep life from being artificially and unrealistically extended. This helps to reduce the costs associated with death. Choosing one's home or a hospice for terminal care can also lower the costs of death.

The death of a wage earner can be financially devastating to that person's survivors. It is important for individuals and families to consider the impact of death on their survivors and to adequately finance these exposures before the loss occurs.

Some individuals choose to retain this loss exposure. They may not have dependents whom they need to protect from financial loss. They may prepay their burial expenses, or they may have enough in their savings and investments to cover their death expenses.

Individuals with dependents and family members generally have life insurance coverage. According to the latest available estimates, 67 percent of all adults in the United States have life insurance. Of these adults, about 43 percent have individual life insurance and 40 percent receive group life insurance as part of an employee benefit package from their employer.[4] In most cases, life insurance benefits are paid to the survivors at the time of the insured's death. Social Security provides funeral and survivorship benefits to spouses and other dependents of covered workers. Workers compensation provides a lump-sum funeral benefit and income to survivors of individuals killed while in the course of employment.

The Retirement Loss Exposure   Although an individual can control the timing of the retirement exposure, retirement cannot often be prevented or avoided. Financing the retirement loss exposure is a must. Several sources of financing are available to individuals and families:

- *Social Security.*   The Social Security program provides a base of monthly retirement income to all covered individuals. The program is not designed to replace, dollar for dollar, the income lost due to retirement. The income provided through Social Security is presumed to allow retirees, their spouses, and any eligible dependents to maintain a minimum standard of living. The benefits depend on annual income over a person's entire working life and may not reflect the most recent level of income earned prior to retirement.

- *Pensions and other retirement plans.* Many retirees also receive retirement income from their former employers under pension and other retirement plans. These plans generally base the amount of retirement income on the attained age, the number of years worked, and the level of earnings in the years just prior to retirement. This helps the retiree to preserve the standard of living maintained while actively employed.

- *Annuities.* Annuities allow the individual to transfer the financial burdens of outliving retirement income, usually to an insurance company, although retirement annuities are also offered by some banks and investment firms. Prior to retirement or at retirement, the individual pays a series of premiums or a single premium to the insurer in return for the promise of retirement income for as long as the individual survives. Because annuities can be modified to provide income for a certain period or to provide a specific amount, an individual can purchase an annuity that meets his or her needs.

Individuals and families can retain the retirement loss exposure. Many people make investments throughout their lives and then liquidate these investments or use the investment return as income for retirement. For example, *Individual Retirement Accounts* (IRAs) are available to individuals as a vehicle for retirement saving. These are special savings accounts that are designed to defer taxes on the contributions to and the investment earnings on the amounts placed in the accounts until the funds are withdrawn for use as retirement income.

The Unemployment Loss Exposure   The loss exposure associated with unemployment may be controlled and financed. For unemployment that does occur, government-sponsored insurance and welfare programs are available.

The possibility of unemployment generally cannot altogether be avoided. However, the unemployment loss exposure can be reduced or prevented in many different ways. Employees can make themselves indispensable to the employers' operations to reduce the possibility that they will be laid off or fired. Individuals may choose to enter expanding fields that have long-term futures. People can get training for several different occupations, so that, in the event that one does not work out, another might.

An individual or family can retain or transfer the unemployment loss exposure or use a combination of the two. Retention may simply mean that the person no longer chooses to work, or it may involve building up savings or investments that will provide the family or individual with income until the breadwinner can locate another job. Transfer generally is achieved through unemployment compensation insurance or welfare programs.

Unemployment compensation insurance is a government insurance program administered by the states at the direction of the federal government. Each state has its own specific rules concerning eligibility and benefit levels. The general rules concerning eligibility ensure that the individual has some prior work experience and that the individual is "unemployed" according to the state's definition—in other words, willing and able to work. In some cases, unemployed persons who refuse to attend job interviews arranged by state unemployment offices may be denied unemployment benefits because they have not shown that they are willing to work.

Benefits are typically paid to the unemployed weekly for a period of twenty-six weeks after a waiting period of one week and generally reflect the level of the worker's prior wages within certain minimum and maximum dollar limits. In recent years, Congress has passed and renewed legislation to extend unemployment benefits periods for an additional twenty or twenty-six weeks for people who have used up the regular twenty-six-week benefits.

Welfare programs are government programs that provide a minimum level of income and other benefits to individuals and families that qualify. Generally, to qualify for welfare, the individual or family must be living on an income that is below poverty level. Benefits are typically paid monthly and include food stamps and housing subsidies.

Implementing the Risk Management Plan

Once the individual or family has determined how best to deal with its loss exposures, the treatments must be put in place. If the individual or family has decided that insurance is necessary to deal with home ownership exposures, a homeowners policy, with the appropriate deductible, should be purchased. If it is believed that a loss exposure can be retained, but it is necessary to maintain a savings account to do so, the savings account must be established. The individual or family should implement all the measures so that the identified loss exposures are effectively and efficiently treated. However, outside help may be needed to install alarms or other risk control measures and to purchase insurance policies or arrange other risk financing measures.

Monitoring and Revising the Risk Management Plan

Individuals and families do not live in a static world. Once appropriate insurance has been purchased or other appropriate risk management techniques have been implemented, it is necessary to be alert to changes in exposures and in available control and financing techniques. For example, home security systems have become available at affordable prices, and insurers provide premium credits for homes with these loss control devices. Knowledge of these changes should prompt the alert individual or family to improve the risk management program by purchasing a security system and obtaining an insurance premium reduction.

Personal Financial Planning as Part of Personal Risk Management

The purpose of **personal financial planning** is to develop plans for reaching the financial objectives of an individual or family. While financial planning is often conducted by specialists in that field, for the purposes of this text, financial planning is considered part of personal risk management. Financial planning helps a family or individual select appropriate loss financing techniques to deal with loss exposures.

Financial Planning Objectives

Each person or family has different financial objectives that must be individually analyzed. However, the following broad objectives are addressed in most situations:

- *Maintaining a standard of living.*   Analyze the spending that is required (such as food and housing costs) as well as desired (travel and entertainment).

- *Saving.*   Set aside money that can be used to meet an emergency or other special need. The ideal level of savings will depend upon personal characteristics such as income, personal risk attitudes, stability of employment, and types of insurance coverages held.

- *Protection.*   Design a program of insurance to provide protection against insurable risks and related losses. Coverage provided through public programs such as Social Security as well as group insurance offered as an employee benefit should be considered.

- *Accumulation or investment.*   Build up capital for future significant financial needs. This objective differs from saving in that a specific financial goal and plan to achieve the goal are formally established.

- *Financial independence at retirement.*   Be able to support oneself, until death, upon retiring. This objective is an important example of the accumulation or investment objective. Social Security and benefits paid by employers should be considered.

- *Estate planning.*   Preserve and distribute wealth after the estate owner dies. This is a complex area of financial planning. Writing a will is the most fundamental act in estate planning. Another important consideration may be the avoidance or minimization of estate taxes.[5]

Not only do objectives vary from person to person, but they also change during the course of one's life. For example, a young, single adult might be most concerned with building a special purpose fund to finance the purchase of a new car. On the other hand, a fifty-year-old couple with an "empty nest" might place the highest priority on a retirement fund. The **life-cycle concept** is illustrated in Exhibit 1-6.

Exhibit 1 6
Role of Life-Cycle Stages in Planning Goals

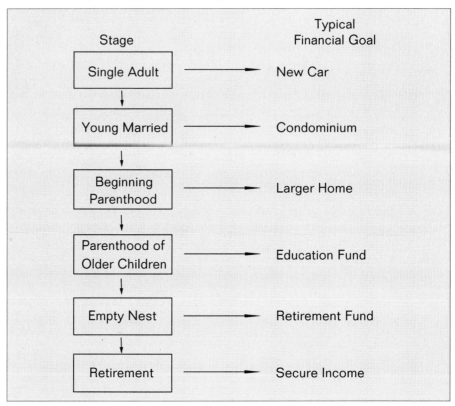

Reprinted with permission from Mark R. Greene and Robert R. Dince, *Personal Financial Management*, Southwestern Publishing Company, 1983, p. 5.

The categories of objectives listed above can also represent areas of loss exposures faced by individuals and families. For example, objectives that deal with standard of living help to establish the financial needs of an individual or family to support its lifestyle. If these objectives cannot be met, possibly because of the death of the primary wage earner, an individual or family cannot live as fully as it desires. The individual or family should make arrangements to deal with the financial consequences of the loss should it occur.

Several financial planning methods are available to help individuals or families meet their financial objectives. Insurance and noninsurance transfers are two financial planning devices. Both of these techniques put at least part of the financial burden of a loss on another entity and help individuals or families meet their financial objectives. Retention is also a financial planning tool and different kinds of retention—including capital appreciation, tax minimization, and estate planning—can be used to meet different financial objectives.

Capital Accumulation

In the context of personal financial planning, the term **capital** refers to assets or worth. When capital is *accumulated*, the net worth of an individual or family increases. Capital can accumulate when people receive gifts or inheritances or when families spend less than their disposable income—in other words, save or invest the remainder. Many people have various semiautomatic plans, such as a pension plan or an employer-sponsored savings plan, that help them both save and invest.

The words "saving" and "investing" often are used interchangeably, but they are not entirely synonymous. **Saving** implies the preservation of funds for use in the future; to save is not to spend. **Investing** means using funds to earn a positive return, thereby increasing the amount of funds held.

Many people accumulate capital in various forms to meet certain contingencies.

- A general *emergency fund* may be established to cover the cost of loss exposures such as a leaky roof that needs to be repaired; the death of a relative, which requires a sudden trip to a distant location; or the replacement of an auto that has no collision insurance.

- A *special purpose fund* may be required to meet specific goals such as purchasing a security door for the garage or having a fence installed around the property.

- An *education fund* may be established to meet children's college expenses.

- A *general investment fund* may be provided as an added measure of security in event of a loss and may also provide an inheritance for one's children or other heirs.
- A *retirement fund* may be established that will pay for living expenses during retirement after the regular flow of earned income ceases.

Thus, capital accumulation can be used to pay for losses when exposures are retained.

Tax Minimization

Tax minimization, the process of keeping tax payments as low as possible, is closely related to capital accumulation. Every dollar paid to the government in taxes is a dollar that cannot be accumulated or consumed by the taxpayer. Two principal means of minimizing taxes exist.

Tax evasion, an illegal action to lower or avoid one's taxes, is a crime. **Tax avoidance**, the use of legal methods to reduce or eliminate one's taxes, is an important part of good financial planning. Tax avoidance is entirely legitimate. In fact, one reason for some provisions in the tax law is to provide tax incentives so that individuals will behave in a specific manner. For example, individuals are allowed to deduct mortgage interest from their gross income for calculating federal income tax. This encourages individuals to buy real estate, thus investing in communities and paying community taxes.

Tax considerations should not outweigh other important objectives. Anything that involves tax savings usually also requires taxpayers to give up some flexibility or control or to forgo some other advantage. For example, many people invest in municipal bonds because they are tax exempt, but this advantage may be offset since municipal bonds pay a lower yield than corporate bonds. Tax laws change, too, and a device that minimizes taxes in the current year might have the opposite effect in subsequent years.

Estate Planning

Estate planning is the process of making arrangements for the orderly transfer of property, during life or at death, from one person to another person (or persons) in anticipation of death. A specialized aspect of overall financial planning, estate planning concentrates on techniques that provide for the orderly and efficient transfer of assets to heirs and survivors. Tax minimization is an important goal of estate planning, and tax planning can make a considerable difference in the size of one's estate, which passes to heirs.

The Personal Financial Planning Process

The **financial planning process** involves the following steps:

1. Gathering information and analyzing the current situation
2. Establishing future financial objectives
3. Identifying alternative courses of action to achieve objectives
4. Developing and implementing a plan that meets the objectives without unacceptable tradeoffs
5. Periodically reviewing the plan and revising it when necessary

It is necessary to accumulate information regarding the current financial standing of an individual or family before any financial plans are made. The types of information needed are as follows:

*   Spouse, dependents, and other family commitments
*   Age, condition of health, and related factors
*   Debts and other liabilities
*   Status under the Social Security program
*   Current employee benefits and available options
*   Current individual insurance
*   Current investments
*   Past and current retirement plans and available options
*   Current and projected income
*   Essential short-term and long-term financial needs
*   Provisions of current will and other estate plans

Much of this information is also necessary for risk management planning, but where the emphasis of risk management is on the entire impact of the loss exposure and how to treat it, financial planning considers the financial impact of the loss exposure and how to prevent financial shortages.

Several sources of information are available to individuals and families. Financial planning questionnaires, similar to the risk management question-naires previously discussed and represented in Exhibit 1-2, help to identify financial facts. Many financial planning questionnaires are oriented toward single-purpose financial planning, such as estate planning questionnaires or investment questionnaires and checklists. Personal financial statements can also provide financial information. Individuals and families file tax returns annually. Bank and investment account statements, paycheck stubs, credit card statements, and loan balances also provide financial information about individuals and families.

Computer programs are available as tools for information gathering and analysis. Several consumer-oriented software packages handle many aspects of personal financial planning, including budgeting, preparing personal financial statements, maintaining tax records, estimating tax payments, and analyzing investments.

Once the present financial situation is known, financial objectives can be set. It is important to ascertain the current situation so that the objectives can focus on the future and do not include goals that have already been met or are impossible to meet. For example, if an individual is already involved in a pension plan that will more than adequately meet his or her retirement needs, it may be more prudent to focus on maintaining the current standard of living than to save for retirement.

With the objectives identified, alternative financial treatments can be formulated and analyzed to develop the best financial plan for the individual or family. The financial plan, just as the risk management plan, must be monitored to make sure that it is achieving the goals it was designed to meet. If not, or if alternatives or other objectives arise, the financial plan should be revised to better deal with the new circumstances.

Risk Managers and Financial Planners for Individuals and Families

In a general sense, personal risk management planning is done by every person who, among other things, purchases insurance, saves for retirement, maintains personal property in proper working order, and installs loss control devices such as security systems and smoke detectors. Personal financial planning is also done by everyone who earns, spends, saves, owns, manages, marries, buys, sells, gives, preserves, inherits, or retires. Everyone is a risk manager of his or her own loss exposures and a financial planner of his or her own finances, although to varying degrees of planning and managing.

Some people are known as **risk managers** or **risk management consultants**, because their occupations involve providing risk management advice and services to others. These professionals work mainly with commercial or business concerns and are generally not concerned with individuals and families. Most personal risk management that is carried out on behalf of an individual or family is performed by a personal financial planner or financial planning consultant.

The business of **financial planners** or **financial planning consultants** involves providing financial planning advice and services to others. Financial planners fall into two broad categories:

- **Single-purpose financial planners** are specialists who function primarily as one of the following:

- Insurance specialists
- Investment specialists
- Tax planners
- Accountants
- Bankers and trust officers
- **Comprehensive financial planners** are generalists who work with a client to do the following:
  - Help set objectives and establish priorities
  - Coordinate the development, implementation, and monitoring of a financial plan—drawing on the resources of specialized, single-purpose financial planners where appropriate.

Summary

Personal risk management involves the development and implementation of total, coordinated plans for achieving the goals of an individual or family. This chapter has introduced the techniques of personal risk management; the personal financial planning process; and the loss exposures that face most individuals and families and how they are treated through risk management and financial planning.

A good risk management plan should address the loss exposures that face almost all individuals and families. In so doing, it should provide the means for controlling the loss exposures and financing losses so that they will not drain the assets of a person or family. The exposures discussed in this chapter include property loss exposures, liability loss exposures, illness and injury loss exposures, the death exposure, the retirement exposure, and the unemployment exposure.

The costs of loss exposures facing an individual or family can be substantial. The importance of good risk management should not be underestimated. The rest of the text deals more specifically with personal risk management techniques, with the focus on personal insurance.

Chapter Notes

1. James J. Lorimer, et al., *The Legal Environment of Insurance*, vol. 2, 4th ed. (Malvern, PA: American Institute for Property and Liability Underwriters, 1993), p. 246.
2. Deborah Chollet, "Health Insurance," a presentation at Understanding Insur-

ance: A Seminar for Legislators, sponsored by the Griffith Foundation for Insurance Education and the National Council of Insurance Legislators, February 6, 1993, Columbus, OH.

3. Many term life insurance policies allow insureds to change their policies to more permanent forms of life insurance (such as whole life insurance) at some point during the term life policies' periods of coverage without proving they still meet the insurer's underwriting requirements. Thus the twenty-year-old could buy a convertible term policy now and change to a permanent policy later, whether or not he or she still meets the insurer's underwriting requirements.

4. *1993 Life Insurance Fact Book Update* (Washington, DC: American Council of Life Insurance, 1993), p. 16.

5. Stephan R. Leimburg, Martin J. Satinsky, and Robert T. LeClair, *The Tools and Techniques of Financial Planning*, 2d ed. (Cincinnati, OH: The National Underwriter Co., 1987), pp. 76-77.

Chapter 2

Homeowners Property Insurance

This chapter describes the treatment of property loss exposures, other than auto-related exposures, faced by individuals and families. Most individuals and families treat these exposures in large part by purchasing homeowners insurance. Homeowners insurance provides coverage for both property and liability loss exposures. This chapter discusses the property coverages, and Chapter 3 deals with the liability coverages.

In some instances, other insurance policies may be used instead of or as a supplement to homeowners coverage. For example, other insurance policies may be needed to cover watercraft, dwellings ineligible for homeowners insurance, and highly valued or rare articles. These additions and alternatives to the homeowners policy are mentioned in this chapter and described in Chapters 3 and 6.

In other instances, some property loss exposures are not covered by homeowners insurance or other property insurance. For example, homeowners policies generally do not cover the loss of an insured's dog, and, unless the pet is also an investment—such as a show dog—other insurance is not typically available either. Alternative risk treatments are identified for certain exposures that are difficult to insure or are excluded from coverage.

Introduction to Homeowners Insurance Policies

Homeowners insurance is the primary source of insurance on dwellings, contents, and other personal property. Homeowners policies are **package policies**, since they provide both property coverage and liability coverage. They are the result of a long development process for personal and private residential property insurance.

The Development of Homeowners Policies

The first American fire insurance policies began appearing in the middle 1700s. It was years before coverage against causes of loss other than fire was offered by property insurers. When additional causes of loss were to be covered, supplemental contracts were purchased from other insurers.

In the mid-1940s, policies were developed that offered residential property owners a combination of coverages on one form that had to be attached to a fire policy. The *dwelling and contents form* covered the dwelling and personal property.

It was not until 1950 that an independent policy combined personal liability coverage with packaged property coverages. This one policy covered most types of personal property and private residences, as well as provided owners of the property with liability insurance. By 1958, a standard homeowners policy program had been developed. Homeowners were finally able to buy standard homeowners policies from any number of insurers. The homeowners program has been revised several times since 1958.

The Insurance Services Office (ISO) and the American Association of Insurance Services (AAIS) develop and *file* (submit policies to insurance departments for notice and approval, depending on state regulations) policies, including homeowners policies, for their member insurance companies. Individual insurance companies also may independently develop and file their homeowners, and other, policies. The homeowners programs offered by the advisory organizations and independent insurers are similar in content and organization, but actual coverages may vary.

This chapter discusses the property coverages available under the ISO homeowners program. While ISO homeowners policies were available before 1976, the current ISO homeowners policies are based on its Homeowners 76 Policy Program. These 1976 policies simplified the language of homeowners policies to make them easier to read and understand by the average policyholder. The ISO homeowners policies have since been revised in 1984 and 1991. This chapter and Chapter 3 analyze the 1991 ISO homeowners policies.

Overview of the ISO Homeowners Program

The ISO homeowners program is available to individuals and families that own or rent and live in a private residence, such as a house, an apartment, or a condominium. Personal liability insurance and medical expense coverage are also included in the homeowners policy; these coverages will be discussed in Chapter 3. There are different forms of homeowners coverage to meet an individual's or family's situation, and, as with any insurance policy, there are certain eligibility requirements.

Homeowners Eligibility

In order to qualify for a homeowners policy, an individual or family must reside in a dwelling used principally for residential purposes. The individual or family may own the property, or may rent it, but must live at the residence.

Homeowners policies allow limited property coverage for **incidental occupancy** (use of the residential premises for other than residential purposes, such as a home office or studio) as long as it meets two requirements. The premises must (1) be occupied principally as a dwelling and (2) not be used for any business purpose other than the incidental occupancy. For example, Keith, a professional portrait artist, uses the extra bedroom of his apartment as his painting studio. He is able to insure his property under a homeowners policy because the studio is incidental to his use of the apartment as a residence.

Three primary types of situations are eligible for coverage under the ISO homeowners program:

1. *Owner-occupants of private homes*—Individuals and families who own the private home in which they reside. These homes typically are single family houses, but two-family houses (and in some state three- and four-family houses) may also be eligible. Prospective owner-occupants can generally purchase a homeowners policy for a residence under construction.

   Generally, state insurance regulations require residences to meet certain construction specifications to be eligible for coverage. The residence must not be a mobile home, and most states also establish size and minimum value requirements. Dwelling and mobilehome policies deal with residences that are not eligible for homeowners policies. These policies are discussed in Chapter 6.

2. *Tenants of residential premises*—Individuals and families who rent or lease the premises where they reside. The residence may be an apartment, a house (either a single-family house or other), a mobile home, a trailer home, a house trailer, or a condominium unit.

3. *Owner-occupants of private condominium units*—Individuals and families who own the private condominium unit in which they live.

In some cases, the owner-occupant or tenant-occupant may still be eligible for a homeowners policy even if renting out part of the residence to others for residential purposes. If the residence premises is a house (single-family to four-family) occupied by an owner or a tenant, the premises is still eligible for coverage with up to two roomers or boarders per family living there. In situations involving tenants of apartments or owner-occupants of condominiums, up to one additional family or two roomers or boarders are allowed.

Homeowners policies can also be used in situations involving long-term installment purchase contracts and life estates. Under a *long-term installment contract* or a *land contract*, the occupant of the home is buying the dwelling by making periodic payments to the seller. The seller retains the title until the contract has been fulfilled. In other words, the seller holds a mortgage on the property. A homeowners policy can be used to insure both the buyer's and the seller's interests in the residence.

In a *life estate*, someone is allowed to reside on a premises for a period of time ending with the death of the individual upon whose life the agreement is based. For example, a life estate may be arranged whereby the occupant is living in the residence at the direction of the previous owner's will and last testament and has the right to live on the premises until he or she also dies. A homeowners policy can be used in this situation to protect the interests of the occupant and the estate in the property.

Different Policy Forms

All homeowners policies are package policies combining property and liability coverage. Essentially the same liability coverage is provided in each of the several homeowners forms. All forms also cover loss of use resulting from damage to insured property and provide similar additional coverages, such as debris removal and fire department service charge. The differences among the forms relate primarily to the property coverage on the dwelling, other structures, and personal property of the insured.

The ISO homeowners program offers six homeowners policies:

- **HO 00 01, Homeowners 1 Basic Form (HO-1)**—Provides limited coverage on buildings and personal property for owner-occupants of homes. It is seldom used because of its relatively narrow coverage and has been withdrawn in many states.

- **HO 00 02, Homeowners 2 Broad Form (HO-2)**—Provides coverage on buildings and personal property for owner-occupants of homes for a range of specifically named perils. An HO-2 is similar to an HO-1, but it provides coverage against more causes of loss.

- **HO 00 03, Homeowners 3 Special Form (HO-3)**—Designed for owner-occupants of homes. It provides coverage on buildings for all causes of loss not otherwise excluded and coverage on personal property for the same perils named in form HO-2.

- **HO 00 04, Homeowners 4 Contents Broad Form (HO-4)**—Designed for tenants, this form provides coverage on the personal property of the tenant-occupant of a residence for the same causes of loss covered in an HO-2.

- **HO 00 06, Homeowners 6 Unit-Owners Form (HO-6)**—Designed for condominium and cooperative unit owners, this form provides coverage on the personal property of the condominium owner-occupant, as well as for certain building items in which the unit owner may have an insurable interest. The policy covers the same specifically named perils as covered by form HO-2.

- **HO 00 08, Homeowners 8 Modified Form (HO-8)**   Provides package coverage to the owner-occupants of homes that do not meet all the eligibility requirements applicable to other homeowners forms. An HO-8 covers the same causes of loss as an HO-1, with some modification, on buildings and personal property of owner-occupants of private homes. The HO-8 is particularly well-suited for older residences whose market value is considerably less than the cost to rebuild them.

Homeowners Policy Format

Each homeowners policy contains three preliminary sections and two coverage sections. The following are the preliminary sections:

- The **declarations** page that contains the policy number, period of coverage, insured's name and address, agent's name, location of insured premises if different from the insured's address as noted, mortgagee (if any), limits that apply to the coverages, any deductible amounts, and premium amount.

- The **general agreement** that serves as a preface to the policy as a whole and makes the insurer's obligations contingent upon the insured's payment of premium and compliance with the policy provisions.

- The **definitions** section that consists of two parts. The first part explains that, throughout the policy, "you" and "your" refer to the named insured, as shown in the declarations, and that person's spouse if resident of the same household; and "we," "us," and "our" refer to the insurance company. The second part lists in alphabetical order certain commonly used terms and their definitions. The terms defined include "property damage," "insured location," and "residence premises."

The declarations page, shown in Exhibit 2-1, can be used with any of the six homeowners policies available through ISO. The general agreement and the definitions are similar for each of the homeowners policies.

The two coverage sections and their component coverages are listed on the declarations page in Exhibit 2-1. Section I deals with property loss exposures and consists of four major coverages:

- Coverage A—Dwelling
- Coverage B—Other Structures
- Coverage C—Personal Property
- Coverage D—Loss of Use

HO-1, HO-2, HO-3, and HO-8 policies have each of these four coverages. An HO-4 policy does not provide property coverage on the dwelling and other structures since the insured does not own this property. Under an HO-6 policy, coverage for other structures is included in Coverage A, and thus there is no Coverage B in an HO-6 policy. These coverages are discussed in greater detail later in this chapter.

Section II coverages include Coverage E—Personal Liability and Coverage F—Medical Payments to Others, and additional incidental coverages. All homeowners policies include Section II coverages. These coverages are discussed in Chapter 3.

Homeowners Section I Property Coverages

The ISO homeowners policies provide property coverage for the dwelling, other structures, personal property, and loss of use. They also cover a variety of other types of property exposures through the "Additional Coverages" portion of Section I. These coverages and the differences among the homeowners policies are discussed in the following paragraphs.

Loss covered under Section I of the homeowners policies is subject to a per occurrence deductible. The standard deductible is $250, but the amount of the deductible, which is stated on the declarations page, can be increased as requested by the insured and agreed to by the insurer. The deductible applies once per occurrence, not per property coverage. For example, Joe has the standard HO-2 policy with a $250 deductible. A fire severely damages Joe's house and its contents. The damage to the house is covered under Coverage A, and the loss to the contents is covered under Coverage C (as discussed below).

Exhibit 2-1
Homeowners Policy Declarations Page

Declarations applicable to all policy forms

Policy Number
Policy Period: 12:01 a.m. Standard time   From: To:
                at the residence premises

Named insured and mailing address

The residence premises covered by this policy is located at the above address
unless otherwise stated:

Coverage is provided where a premium or limit of liability is shown for the coverage.

	Limit of Liability	Premium
SECTION I COVERAGES		
A. Dwelling		
B. Other structures		
C. Personal property		
D. Loss of use		
SECTION II COVERAGES		
E. Personal liability: each occurrence		
F. Medical payments to others: each person		

Total premium for endorsements listed below

Policy Total

Forms and endorsements made part of this policy:

Number	Edition Date	Title	Premium

[Special State Provisions: South Carolina: Valuation Clause (Cov.A) $
                            Minnesota Insurable Value (Cov.A) $
                            New York: Coinsurance Clause Applies ___Yes___No]

DEDUCTIBLE - Section I: $
In case of a loss under Section I, we cover only that part of the loss over the deductible stated.
Section II: Other insured locations:

[Mortgagee/Lienholder (Name and address)]

Countersignature of agent/date   Signature/title - company officer

Ed.4/84

The deductible applies *once* to all covered loss caused by the fire. It does *not* apply *separately* to the damage to the house and also to the contents.

For the purposes of Section I property coverages, the definition of **insured** includes the following:

1. The person named in the declarations as the insured
2. Relatives who reside in the named insured's household
3. Other persons under the age of twenty-one and in the care of the people described in item 1 or 2

This definition is the same for all the homeowners forms.

Coverage A—Dwelling

Exhibit 2 2 provides examples of the policy clauses that establish the property covered under Coverage A for an HO-3 and an HO-6 policy. (The clause included in an HO-1, HO-2, or HO-8 policy is essentially the same as that for the HO-3.) The major property coverage for the forms insuring owner-occupants (HO-1, HO-2, HO-3, and HO-8) is protection for the one- or two-family dwelling used as a private residence and described in the policy declarations. Included as part of the dwelling is any structure attached to it, such as a garage or tool shed. A structure attached to the main part of the dwelling by only a fence, utility line, or similar connection is not considered part of the dwelling, but a separate structure subject to Coverage B.

The definition of "residence premises" is important in determining the extent of coverage available under Coverage A. According to the policy definitions, the **residence premises** is the place where the insured resides as identified in the policy declarations. A "residence premises" may include any of the following:

1. A one-family dwelling, other structures, and grounds
2. One unit of a two-family dwelling and its other structures and grounds
3. A part of any other building

Coverage is provided for two other classes of property. Specifically covered are materials and supplies located on or next to the "residence premises" for use in the construction, alteration, or repair of the dwelling or other structures. By implication, fixtures attached to the dwelling and considered part of the realty are covered as part of the dwelling. Examples of such fixtures include built-in appliances, plumbing and heating systems, and electrical wiring.

The policy specifically excludes coverage for land. If land on which the house sits is somehow damaged by an insured peril, such as a volcanic eruption, the insurer is under no obligation to replace or restore the land.

Exhibit 2-2
Property Covered Under Coverage A—Dwelling

HO-3 COVERAGE A—Dwelling

We cover:

1. The dwelling on the "residence premises" shown in the Declarations, including structures attached to the dwelling; and

2. Materials and supplies located on or next to the "residence premises" used to construct, alter or repair the dwelling or other structures on the "residence premises."

This coverage does not apply to land, including land on which the dwelling is located.

HO-6 COVERAGE A—Dwelling

We cover:

1. The alterations, appliances, fixtures and improvements which are part of the building contained within the "residence premises";

2. Items of real property which pertain exclusively to the "residence premises";

3. Property which is your insurance responsibility under a corporation or association of property owners agreement; or

4. Structures owned solely by you, other than the "residence premises," at the location of the "residence premises."

This coverage does not apply to land, including land on which the "residence premises," real property or structures are located.

We do not cover:

1. Structures used in whole or in part for "business" purposes; or

2. Structures rented or held for rental to any person not a tenant of the "residence premises," unless used solely as a private garage.

Coverage on the dwelling is different for owner-occupants of condominium units and cooperative apartments. These individuals and families are insured under an HO-6. As can be seen in Exhibit 2-2, this policy provides the unit owner with coverage for alterations, appliances, fixtures, and improvements made a part of the building within the unit. Other structures at the location of the condominium unit, other than the unit itself, are also covered under Coverage A of the HO-6 if they are owned solely by an insured or if an insured has accepted insurance responsibility for them under a contract with the cooperative or condominium association. Thus a condominium unit owner who owns a detached shed would find coverage under Coverage A—Dwelling, whereas an owner-occupant of a family home would find coverage for a detached shed in Coverage B—Other Structures.

Tenants do not own the dwelling in which they reside; thus the HO-4 does not provide Coverage A. Tenants may, however, have a use interest in fixtures, improvements, additions, and alterations installed in the dwelling at their own expense. Accordingly, form HO-4 covers building additions and alterations in its Additional Coverages.

The property covered under Coverage A—Dwelling is not subject to any minimum values in an HO-1, HO-2, HO-3, or HO-8. The decision to insure a privately owned and occupied residence, and for how much, is left to the insurer, subject to any state requirements for minimum standards of property value. For an HO-6, an owner-occupant of a private residential condominium or a cooperative apartment must insure property under Coverage A for at least $1,000. Higher limits are available upon request for an additional premium. These limits are summarized in Exhibit 2-3.

Exhibit 2-3
Standard Minimum Coverages and Limits for ISO Homeowners Policies

COVERAGES	HO-1	HO-2	HO-3	HO-4	HO-6	HO-8
A—Dwelling	no minimum	no minimum	no minimum	not covered	$1,000, higher optional	no minimum
B—Other Structures	10% of dwelling limit	same as HO-1	same as HO-1	additional coverage	covered in A	same as HO-1
C—Personal Property [1,2]	50% of dwelling limit	same as HO-1	same as HO-1	no minimum	no minimum	same as HO-1
D—Loss of Use	10% of dwelling limit	20% of dwelling limit	same as HO-2	20% of personal property limit	40% of personal property limit	same as HO-1

1. If personal property is usually located at another residence, it is subject to a limit of 10 percent of the limit on Coverage C or $1,000, whichever is greater.
2. Special limits apply to certain types of property.

Coverage B—Other Structures

Exhibit 2-4 contains an example of the clause describing the property covered under Coverage B—Other Structures. It is from an HO-3 policy, but the clauses in HO-1, HO-2, and HO-8 forms are similar. The tenants and unit-owners forms do not include Coverage B.

Covered as separate items under the HO-1, HO-2, HO-3, and HO-8 home-owners forms are structures on the residence premises (1) separated from the dwelling by a clear space or (2) connected to the dwelling by a fence, wall, wire, or other form of connection, but not otherwise attached. Examples of other structures include a detached garage or tool shed, fences, driveways, sidewalks, patios, and piers.

Exhibit 2-4
Property Covered Under Coverage B—Other Structures

COVERAGE B—Other Structures

We cover other structures on the "residence premises" set apart from the dwelling by clear space. This includes structures connected to the dwelling by only a fence, utility line, or similar connection.

This coverage does not apply to land, including land on which the other structures are located.

We do not cover other structures:

1. Used in whole or in part for "business"; or

2. Rented or held for rental to any person not a tenant of the dwelling, unless used solely as a private garage.

The limit of liability for this coverage will not be more than 10% of the limit of liability that applies to Coverage A. Use of this coverage does not reduce the Coverage A limit of liability.

In two situations, other structures are not insured under the policy. If a structure is used partially or completely for business purposes, or if it is leased or rented out, it is not covered. The only exceptions to this exclusion are (1) any structure rented or leased to a tenant of the described dwelling for other than business purposes, or (2) a structure rented for use solely as a private garage.

If the named insured rents or leases other structures to a person who is not a tenant of the described dwelling, protection for this situation may be obtained by the homeowner for an additional cost by using the *structures rented to others endorsement*. This endorsement adds coverage for a structure on the residence premises, such as a garage apartment or a small cottage, for use only as a private residence. The same garage apartment or cottage, rented to an artist as a studio, would not be covered.

The amount of coverage provided for other structures under forms HO-1,

HO-2, HO-3, and HO-8 is limited to 10 percent of the amount of insurance on the dwelling. This coverage is in addition to Coverage A, not a part of it. For example, if Beth insures her dwelling for $100,000, she also has coverage for $10,000 on other structures. Because the 10 percent limit is provided in the Coverage B agreement, it is not always shown as a dollar limit on the declarations page.

A named insured who owns other structures valued at more than 10 percent of the dwelling coverage might want to purchase additional protection. The *other structures endorsement* can be used to purchase additional, specific coverage. This endorsement provides coverage *in excess of* the 10 percent limit—the coverage of the endorsement will apply to a loss after the homeowners policy has covered the loss up to the Coverage B limit, as needed.

For example, if John purchases $60,000 of coverage on a dwelling under an HO-3, he has $6,000 of protection on other structures. If the other structures are valued at $9,000, he could use the other structures endorsement to provide the needed additional $3,000 of protection. If a loss occurs, the endorsement will provide coverage only if the loss exceeds the $6,000 limit that exists under Coverage B of John's HO-3.

Coverage C—Personal Property

Exhibit 2-5 shows the Coverage C—Personal Property clause that describes the property covered under the homeowners policies. This clause is common to all the forms, including the HO-4 and the HO-6.

Exhibit 2-5
Property Covered Under Coverage C—Personal Property

COVERAGE C—Personal Property

We cover personal property owned or used by an "insured" while it is anywhere in the world. At your request, we will cover personal property owned by:

1. Others while the property is on the part of the "residence premises" occupied by an "insured";

2. A guest or a "residence employee," while the property is in any residence occupied by an "insured."

Our limit of liability for personal property usually located at an "insured's" residence, other than the "residence premises," is 10% of the limit of liability for Coverage C, or $1000, whichever is greater. Personal property in a newly acquired principal residence is not subject to this limitation for the 30 days from the time you begin to move the property there.

Most personal property owned or used by an insured is covered anywhere in the world. Personal property includes not only what is ordinarily contained within a dwelling—such as furniture, appliances, and clothing—but also property stored in the garage, in other structures, or outdoors. A lawn mower and other tools for maintaining the premises, a child's tricycle left in the driveway, and luggage accompanying an insured on a trip to China are all personal property.

At the option of the insured, personal property owned by a guest or residence employee is covered when the property is at any residence occupied by any insured. For example, Elliott could request that his insurer—after a loss—cover his mother-in-law's property when she is his guest at his home, a summer cottage, or a motel or hotel. Personal property owned by persons other than guests and residence employees also is covered, but only when their property is on the part of the "residence premises" occupied by the insured. An example of covered property could include a friend's personal property temporarily stored in the insured's attic until the friend moves into a new apartment.

For HO-1, HO-2, HO-3, or HO-8 policies, the limit of coverage for personal property is 50 percent of the amount of insurance on the dwelling. Like the limit on Coverage B, the amount of coverage offered under Coverage C is in addition to the amounts of coverage under Coverage A and Coverage B; it is not included in these limits. Since the amount of coverage on personal property is determined by the amount of coverage on the dwelling, the limit for Coverage C may not be, but usually is, shown on the declarations page.

The limit for personal property coverage under an HO-4 or an HO-6 is determined by the insurer and the insured. No minimum standard value applies in these homeowners policies. The insurer may have its own minimum qualifications, and these standards may be subject to state requirements.

Under all forms except an HO-8, personal property *usually located* at any residence other than the residence premises is subject to a maximum of 10 percent of Coverage C or $1,000, whichever is greater. (The HO-8 limits the amount of coverage on *all* property off-premises to 10 percent of the Coverage C limit or $1,000, whichever is greater.) "Usually located" connotes a location with some degree of permanency, such as an undeclared secondary residence, like a cabin, where furniture and other property are kept. This limitation does not apply to a temporary residence—such as a student's dormitory room or a traveler's hotel room. Furthermore, the type of personal property subject to the limitation is that which is *usually* located at the other residence, and not property taken to those locations for the period of occupancy. The purpose of the limitation is to prevent the insured from using one homeowners policy to insure in full the contents of two major residences. This limit can be increased, for an additional premium, with the *increased limit on personal property in other residences endorsement.*

If the insured should move to a new principal residence, full coverage applies to personal property for thirty days after the move begins. This means that the insured's personal property is covered for the insured perils while the property is in transit, as well as at the new principal residence. After the thirty-day period, the newly acquired residence must be specifically declared if the full protection of the homeowners policy is desired.

Special Limits on Personal Property

The homeowners forms contain special limits on certain kinds of personal property. The following limitations apply under each of the homeowners policies, except an HO-8, for each loss:

1. Money, bank notes, bullion, gold other than goldware, silver other than silverware, platinum, coins, and medals are subject to a $200 limit.

2. Securities, accounts, deeds, evidences of debt, letters of credit, notes other than bank notes, manuscripts, personal records, passports, tickets, and stamps are subject to a limit of $1,000, regardless of whether printed on paper or stored on computer disks.

3. Watercraft—including outboard motors, furnishings, equipment, and trailers—are subject to a limit of $1,000.

4. Any trailer not used with watercraft, such as a utility or camping trailer, is subject to a limit of $1,000.

5. The following types of property are subject to limits for only loss by theft:

   a. Jewelry, watches, furs, and precious and semiprecious stones are subject to a limit of $1,000.

   b. Firearms of any type are limited to $2,000.

   c. Silver and silver-plated ware, gold and gold-plated ware, and pewterware are limited to $2,500.

6. Property used at any time, in any manner, for any business purpose is subject to a limit of $2,500 on premises and $250 off premises. This limit does not apply to the electronic apparatus discussed below in item 7.

7. Electronic apparatus, such as a citizens' band radio or a tape deck that can be plugged into the cigarette lighter, while in or upon a motor vehicle or other motorized land conveyance, if it can be powered by the electrical system of, or another source of power within, the vehicle or conveyance, is subject to a limit of $1,000. The limit includes accessories, antennas,

tapes, wires, records, discs, or other media for use with this electronic apparatus. If the apparatus is not in or upon the vehicle or conveyance, it is subject to the $1,000 limit only if it is away from the residence premises and is used at any time or in any manner for business purposes.

Exhibit 2-6 illustrates how these limitations function. Susan's house is burglarized, and several items are stolen. They are listed, along with their value, in Exhibit 2-6. Since Susan has an HO-2, her insurer will provide only limited coverage for most of these items. The amount paid by the insurer and the amount of the loss that Susan will be forced to retain are calculated. Due to the special limits, the insurer is responsible for $2,200 of the $4,600 loss. Susan must retain the remaining loss of $2,400.

An HO-8 carries the same limits as those listed, with the exception of the special theft limits in item 5. HO-8, as detailed later, provides limited coverage for theft, and the limits placed on jewelry, firearms, silver and goldware, and the like, are not necessary.

Exhibit 2-6
Hypothetical Theft Loss—Items Taken and Amount Paid

	Loss	Amount Paid by Insurer	Amount Retained by Insured
Susan's home is burglarized. The list and value of the items taken, the amount paid by the homeowners insurer, and the amount retained by Susan are shown below.			
Money	$ 400	$ 200	$ 200
Coin collection	2,000	(no additional coverage since money and coins are in the same category)	2,000
Jewelry	800	800	0
Fur coat	400	200 (balance of $1,000 limit on jewelry and furs)	200
Silverware	1,000	1,000	0
Total	$4,600†	$2,200	$2,400

†Any deductible in the policy will be subtracted from the total loss.

Whenever an insured owns personal property subject to these limitations, special care must be taken to insure these items as desired. This extra coverage can be added to the homeowners policy by endorsement or purchased under a separate policy. The *Coverage C increased special limits of liability endorsement* allows the insured to increase the limits for property included in items 1, 2, 5, or 7. The coverage limit on business personal property can be increased for an additional premium with an *increased limits on business personal property endorsement*. Another common form of coverage, the *scheduled personal property endorsement*, allows the insured to list specific pieces of property at their dollar value; it is discussed in Chapter 3.

Personal Property Not Covered

The homeowners policies do not cover all types of personal property. Property that cannot be easily valued or that is generally insured under other forms of coverage are typically excluded from coverage under the homeowners policies. The following paragraphs identify the types of property excluded by all the homeowners forms and briefly explain why coverage is not provided.

Separately Described and Insured Property

Property that is separately described and specifically insured on another policy or on an endorsement attached to the homeowners policy is not covered by the homeowners, not even on an excess basis. For example, Rita owns a $10,000 diamond necklace that is subject to the $1,000 special limit for loss by theft under her homeowners policy. Therefore, she purchases $9,000 of insurance that specifically covers theft of her $10,000 diamond necklace. However, her homeowners policy, due to the exclusion, will *not* help pay for the theft of her diamond necklace once the additional policy is in effect. If her necklace is stolen, Rita will collect only $9,000 from the insurer of the policy specifically covering the necklace for theft. Therefore, to cover the entire cost of the necklace, Rita would have to purchase $10,000 of insurance that specifically covers her diamond necklace.

The coverages provided under the homeowners policy for certain types of personal property are meant to provide protection when exposures are minimal. When exposures to loss exceed the protection provided by the homeowners policy, specific coverage should be purchased to cover the exposure(s) fully.

Animals, Birds, and Fish

Pets are excluded because they are difficult to value. When animals, birds, and fish are of a special pedigree, rare specimen, or otherwise of special value to their owners, specialized coverages are available for insuring them.

Motorized Land Vehicles

While most motorized land vehicles are not covered, the policy does cover vehicles such as rider lawn mowers, unlicensed autos used on the insured's estate, and electric wheelchairs. Other motorized land vehicles are insured under other forms of coverage—such as auto and recreational vehicle policies.

Equipment and electronic apparatus, and their accessories, that are powered only by the electrical system of a motorized land vehicle, may also be excluded while in or upon a vehicle. If these types of items are permanently installed in the dashboard or console of a motor vehicle, they are generally covered under the physical damage insurance of a personal auto policy. If not permanently installed, these types of property are subject to the special limit for electronic apparatus, and may be eligible for endorsements and policies that will be discussed in later chapters.

The purpose of this exclusion is to prevent overlapping coverage with auto and other policies and to require separate coverage for specialized sound equipment in motor vehicles. The loss exposure differs when such equipment is in a motor vehicle rather than on the "residence premises." These devices are covered by the homeowners policy when they are removed from the auto for safekeeping.

Aircraft and Parts

Aircraft and their parts are excluded property under the homeowners policy, because they should be covered under a separate aircraft policy. This exclusion does not apply to model aircraft.

Property of Roomers, Boarders, and Other Tenants

No coverage exists for loss to property of roomers, boarders, or other tenants. This exclusion encourages these people to obtain their own insurance on their personal property and ensures that the insurer does not assume additional unanticipated loss exposures. The property of roomers or boarders related to the insured—such as when a cousin rents a room—may, however, be covered at the insured's option.

Property in Regularly Rented Apartments

Any furniture, appliances, and other personal property contained in an apartment regularly rented or held for rental to others by the insured are also not covered. This is intended to exclude property in apartments rented out by the insured, not those rented to the insured. When acting as a landlord, the insured is involved in a form of business, and the personal property contained in the rental unit is business personal property that should be separately insured. The exclusion does not apply if an apartment is occasionally rented. For example, if Jan, the insured, owns a seaside apartment that she occupies for a month or so each year and rents to others for the remainder of the year, she is affected by this exclusion and her property at the apartment would be excluded. If Jan usually lives in the apartment but rents it to Bill for a month while she is away on business, her property contained in the apartment would not be excluded from coverage.

Other Business Property

The remaining types of personal property are not covered under the homeowners policy because they are kinds of business personal property:

1. Property rented or held for rental to others away from the residence premises. If Becky rents one of her typewriters to another person, that typewriter would not be covered by Becky's homeowners policy.

2. Paper records or software media, such as tapes or discs, containing business data. Since the cost of blank records, media, and prerecorded computer programs available on the retail market are covered, the effect of this exclusion is to eliminate coverage for the expense of reproducing business records.

Coverage D—Loss of Use

Under the loss of use coverages, two forms of protection are provided: (1) additional living expense and (2) fair rental value. These two coverages are provided on all homeowners policy forms.

If the dwelling described in the policy is damaged by an insured peril and becomes uninhabitable, the named insured and the insured's family will be reimbursed for additional living expense actually incurred and for fair rental value actually lost. **Additional living expense** is the cost of maintaining the insured's normal standard of living after a covered loss, which is above the insured's usual amount of expenses prior to the loss. **Fair rental value** is the amount of rent, less any discontinued expenses, that the insured would have received for the residence or any part of the residence rented to another individual for residential purposes, if the residence had not been damaged. Under either form, reimbursement is made only for the period necessary to repair or replace the damaged residence or to move to a different, permanent residence.

The following example illustrates how additional living expense coverage can aid an insured. After Sally's apartment is damaged by fire, she and her family move into temporary quarters. The repairs to the apartment take sixty days. During this time, Sally rents a duplex at a cost of $750 per month. The utilities for the duplex are listed in Exhibit 2-7. Sally has to pay $25 to have the phone installed at the duplex, and her laundry bill increases from $15 a month to $40 a month because she has to use a coin-operated laundry. All utilities in Sally's damaged apartment have been shut off, resulting in the savings listed in Exhibit 2-7. Although Sally does not have to pay rent for the apartment while she is awaiting its repair, her rent has increased from $600 per month to $750 per month. The expenses paid by the insurer are calculated in Exhibit 2-7 and amount to $325.

Exhibit 2-7
Additional Living Expense Paid by the Insurer

	Actual Expenditure While Located in Temporary Quarters (per month)	What Normal Living Expenditures Would Have Otherwise Been (per month)
Rent	$750.00	3000.00
Water	27.00	34.00
Electricity	90.00	140.00
Gas	32.00	0.00
Telephone	12.50	12.50
Laundry	40.00	15.00
Monthly total	$951.50	$801.50

Covered Costs (per month) = $951.50 – $801.50 = $150.00

Additional Living Expense Paid by the Insurer:

	Covered costs
Two months, $150.00 covered each month	$300.00
Telephone installation at duplex	25.00
Total Covered by Insurer Under Coverage D	$325.00

In the homeowners policies, fair rental value applies to situations in which the named insured suffers a loss of rent. If the named insured is renting out or is holding for rental a portion of the described dwelling or other structure on the premises, the fair rental value of the rented space is reimbursed by the insurer under this coverage. Noncontinuing expenses are excluded.[1]

For example, Seth rents a room over his unattached garage to a college student for $100 a month. Seth's garage is damaged by a fire and the room is uninhabitable for the three months it takes to repair the damage. Because the student is unable to live in the room for three months, Seth has suffered a $300 loss of fair rental value ($100 x 3). This loss will be covered by his HO-3 Coverage D.

An insured under a homeowners policy might incur additional living expenses *and* lose fair rental value as the result of the same occurrence. In such a situation, a homeowners policy Coverage D will cover both types of loss up to the policy limit. Thus, suppose the fire that damaged Seth's garage also damaged his house, making it uninhabitable. Seth moved into an apartment for the three months needed to repair his home and garage, incurring $500 of additional living expenses per month. He will receive a total of $1,800 under Coverage D—$1,500 additional living expenses ($500 x 3) plus the $300 loss of fair rental value.

Both additional living expense and fair rental value may be paid even when direct loss has not damaged the described dwelling or other structure. When access to the described residence is barred by civil authority, both coverages are applicable. However, the action taken by civil authority must be due to damage to neighboring premises caused by a peril covered by the policy.

For example, a tornado devastates a large section of a housing development where Nancy resides. Although Nancy's dwelling miraculously escapes damage, a large part of the development where she resides is cordoned off for two days by police and town officials who order that no one is to enter the area, not even the people who reside there. Since the neighboring premises were damaged by the insured peril of windstorm, Nancy's additional living expenses and any fair rental value loss would be covered.

The policy does not cover any loss or expense resulting from cancellation of any lease or agreement. For example, following extensive fire damage to an apartment building, John, the owner, decides not to rebuild and cancels all leases. Andy, an occupant of John's building who has a homeowners policy, would have protection for any additional living expenses and fair rental value losses incurred for the period it would have taken to rebuild. If Andy should need extra time beyond the covered period to locate other permanent living quarters, no additional coverage would be provided by the homeowners policy. Likewise, the higher cost of comparable permanent living quarters is not covered beyond the time it normally would have taken for John to rebuild the apartment building. The tenant of a private residence or two-family dwelling is similarly affected if the residence is not rebuilt following a loss and his or her lease is canceled.

The amount of coverage provided for additional living expense and fair rental value is a percentage of the limit for Coverage A in HO-1, HO-2, HO-3, and HO-8 policies and a percentage of the limit for Coverage C in HO-4 and HO-6 policies. The percentages are shown in Exhibit 2-3.

Additional Coverages

All the homeowners forms contain **additional coverages**, which expand the coverage. Additional coverages generally expand the types of losses covered. The amount of loss covered may be in addition to coverage limits or may be included within coverage limits. *Unless otherwise noted, each homeowners form contains the additional coverages discussed below.* The additional coverages provided by each of the homeowners policies are outlined in Exhibit 2-8.

Debris Removal

If property is damaged by an insured peril, the insurer agrees to pay the insured's reasonable expenses for removal of debris of the covered property. For example, if a garage is struck by a garbage truck, the policy will cover the costs of removing the pieces of brick, board, and glass that had been the garage door and wall. The insurer also agrees to pay the expense of removing ash, dust, or particles from volcanic eruption that has caused direct loss to a building or property contained in the building.

Generally, debris removal expense is included as part of the coverage amount applying to the damaged property. If the garage referred to above were attached to the house, the costs of debris removal fall under Coverage A. If the garage were unattached, the cost to remove the debris would be considered part of Coverage B. If, however, damage to the covered property plus the expense for removing the debris exceeds the limit on the property, the policy provides an additional 5 percent of the coverage limit toward the costs of debris removal.

The debris removal clause also contains a provision that allows up to $500 per loss to cover the removal of trees that have damaged a covered structure. The coverage applies to the named insured's trees felled by windstorm or hail. Forms HO-2, HO-3, HO-4, and HO-6 also cover the cost of removing trees felled by the weight of ice, snow, or sleet. Removal of debris is also covered if a neighbor's tree falls onto the insured's property due to any cause of loss covered under Coverage C, such as fire or explosion. In each case, the fallen tree must have damaged an insured structure.

Reasonable Repairs

The cost of reasonable repairs, made by the insured solely to protect covered property from further damage after a loss by an insured cause of loss, is covered. These repair costs are not an additional amount of insurance—they are included in the limits of the coverage applicable to the damaged property. For example, the cost of a tarpaulin placed over a fire-damaged opening in a

Exhibit 2-8

Additional Coverages and Limits Offered by Each Homeowners Policy

COVERAGES	HO-1	HO-2	HO-3	HO-4	HO-6	HO-8
Debris Removal	to 5% above coverage limit	*	*	*	*	*
Reasonable Repairs	included in limit	*	*	*	*	*
Trees, Shrubs, and Other Plants	to 5% above A's limit, max. $500 per item	*	*	*	*	to 5% above A's limit, max. $250 per item
Fire Department Service Charge	to $500	*	*	*	*	*
Property Removed	included in limit	*	*	*	*	*
Credit Card, Fund Transfer Card, Forgery, and Counterfeit Money	to $500	*	*	*	*	*
Loss Assessment	to $1,000	*	*	*	*	*
Collapse	not covered	included in limit	**	**	**	not covered
Glass and Safety Glazing	included in limit	*	*	*	*	*
Landlords Furnishings	to $2,500	*	*	not covered	not covered	not covered
Building Additions and Alterations	covered in A or B	*	*	to 10% of C's limit	covered in A	*
Ordinance or Law Coverage	to 10% of Coverage A limit	*	*	to 10% of Building Additions and Alterations limit	*	not covered

*Same as HO-1   **Same as HO-2

house's roof to reduce damage by rain would be covered under this provision subject to the available limits under Coverage A.

Trees, Shrubs, and Other Plants

Additional insurance is provided on loss to trees, shrubs, plants, and lawns on the residence premises. Coverage is limited to loss caused by fire, lightning, explosion, riot or civil commotion, aircraft, vehicles not owned or operated by a resident on the insured premises, vandalism, malicious mischief, and theft. No coverage applies to damage caused to these items by windstorm, hail, and smoke.

A limit of $500 ($250 for an HO-8 policy) exists for any one tree, shrub, or plant, but there is no special limitation applicable to lawns. The maximum limit on this additional coverage is 5 percent of the coverage limit on the dwelling. This provision does not apply to vegetation grown for business purposes, which is excluded, nor to houseplants, since they are covered as personal property. The tree, shrub, or other plant need not be replaced.

This coverage is designed to pay for the reduction in value of the trees, shrubs, plants, or lawn that has been damaged. The costs of removing the debris of such losses is covered under the additional coverage for debris removal in the event an insured structure is damaged, as discussed earlier. The following are examples that consider both of these additional coverages:

- If windstorm or hail, or the weight of ice, snow, or sleet causes a tree of the insured's to fall onto an open area in the insured's yard, the cost of removing the debris of the tree is not covered because the tree has not damaged a covered structure. Any damage to the tree is not covered because the perils named are not covered perils for trees.

- If windstorm or hail, or the weight of ice, snow, or sleet causes an insured's tree to fall onto the insured's house or other structure, the cost of removing the tree is covered up to $500 under the debris removal clause. The damage to the tree is not covered, because the perils named are not covered perils for trees.

- If any peril insured against under Coverage C causes a neighbor's tree to fall onto the insured's house or other structure, the cost of removing the debris of the tree is covered up to $500 under the debris removal clause.

- If the insured's tree is damaged by vandalism, or any other covered peril for trees, the value of the tree is covered up to $500 ($250 for an HO-8 policy), and the value of the tree plus the cost of removing debris of the tree is covered up to 5 percent above the $500 limit on the tree value, or a total of $525 ($262.50 for an HO-8 policy due to the $250 limit).

Fire Department Service Charge

When an insured uses fire-fighting services from a territory or fire protection district in which he or she does not live, the insured may have to pay a service charge. In response to this exposure, the insurer agrees to pay up to $500 of this service charge. This coverage is over and above the policy limits and is not subject to a deductible.

Property Removed

Covered property (1) while being removed from the premises when endangered by loss from an insured peril and (2) while stored at other locations for up to thirty days is covered for direct loss from any cause (even those causes normally excluded by the policy). This coverage is included in the limits of coverage that apply to the property being removed.

Credit Card, Fund Transfer Card, Forgery, and Counterfeit Money

Up to $500 in additional coverage is available for losses that result from the following:

- Theft or unauthorized use of credit cards or fund transfer cards issued or registered to any insured
- Forgery or alteration of any check or other negotiable interest
- Acceptance in good faith of United States or Canadian counterfeit currency

The coverage does not apply when credit cards or fund transfer cards are misused by a resident of the insured's household or by an individual to whom the insured has entrusted a credit card or fund transfer card. The additional coverage also excludes coverage for the following losses:

1. Losses resulting from an insured's failure to abide by the credit card or fund transfer card conditions
2. Losses arising out of business activities
3. Losses due to an insured's dishonesty

A series of acts by or involving any one person is considered one loss. For example, a babysitter steals a checkbook from an insured, and over the course of a month forges twenty checks totaling $2,000. All twenty checks are considered one occurrence by the additional coverage, and thus the insurer will cover the $500 limit and the insured retains the remaining $1,500 loss.

A series of acts can also involve the unauthorized use of credit cards. Suppose Terry's wallet, containing five credit cards, is stolen. Eventually the cards are used by someone other than Terry. Terry is legally obligated to pay only the first $50 of the unauthorized charges for each card. Terry's legal obligation is covered by the additional coverage, so the insurer will pay $250 in this case. If Terry had had more than ten credit cards stolen, the coverage limit would apply—the insurer would cover Terry's legal obligation only to $500.

Defense protection is an additional feature of this coverage. Under the defense coverage, the insurer retains three rights:

1. First, the insurer has the right to settle any claim or suit against the insured as the insurer deems appropriate.
2. Second, the insurer has the right to defend the insured in any claim or suit alleging the insured's liability for unauthorized use of the insured's credit card or fund transfer card.
3. Third, the insurer has the right to defend the insured's bank in a suit alleging the bank's liability for payment of a forged check drawn on the insured's account.

If the insurer does provide defense, the insurer chooses the counsel and pays all costs involved in the defense, investigation, and settlement, other than the amounts for which the insured is liable that exceed the coverage limit. The insurer will not provide defense in those situations that involve losses not otherwise covered by the additional coverage (for example, if the forger is a resident of the insured's household), or when the coverage limit has already been totally depleted.

No deductible applies to the credit card, fund transfer card, depositor's forgery, and counterfeit currency coverages. If the basic limit that applies to all coverages is deemed inadequate, coverage can be increased by using the credit card, fund transfer card, forgery, and counterfeit money—increased limits endorsement.

Loss Assessment

Many homeowners and condominium unit owners belong to an association of property owners. A condominium unit-owners association owns the condominium buildings and may also own other property, such as a clubhouse or swimming pool. A homeowners association may own property such as a neighborhood swimming pool or clubhouse. Generally, such property is insured by the association. However, the insurance may not cover some perils; the amount of insurance may be inadequate or, through some error or omission, the property may be uninsured.

If association property is damaged and insurance is inadequate or nonexistent or the association's property insurance requires that a large deductible be paid, restoration of the property can usually be financed only by levying an assessment against association members. When joining such an association, members agree to pay such assessments.

Loss assessment coverage provides up to $1,000 of coverage under the following circumstances:

1. The assessment results from damage to collectively owned property covered by a peril insured against under Coverage A (Coverage C of an HO-4 policy), except earthquake.

2. The insured, as owner or tenant of the residence premises, is charged an assessment by a corporation or association of property owners.

3. The assessment is not charged against the insured or the association by a governmental body.

By requiring the insured to be an owner or tenant, the homeowners policy prevents property coverage for the members of a swim club or a church. Without eliminating coverage for assessments made by governmental bodies, the policy might be construed to provide coverage when damage to a municipally owned property necessitates a tax increase. Taken together, these provisions limit the additional coverage to homeowners and condominium unit-owners association situations.

Coverage for loss assessments is triggered when the assessment is charged against the insured. That is, the policy in effect at the time the loss assessment is actually charged to the insured is the policy that applies to the claim, even if the loss that results in the loss assessment occurs in an earlier policy period. All other Section I homeowners coverages apply only to loss that occurs during the policy period.

Glass or Safety Glazing Material

The breakage of or damage to glass or safety glazing material that is part of an insured building, storm door, or storm window is covered by the policy. The coverage also applies to direct damage to covered property caused by pieces, fragments, or splinters of the broken glass or safety glazing material. The coverage does not apply if the building has been vacant for more than thirty consecutive days immediately before the loss. The dwelling is **vacant** if all furniture and other property are absent from it. The dwelling is only **unoccupied** if it contains furniture and fixtures, but has no occupants. For example, if Al leaves his home for two months while on vacation, his home is unoccupied and he is covered for loss involving glass breakage. If Al vacates his dwelling and moves to another location, he has no coverage at the vacant premises after thirty days.

The policy will pay for increased costs to replace safety glazing materials where required by building ordinances or laws, but the coverage is included in the limit of the coverage that applies to the property sustaining the damage. Furthermore, forms HO-1 and HO-8 limit the amount of coverage to $100 for the entire loss.

Landlord's Furnishings

In some instances, an apartment on the insured residence premises is normally rented or held for rental to people other than the insured. The insured may have provided appliances, carpeting,.and other household furnishings with the rental. The HO-1, HO-2, and HO-3 forms provide coverage for these furnishings that are owned by the insured but used by a tenant of the insured in the rental apartment on the residence premises. The furnishings are covered for broad named perils, with the exception that theft is not covered, and the most the insurer will pay for a covered loss is $2,500.

Collapse

The HO-2, HO-3, HO-4, and HO-6 policies provide an additional coverage that insures losses "involving" collapse and caused by a Coverage C covered peril. This additional coverage does not increase the limits of coverage for the policy.

To some extent, this provision is redundant since, for example, a fire "involving" collapse is covered without the collapse extension. However, the additional coverage also insures against collapse resulting from the following factors:

- Hidden decay
- Hidden insect or vermin damage
- Weight of contents, equipment, animals, or people
- Weight of rain that collects on a roof
- Use of defective material or methods in construction, remodeling, or renovation if the collapse occurs in the course of the work

Collapse does not include mere settling, cracking, shrinking, bulging, or expansion. Losses to awnings, fences, patios, pavement, swimming pools, underground pipes, flues, drains, cesspools, septic tanks, foundations, retaining walls, bulkheads, piers, wharves, or docks are not included for these additional perils unless they, in turn, result in the collapse of a building.

Building Additions and Alterations

An HO-4, although it does not include coverage for the dwelling or other structures, does provide coverage for building improvements or installations made or acquired at the insured's expense and made to the part of the residence premises that the insured exclusively rents or leases. This coverage is in addition to other coverages contained in the policy and is subject to a limit equal to 10 percent of the limit applying to Coverage C. If this limit is inadequate, the insured may increase it for an additional premium with the *building additions and alterations increased limit endorsement.*

Ordinance or Law Coverage

Many jurisdictions have laws or building codes that affect the reconstruction of a damaged building. A building may not meet current safety codes if it was built years ago. The ordinance may specify that, if a building in violation of current building codes is 50 percent, or more, damaged, it must be razed rather than repaired. To the building owner, this requirement significantly increases the loss exposure. The costs of demolishing the undamaged portion and removing the debris, as well as the increased costs to rebuild under the requirements of existing laws and ordinances, may be steep. Most such laws are more likely to affect commercial buildings than private dwellings. However, the law in some jurisdictions states that a substantially damaged dwelling located on a plot of land smaller in size than required by present law may not be repaired or replaced.

As of October 1994, an ISO multistate endorsement adds ordinance or law coverage to HO-1, HO-2, HO-3, HO-4, and HO-6 policies, as a standard additional coverage. The ordinance or law coverage applies to the increased construction costs resulting from enforcement primarily of building codes in repairing or replacing covered buildings or structures damaged by a covered cause of loss. The coverage can also be used to cover the additional debris removal costs resulting from enforcement of such ordinances or laws. The coverage does not apply to ordinances or laws that do not deal with building and safety codes, and specifically excludes coverage for increased costs required to deal with the effects of pollutants.

The ordinance or law coverage is provided in addition to other coverages contained in the policies. For HO-1, HO-2, HO-3, and HO-6, it is subject to a limit equal to 10 percent of the limit for Coverage A. For HO-4, it is subject to a limit equal to 10 percent of the limit for Building Additions and Alterations. If the 10 percent limit is inadequate, it can be increased—to 25 percent, if needed—with the *ordinance or law coverage endorsement.*

Perils Insured Against in the Homeowners Forms

Two approaches are used in describing covered causes of loss—(1) named perils and (2) "all-risks." **Named perils** protection covers property only against losses caused by a list of causes of loss actually named in the policy. Exclusions and limitations usually apply to these perils. "**All-risks**" protection covers property for all losses that are not specifically excluded by the policy form.

The term "all-risks" is still used by insurance people when referring to coverage that covers all losses except those excluded, but "all-risks" is not considered appropriate when relating to the general public. In the late 1970s and early 1980s, courts interpreted the policy literally to cover all risks' and many insurers were required to cover causes of loss they did not expect. The term "all-risks" has been dropped from the homeowners policies, but this text uses the term, sparingly, to refer to such coverage.

Two forms of named perils coverage are available under the homeowners policy program: **basic**, which covers a limited list of causes of loss, and **broad**, which covers the same causes as basic plus six additional named causes of loss. The HO-1 and HO-8 provide all property coverages on a basic named perils basis. The covered causes of loss under an HO-8 are more restricted than under an HO-1. Forms HO-2, HO-4, and HO-6 cover all property on a broad named perils basis. HO-3 is referred to as the **special form**, because it covers the dwelling, other structures, and loss of use of the dwelling and other structures on an "all-risks" basis and covers personal property on a broad named perils basis. This information is outlined in Exhibit 2-9.

Basic Named Perils

Policy coverage written on a basic named peril basis covers the twelve causes of loss discussed below:

Fire

Although it is one of the leading causes of loss to property, fire is not defined in the policy. Through court decisions over the years, *fire* has come to mean "oxidation sufficiently rapid to cause a flame or glow." Thus oxidation that occurs without causing a flame, such as heating, scorching, or charring, is not considered a fire. The fire must also be *hostile* (one that is where it is not supposed to be), such as a spark jumping from a fireplace that ignites the carpeting or a forest fire started by lightning.

Although the peril of fire is insurable, loss control measures can be used. Smoke detectors and alarms help to reduce the potential cost of the loss as well

Exhibit 2-9
Covered Causes of Loss by Homeowners Policy Coverages

COVERAGE	HO-1	HO-2	HO-3	HO-4	HO-6	HO-8
A—Dwelling	basic	broad	"all-risks"	NA	broad	basic
B—Other Structures	basic	broad	"all-risks"	NA	NA	basic
C—Personal Property	basic	broad	broad	broad	broad	basic
D—Loss of Use	basic	broad	"all-risks" or broad*	broad	broad	basic

* Depends on type of property damaged. If real property, "all-risks" coverage; if personal property, broad named perils coverage.

Basic and broad named perils are as follows:

Basic:	fire	lightning	windstorm and hail
	explosion	riot or civil commotion	aircraft
	vehicles	smoke	vandalism and mali-
	theft	volcanic eruption	cious mischief
Broad:	basic perils	falling objects	weight of ice, snow,
	accidental discharge	sudden and accidental	or sleet
	or overflow of	tearing apart,	freezing
	water or steam	cracking, burning,	sudden and acciden-
		or bulging	tal damage from
			artificially gener-
			ated electrical
			current

as prevent loss of life. Sprinkler systems and fire extinguishers help to put out a fire once it has started and, thus, reduce the severity of a loss. Safe habits, such as keeping gasoline and other flammables in airtight containers away from heat sources and not overloading electrical outlets, prevent the occurrence of fires. Some appliances are equipped with their own fire prevention measures. Appliances, such as coffee makers and irons, can be purchased that include switches or circuits that automatically shut the appliance off after a certain period of time or if the appliance begins to get too hot.

Lightning

Lightning is also not defined in the policy, but is generally considered the discharge of atmospheric electricity. It does not include artificially generated electricity, such as a power surge that damages a television.

The threat of lightning damage to a house can be reduced by installing lightning rods on the roof of the dwelling (though doing so is not as common as it was in earlier decades). Electronics can be protected from loss caused by lightning by using a surge protector that will prevent an electrical surge from reaching the equipment through a power cord plugged into the electrical system.

Windstorm

Windstorm has come to mean wind, with or without rain, of sufficient velocity to cause damage, or wind of a certain specified velocity. Generally, if wind is strong enough or severe enough to cause damage to property in a normal state of repair, it is considered to be a windstorm regardless of the atmospheric conditions prevailing at the time. Windstorm includes tornadoes or cyclones, and hurricanes, and is broad enough to cover direct loss by the force of wind, as well as by debris carried by the wind. Specifically covered by the windstorm peril is loss to any watercraft, subject to the special limits, but only while inside a fully enclosed building. Thus, if a tornado destroys both the shed in which Tim's boat was stored and Tim's boat, Tim's homeowners policy would pay for the windstorm damage to the boat and the shed. However, if the boat was destroyed but was not in the shed at the time of the tornado, Tim's homeowners policy would not pay for the damage to the boat.

The windstorm peril contains an exclusion with an exception. Windblown rain, snow, sleet, sand, or dust that causes loss to the inside of a building or to property within a building is not covered, *unless* the direct force of the wind first creates an opening in the roof or wall of the building through which the elements can enter. This exclusion prevents coverage of loss caused by leaving a window or door open. If a closed window or door is damaged by a windstorm, coverage applies to loss within the building because closed windows and doors are considered part of the wall.

Hail

Large hailstones can be especially destructive to property. The peril of *hail* is subject to the same exclusion and coverage limitations as windstorm.

Explosion

Explosion is not easily defined, and the clause makes no attempt to describe or limit the cause of loss. A covered loss by explosion can therefore be caused by an explosion outside the dwelling, such as a nearby industrial explosion or blasting work. Explosion losses inside the dwelling or other structures could stem from rupture or bursting of pipes and water heaters; rupture or bursting of pressure relief valves, such as on water heaters and furnace explosions. Loss due to explosion can be prevented by proper maintenance of heating and cooling systems.

Riot or Civil Commotion

Neither riot nor civil commotion is defined by the homeowners forms. Although common law and statutory definitions vary, *riot* is generally deemed to be an activity involving three or more persons with a common purpose who carry out that purpose in a violent or turbulent manner, and, when these circumstances exist, any resulting loss may be considered caused by a riot. *Civil commotion* is commonly held to be an uprising of citizens and may be viewed as a large or prolonged riot.

Aircraft

Loss to insured property caused by *aircraft*, including self-propelled missiles and spacecraft, is covered in the homeowners forms. Damage from parts or equipment that fall from aircraft or from a disintegrating spacecraft is also covered. Since no direct contact is required, loss caused by a sonic boom is also covered under this peril.

Vehicles

This peril includes damage from loss caused by *vehicles*, with one or two exclusions. The HO-1 and HO-8 do not cover "loss caused by a vehicle owned or operated by a resident of the residence premises," but they do cover loss by vehicles owned and operated by others. Under an HO-6, this peril does not include "loss to a fence, driveway or walk caused by a vehicle owned or operated by a resident of the resident premises."

Smoke

Smoke is defined as "sudden and accidental damage from smoke...[other than] smoke from fireplaces or agricultural smudging or industrial operations." Since smoke damage resulting from a hostile fire is considered *fire* damage, the *smoke* peril extends coverage so that it applies to circumstances that are not hostile-fire-related. Examples are smoke and soot suddenly and accidentally discharged from a faulty fuel oil furnace, or smoke damage caused by a neighbor's burning leaves.

Vandalism or Malicious Mischief

These perils have come to mean willful or malicious damage or destruction of property, caused by a person or several persons, without the tumult associated with a riot. Examples of losses include damage to a dwelling and other structures by pranksters or personal property intentionally destroyed in anger by an adult guest in the household. *Vandalism or malicious mischief* may also encompass willful damage to the premises and its property by burglars. The peril also includes vandalism to a house under construction.

Specifically excluded from coverage under this peril is loss to property on the residence premises if the dwelling has been vacant for more than thirty consecutive days. A house that is merely unoccupied or is under construction is not considered vacant.

Theft

Theft is not defined in the policy, but includes "attempted theft and loss of property from a known location where it is likely that the property has been stolen." Therefore, the peril covers loss by burglary, robbery, and larceny. Loss due to theft also may be covered when the circumstances at least show the likelihood or presumption that property was stolen and not merely misplaced. The burden of proof falls on the insured.

Loss by theft is subject to the following three exclusions:

1. Theft committed by an "insured"
2. Theft in or to a dwelling under construction, or of materials and supplies for use in the construction until the dwelling is finished and occupied
3. Theft from that part of the "residence premises" rented by an "insured" to other than an "insured"

"Insured" and "residence premises" refer to the policy definitions previously discussed.

Also, when theft occurs off the "residence premises," the following limitations exist:

*   No coverage applies for property stolen from any other residence owned by, rented to, or occupied by any insured, unless the insured is temporarily living there. Betty, an insured who rents a hotel or motel room, is considered to be temporarily occupying it and would have theft coverage on her personal property, while it is located in the hotel or motel room. But property contained at Betty's summer home would not be covered against theft loss while she is not living there. Any insured who is a student living away from home has coverage against theft of his or her personal property, provided he or she had been at the secondary residence at any time during the forty-five day period immediately preceding the loss.

*   No coverage applies to theft of trailers, campers, or watercraft, including their equipment, furnishings, and outboard motors, if stolen while off the residence premises.

An HO-8 limits the coverage available for the peril of theft. In an HO-8, property off the residence premises—unless it is contained in a bank, trust or safe deposit company, or public warehouse—is not covered for loss by theft. The most the insurer will pay for any covered theft loss under an HO-8 policy is $1,000. This limit can be increased, for an additional premium, with a *theft coverage increase endorsement.*

Loss due to theft can be controlled in a number of ways. Among the more common treatments are the following:

- Using a security system within the dwelling that will sound an alarm if an unlawful entry is attempted

- Installing dead bolts on all doors of the dwelling

- Keeping motor homes locked when unoccupied

- Keeping valuable items in a safe on the premises or in a safe deposit box or vault at a bank

- Recording all serial numbers of electronic equipment and storing them in a safe place

- Scratching initials, driver's license number, or other identification on valuables and equipment

Volcanic Eruption

Loss caused by volcanic eruption is covered. However, loss caused by earthquake, land shock waves, or tremors is not covered. Coverage for earthquake damage can be endorsed onto the policy, for an additional premium, with the *earthquake endorsement.* This endorsement is further discussed in Chapter 3.

Broad Named Perils

Coverage written on a broad named perils basis covers the causes of loss described under the basic named perils and six additional causes of loss. The six added perils are discussed below.

Falling Objects

The peril of *falling objects* refers to items that fall onto or into a building and cause some damage to the building. Coverage applies to direct damage to the exterior of the building or other structures, including attached fixtures such as awnings and antennas. Fences, walks, outdoor equipment, and other personal property that is outdoors is also covered. Property inside the building is not covered unless the falling object first damages the building's roof or at least one of its walls. The falling object itself is not covered.

Weight of Ice, Snow, or Sleet

If the weight of ice, snow, or sleet damages the exterior of a building, any loss resulting to the building and its contents is covered. The peril does not include loss to property susceptible to such an exposure, such as awnings, fences, patios, foundations, piers, or docks. Since HO-4 covers only personal property, it covers only damage to property inside a building that is caused by the weight of ice, snow, or sleet.

Accidental Discharge or Overflow of Water or Steam

Coverage is provided for accidental discharge or overflow of water or steam "from within a plumbing, heating, air conditioning or automatic fire protective sprinkler system or from within a household appliance." A plumbing system does not include "a sump, a sump pump or related equipment." The coverage is further limited in that it does not include the following types of loss:

- Loss to the system or appliance that produced the discharge or overflow
- Loss due to freezing
- Loss on the residence premises resulting from discharge or overflow that occurs off the premises

Except for HO-4, the costs of tearing out and replacing any part of the building on the residence premises to repair or replace the faulty pipe or appliance are also covered. These policies do not cover a loss due to accidental discharge or overflow of water or steam if the dwelling has been vacant for more than thirty consecutive days immediately preceding the loss. A dwelling under construction is not considered vacant.

Loss caused by accidental discharge or overflow of water or steam can be controlled. Plumbing, heating, air conditioning, and sprinkler systems should be properly maintained and serviced. Appliances that use water, such as a dishwasher or a refrigerator with an automatic ice maker, should be periodically checked to ensure that the connections to the water supply are dry and in good condition. Hoses from a clothes washer to water faucets should be replaced as soon as cracks begin to appear.

Sudden and Accidental Tearing Apart, Cracking, Burning, or Bulging

The "sudden and accidental tearing apart, cracking, burning, or bulging of a steam or hot water heating system, an air conditioning or automatic fire protective sprinkler system, or an appliance for heating water" is covered. This does not include loss resulting from freezing. The damage caused both to and by the system or appliance is covered under this peril. These losses can be prevented by proper servicing and maintenance of the system or appliance.

Since a sudden and violent tearing apart of an object, accompanied by a loud noise and fragmentation of the object, could also be considered an explosion, portions of this peril would probably also be covered under the explosion peril. However, this coverage is broader than explosion, since it also includes cracking, burning, and bulging.

Freezing

When a household appliance or a plumbing, heating, fire sprinkler, or air conditioning system freezes, resulting in damage to the appliance or system, as well as to the dwelling or its contents, it is covered under the freezing peril. However, coverage does not apply while a dwelling on the residence premises is vacant, unoccupied, or being constructed unless the insured either (1) takes reasonable measures to maintain heat in the building or (2) turns off the water supply and drains the system or appliance. In this case, the insurer is requiring the insured to use loss control methods. If the insured does not perform one of these specified loss prevention techniques, no coverage is provided for loss caused by freezing in a building that is vacant, unoccupied, or under construction.

Sudden and Accidental Damage from Artificially Generated Electrical Current

With the exception of any tube, transistor, or similar electronic component, property is covered against the peril of sudden and accidental damage from artificially generated electrical current. Losses here include damage caused by a power surge or a brownout (lower level of power or voltage reaching a piece of equipment or an appliance than generally recommended and required to operate it). Lightning can also cause power surges that damage electrical or electronic equipment; lightning damage is covered without qualification under the lightning peril.

Surge protectors are useful in preventing losses caused by artificially generated electrical surges.

Special Form Coverage

The HO-3 special form applies "all-risks" coverage to the dwelling and other structures, and covers personal property on a broad named perils basis. If real property is not able to be used, loss of use is covered on an "all-risks" basis, and if personal property is not available for use, loss of use is covered for broad named perils. An example of the "all-risks" coverage as it appears in an HO-3 policy is shown in Exhibit 2-10.

Several of the exclusions included in the "all-risks" coverage have been discussed under the basic and broad named perils clauses. Clause 2a excludes

Exhibit 2-10

Section I—Perils Insured Against   HO 00 03 04 91

COVERAGE A—DWELLING and COVERAGE B—OTHER STRUCTURES

We insure against risk of direct loss to property described in Coverages A and B only if that loss is a physical loss to property. We do not insure, however, for loss:

1. Involving collapse, other than as provided in Additional Coverage **8.**;

2. Caused by:

    a. Freezing of a plumbing, heating, air conditioning or automatic fire protective sprinkler system or of a household appliance, or by discharge, leakage or overflow from within the system or appliance caused by freezing. This exclusion applies only while the dwelling is vacant, unoccupied or being constructed, unless you have used reasonable care to:

       (1) Maintain heat in the building; or

       (2) Shut off the water supply and drain the system and appliances of water;

    b. Freezing, thawing, pressure or weight of water or ice, whether driven by wind or not, to a:

       (1) Fence, pavement, patio or swimming pool;

       (2) Foundation, retaining wall, or bulkhead; or

       (3) Pier, wharf or dock;

    c. Theft in or to a dwelling under construction, or of materials and supplies for use in the construction until the dwelling is finished and occupied;

    d. Vandalism and malicious mischief if the dwelling has been vacant for more than 30 consecutive days immediately before the loss. A dwelling being constructed is not considered vacant;

    e. Any of the following:

       (1) Wear and tear, marring, deterioration;

    (2) Inherent vice, latent defect, mechanical breakdown;

    (3) Smog, rust or other corrosion, mold, wet or dry rot;

    (4) Smoke from agricultural smudging or industrial operations;

    (5) Discharge, dispersal, seepage, migration, release or escape of pollutants unless the discharge, dispersal, seepage, migration, release or escape is itself caused by a Peril Insured Against under Coverage C of this policy.

    Pollutants means any solid, liquid, gaseous or thermal irritant or contaminant, including smoke, vapor, soot, fumes, acids, alkalis, chemicals and waste. Waste includes materials to be recycled, reconditioned or reclaimed;

    (6) Settling, shrinking, bulging or expansion, including resultant cracking, of pavements, patios, foundations, walls, floors, roofs or ceilings;

    (7) Birds, vermin, rodents, or insects; or

    (8) Animals owned or kept by an "insured."

If any of these cause water damage not otherwise excluded, from a plumbing, heating, air conditioning or automatic fire protective sprinkler system or household appliance, we cover loss caused by the water including the cost of tearing out and replacing any part of a building necessary to repair the system or appliance. We do not cover loss to the system or appliance from which this water escaped.

3. Excluded under Section I - Exclusions.

Under items **1.** and **2.**, any ensuing loss to property described in Coverages A and B not excluded or excepted in this policy is covered.

loss due to freezing of plumbing, heating, air conditioning and fire sprinkler systems, or of appliances unless the insured has taken reasonable care to prevent this type of loss while the building is not in use. Clause 2b states that coverage will not be provided for losses to items outside the building caused by weather and other natural conditions such as freezing, wind, and weight of water or rain. Clauses 2c and 2d eliminate coverage for loss due to theft, vandalism, and malicious mischief once a building has been vacant for at least thirty consecutive days immediately prior to the loss. Clause 2e(4) contains an exclusion for smoke from agricultural or industrial operations that is also eliminated in the basic smoke peril.

The rest of clause 2e excludes coverage for loss due to a variety of perils that are generally not accidental, sudden, or unexpected. Of particular importance is exclusion 2e(5), which deals with pollution. The purpose of this exclusion is to remove coverage for those situations in which pollution has occurred gradually, and that should probably have been identified and corrected by the insured. The policy will cover pollution losses that result from those perils covered under the HO-3's Coverage C—Personal Property—broad named perils. Thus, if the insured's oil tank explodes and oil seeps into the water table in the neighborhood, the policy will cover the loss. Notice that the word "pollutant" may also include solid, gaseous, or thermal contaminants and irritants.

The last paragraph in clause 2e adds coverage for accidental discharge or overflow of water. As with the coverage provided in the broad named perils, the "all-risk" form covers only damage to the dwelling or other structure, including the cost to tear out and replace part of the building while repairing or replacing the faulty system or appliance. The system or appliance is not covered.

Clause 3 emphasizes that the exclusions listed for Section I (discussed in the next section of this chapter) are definitely excluded. Even though they are not listed in the "all-risks" coverage exclusions, these losses will not be covered under Coverage A or Coverage B.

The final paragraph of Exhibit 2-10 reiterates that any losses not excluded by exclusions 1 or 2 are covered by the policy. In essence, what is not otherwise excluded is covered by the special form. The following actual building losses have been covered under "all-risks" coverage:

- Loss caused by wind-driven rain through open doors or windows
- Condensation on attic insulation causing water stains on the ceiling of the room below
- Damage to draperies that froze to a large plate glass window

- Damage to the counter top by an overheated coffee pot
- Seepage of water from a Christmas tree stand, which stained the carpet
- Accidental puncture of a septic tank system while digging next to it
- The dropping of an object in the bathtub and chipping the enamel
- Damage to a house caused by a deer's breaking into it
- The malfunctioning of a furnace thermostat during the insured's absence, with the resulting continuous heat's damaging the carpeting and the wallpaper

"All-risks" coverage can be extended to personal property covered under form HO-3 with the *special personal property coverage endorsement*. The exclusions of this endorsement are quite similar to those discussed above with some modification to reflect the differences in the property exposed to loss. For example, the endorsement limits the coverage for breakage of eyeglasses, porcelain, and other fragile articles to specific named perils such as fire, explosion, and theft. The endorsement also excludes loss due to refinishing, renovating, or repairing property other than jewelry, watches, and furs.

"All-risks" coverage can also be endorsed onto the HO-6 for either Coverage A or Coverage C or both for an additional premium. The *unit-owners Coverage C special coverage endorsement*, and the *unit-owners Coverage A special coverage endorsement*, provide "all-risks" coverage, similar to that discussed, for the personal property and the dwelling, respectively, of a condominium unit owner.

General Exclusions

Section I property coverages are subject to several general exclusions listed in all homeowners policies. The exclusions preclude coverage even under circumstances in which a concurrent cause or event is not excluded. The general exclusions are described in the following paragraphs.

Ordinance or Law

Any loss due to ordinances and other laws, except as provided by the additional coverage for glass and safety glazing material and the ordinance or law additional coverage, is not covered by the homeowners policies. As mentioned earlier, if the coverage provided under the ordinance or law additional coverage is inadequate, an *ordinance or law coverage endorsement* can be purchased.[2]

Earth Movement

Loss caused by earth movement—such as earthquake, mudflow, and the

sinking, rising, or shifting of earth—is not covered. Although volcanic eruption is a covered cause of loss under all the homeowners forms, earthquakes
relating to volcanic eruptions are not covered. As mentioned earlier, earthquake coverage can be added for an extra premium through the *earthquake
endorsement*. This endorsement is discussed in Chapter 3.

Specifically excepted from the earth movement exclusion—and therefore
covered—is any loss by fire, explosion, or theft that results from earth movement. Thus, for example, if an earthquake causes the basement of a dwelling to
sink or shift and a natural gas supply line to the furnace to leak and explode, all
loss to the property would be covered except for the structural damage to the
dwelling caused by the earth movement.[3]

Water Damage

Three categories of water damage are specifically excluded.

1. Flood, surface water, waves, tidal water, overflow of a body of water, or
    spray from any of these, whether or not driven by wind
2. Water that backs up through sewers or drains or that overflows from a
    sump pump
3. Water below the surface of the ground, including water that exerts
    pressure on or seeps or leaks through a building, sidewalk, driveway,
    foundation, swimming pool, or other structure

Coverage for floods as described in item 1 above can be obtained through flood
insurance, which is discussed in Chapter 6. The loss described in item 2 is fairly
common, especially in periods of excess rainfall or because of improper
maintenance. Some states require that coverage against this loss be offered by
insurers, and such coverage is available in many states through a *water back up
and sump overflow endorsement*.

Any direct loss by fire, explosion, or theft resulting from water damage is
covered. As an example, looters often steal from buildings during or after a
flood. If the building is insured under a homeowners policy, such theft losses
are covered.

Power Failure

Any loss resulting from the interruption of power occurring off the residence
premises is excluded unless a peril insured against later occurs on premises. In
that case, coverage exists only for the resulting loss. Such losses as flooding of
a basement due to failure of a sump pump caused by an off-premises power
outage, or loss of use of a dwelling from lack of heat because of an off-premises
power outage, would not be covered. However, if an off-premises power outage

causes freezing of plumbing pipes, for example, coverage under homeowners policies other than HO-1 and HO-8 should apply. Also, if a power outage is caused by a windstorm that breaks a utility line on the premises, or if vandals sever a line on the premises, any resulting loss should be covered.

Neglect

Property insurance policies recognize the insured's obligation to preserve property during and after a loss. Homeowners policies even cover reasonable repairs as an additional coverage. If an insured fails to use reasonable means to protect the property from further damage during and after a loss, no coverage applies. This does not mean that an insured must make repeated trips into a burning building, risking life and limb to salvage various items. The insured is expected to take only the *reasonable* steps possible to keep property from further damage.

War

Loss caused by war and its consequences, being catastrophic in nature, is not generally insurable and is not covered by homeowners policies. War includes undeclared war, civil war, rebellion or revolution, warlike acts by military force or personnel, and destruction, seizure, or use for military purposes. Also, the discharge, even accidental, of a nuclear weapon is considered war, and any resulting damage is not covered.

Nuclear Hazard

Nuclear hazard is also excluded. According to the nuclear hazard clause listed in the Section I conditions, **nuclear hazard** means "any nuclear reaction, radiation, or radioactive contamination, all whether controlled or uncontrolled or however caused, or any consequence of these." By exception to the nuclear hazard clause, direct loss by fire resulting from nuclear hazard is covered.

Intentional Loss

The homeowners policies exclude coverage for loss arising out of an act committed by or at the direction of any insured with the intention of causing loss. This attempts to eliminate coverage for any insured—meaning the named insured and his or her spouse, resident relative, and resident dependent under the age of 21—even if not involved in committing the act out of which the loss arises. For example, if a husband burns down a covered dwelling, the wife, even if not involved in the husband's act of arson, may not receive payment for the loss from the insurer.

Jurisdictions vary on the enforcement of this provision against an innocent party. Some jurisdictions do allow recovery by the innocent party. Often recovery is limited to the innocent party's proportion of insurable interest in the property.

Additional Exclusions in HO-3

Form HO-3 has three additional exclusions that apply to property described in Coverages A and B:

1. Weather conditions, if they contribute in any way to the exclusions listed above

2. Acts or decisions, including the failure to act or decide, of any person, group, organization, or governmental body. Thus, an insured cannot claim that a specific loss by flood, an otherwise excluded peril, is covered because the loss was really caused by the governmental authorities' failure to implement flood control measures

3. Activities or materials found to be faulty, inadequate, or defective, which include the following:

   • Planning, zoning, development, surveying, or siting

   • Design, specifications, workmanship, repair, construction, renovation, remodeling, grading, or compaction

   • Maintenance of part or all of any property whether on or off the residence premises

   • Material used in repair, construction, renovation or remodeling

These additional exclusions do not apply to ensuing loss that would otherwise be covered. For example, if faulty installation of a furnace resulted in fire damage to the dwelling, the fire damage would not be excluded.

Valuation (Loss Settlement)

Discussion to this point has concentrated on *whether* the various homeowners policies provide coverage. This section analyzes the *extent of coverage* provided on the various types of property specified in the loss settlement clause of the policy that is contained in the Section I conditions. The **loss settlement clause** identifies (1) property that will be valued at actual cash value and (2) property that will be valued at replacement cost subject to compliance with certain conditions. **Actual cash value** is not defined by the policy but is generally held to mean replacement cost less any reduction resulting from depreciation and obsolescence or the market value, especially for personal property for which a "used" market exists. **Replacement cost** refers to the dollar amount necessary to repair or replace the item lost. It does not consider depreciation or obsolescence.

For example, consider a twenty-year-old television in good working order. This television probably does not have stereo speakers or a remote control, nor is it likely to be cable-ready. All of these features are standard on many newer televisions. Moreover, its parts have been in use for twenty years. If this television had to be replaced today, its actual cash value would be much less than its replacement cost because twenty years of depreciation and obsolescence must be considered.

Actual Cash Value

All standard homeowners forms, unless otherwise endorsed, cover personal property on an actual cash value (ACV) basis, not to exceed the amount necessary to repair or replace. Forms HO-1, HO-2, and HO-3 also cover on an ACV basis certain items that fall within Coverage A—Dwelling and Coverage B—Other Structures and are especially susceptible to depreciation and obsolescence. These types of property include carpeting, household appliances, awnings, and outdoor antennas and equipment, whether or not they are attached to buildings. Structures that are not buildings (such as swimming pools, fences, or docks) are valued at ACV as well. HO-6 requires that loss to property covered in Coverage A be valued at ACV if the damaged property is not repaired or replaced. HO-8 provides coverage for dwellings and other building structures at ACV or market value if the building is not restored for the same occupancy and use, on the same site, within 180 days of the loss.

Determining ACV requires consideration of the replacement cost of the property, its condition immediately before the loss, its age, its use, and its life span. ACV can be difficult to measure. Nevertheless, ACV has long been the primary standard used for property loss settlement. In practice, most ACV claims are settled without difficulty.

Replacement Cost

Dwellings and other building structures are the only property eligible for replacement cost (RC) coverage on the unendorsed homeowners policies. Personal property can be covered on an RC basis by purchasing a *personal property replacement cost endorsement*.

Forms HO-1, HO-2, and HO-3 deal with RC coverage on the dwelling and other building structures in the same way. The part of the loss settlement clause that applies to Coverage A or B is designed to provide strong incentive for homeowners to purchase adequate amounts of insurance, despite the fact that most losses are fairly small.

To qualify for settlement of building losses (even partial losses) on an RC basis, the insured must carry insurance equal to at least 80 percent of the replacement cost of the building at the time of the loss. If it takes $150,000 to rebuild a house, the insured must have at least $120,000 (80 percent of $150,000) of coverage on the dwelling in order to have losses covered on an RC basis. But, even if the insured meets this requirement, the insurer will not cover any costs above the three listed below, *whichever is the least*:

1. The policy coverage limit

2. The cost to repair, replace, or rebuild a dwelling of the same type on the premises, and for the same use

3. The actual cost to replace or repair the damaged building

Note that the insurance must be equal to at least 80 percent of the building value *at the time of the loss*, not at policy inception. Thus if the value of the replacement cost increases, the coverage limit must also increase in order for the insured to remain eligible for RC coverage. Insurance written during a period of positive inflation may prove inadequate later in the policy period. An *inflation guard endorsement*, which is discussed in Chapter 3, can be used to help prevent inadequacy of insurance.

When determining how much insurance to buy, an insured can exclude the following types of property described in the loss settlement clause:

*   Excavations, foundations, piers, or any other underground supports below the lowest basement floor, or below the surface of the ground inside the foundation walls, if there is no basement

*   Underground flues, pipes, wiring, and drains

This property is immune from damage for most insured perils. However, the property is not excluded (in most states) if it is damaged or destroyed, except for certain perils such as "weight of ice, snow, or sleet."

The value of the land on which the home is built is not included in the RC calculation. The RC is usually lower than the purchase price of a new house, since this price includes land and underground items.

If the insured fails to meet the 80 percent requirement at the time of loss, the insurer will pay the greater of (1) the actual cash value of the loss (loss ACV) or (2) a proportion of the replacement cost of the loss (loss RC) less the applicable deductible, but no more than the coverage limit. The proportion of the loss RC is calculated as follows:

$$\frac{\text{Amount of Coverage Carried}}{\text{on the Damaged Property}} \times (Loss\ RC - deductible)$$
$$\frac{\text{80 Percent of the Total}}{\text{Replacement Cost of the Damaged Property}}$$

This proportion is then multiplied by the loss RC less the deductible. A shorthand version of this formula is:

$$\frac{Did}{Should} \times (Loss\ RC - deductible)$$

The final figure is compared to the loss ACV, and the insurer pays the *greater* of the two as long as it does not exceed the limit of coverage for the damaged property.[4]

Consider two examples—one with Sandra, an insured who has met the 80 percent rule, and one concerning Tom, who has not met the requirement.

Sandra purchased $120,000 of coverage on her dwelling a year ago under an HO-3. Yesterday her house was struck by lightning and suffered damage because of an ensuing fire, which will cost $40,000 to repair. At today's prices, it would take $124,000 to rebuild her house (exclusive of land and below-ground foundations or supports). Since $120,000 is greater than 80 percent of $124,000, or $99,200, the insurer will pay the $40,000 needed to repair the home less any deductible that applies.

If Sandra's house had been totally destroyed by the fire, the most the insurer would pay to rebuild it is $120,000—the limit of coverage. If Sandra had decided to replace her house with a cottage that requires only $90,000 to build, the insurer would pay the greater of (1) $90,000, the actual amount to replace the dwelling, or (2) the actual cash value of the destroyed home. Sandra is entitled to at least the ACV of her loss, even if the cost to replace the destroyed dwelling is less than its actual cash value. However, Sandra will be responsible for the deductible.

Tom owns a home insured for $70,000 under an HO-3 policy with a $250 deductible. At the time the insurance was purchased, the house had a replacement cost of $85,000. Tom's house is damaged by fire and sustains a loss valued at $12,000 ACV but will cost $14,650 to repair. At the time of the loss, the house had a replacement value of $90,000. Since $70,000 is less than 80 percent of $90,000, or $72,000, the insurer will cover the *greater* of the loss ACV—$12,000—or a proportion of the loss RC, calculated as follows:

$$\frac{Did}{Should} \times (Loss\ RC - deductible)$$
$$= \quad \$70,000/\$72,000 \times (\$14,650 - \$250)$$
$$= \quad \$14,000$$

$14,000 is greater than the $12,000 ACV and below the $70,000 limit; thus the insurer will pay $14,000 to repair the property, and Tom will retain a loss of $650.

In either case, before an insured can recover on an RC basis, repair or replacement must actually occur. As explained in the loss settlement clause, the insurer will pay no more than the ACV of the loss before the actual repairs or replacement is finished. An exception to this requirement takes effect when the cost to repair or replace the damaged property is both less than $2,500 and less than 5 percent of the limit of insurance coverage.

Suppose Carl has an HO-2 policy for $64,000 on a dwelling with an actual cash value of $60,000 and a replacement cost of $78,000. His dwelling sustains windstorm damage that amounts to $500 ACV but will cost $800 to repair. Since $64,000 is greater than 80 percent of the $78,000 replacement cost at the time of the loss, or $62,400, Carl is entitled to replacement cost coverage. Moreover, $800 is less than $2,500 and less than 5 percent of the $64,000 limit on Coverage A. Carl will therefore receive $800, less the deductible, from his insurer without first making the necessary repairs.

If, however, the damage was $2,100 on an ACV basis and $3,000 on an RC basis, Carl will not automatically receive the full replacement cost of the loss. The loss RC exceeds $2,500. Carl will receive the $2,100 ACV, less the deductible, at once, and another $900 if the repairs are completed.

The loss settlement clause also deals with cases in which an insured suffers a loss to insured property and is undecided as to whether to repair or replace the damage. The insured is not required to make repairs and may disregard a replacement cost settlement, accepting settlement on an ACV basis. If the insured later decides to make repairs or replacement, he or she can claim the difference between the ACV and the RC. However, this claim must be made within 180 days after the loss.

The HO-6 and HO-8 address replacement cost differently than do forms HO-1, HO-2, and HO-3. An HO-6 provides RC coverage for property within Coverage A as long as any property damage is repaired or replaced within a "reasonable time," which is determined by conditions at the time of the loss. For example, in the wake of Hurricane Andrew, many dwellings were not repaired or replaced even six months after they were damaged or destroyed. This was not unreasonable, given the massive amount of destruction and the shortage of supplies. But, if a single condominium unit that is damaged by fire is not repaired within six months, the insurer may find this to be unreasonable.

The HO-8 modifies the method by which replacement cost is measured. The policy covers the cost of only common materials and methods used to repair or replace the damaged property. This is meant to exclude coverage for obsolete and costly materials and methods such as hand-carved stair railings or satin-paneled walls.

The HO-8 also puts a time limit on the availability of RC coverage for the dwelling and other building structures. If repairs or replacement are made within 180 days of the loss, the loss will be covered on the modified RC basis, subject to the limits of coverage.

An HO-8 is especially useful for situations in which a home has a much greater replacement cost than it has an actual cash value—such as a home built during the Victorian Era, which has ornate woodwork and hand-painted plaster ceilings. Requiring an insured to purchase, for example, $200,000 of insurance to meet replacement cost requirements for a house with a market value of $50,000 can create hardship and may seem illogical to many homeowners. The HO-8 is designed, in event of damage to the insured dwelling, to functionally restore the home. The insurer would not pay for the added cost of restoring it to its pre-loss condition but would pay to return it to a livable condition.

Other Valuation Considerations

In addition to the loss settlement clause listed in the Section I conditions, two other Section I conditions influence the value at which property is covered. These are (1) the loss to a pair or set clause and (2) the glass replacement clause.

Loss to a Pair or Set

If there is a loss to an item that is part of a pair or set, the insurer may settle the loss based on (1) the difference between the actual cash value of the pair or set before and after the loss or (2) the cost of repair or replacement of any part of the pair or set to restore the pair or set to its value before the loss. The insurer has the option of deciding which basis will be used. This clause applies to personal property—such as a pair of earrings or a set of dining room chairs—and to real property—such as a pair of ornate gateposts or a set of shutters.

For example, vandals destroy one chair in a set of four antique chairs valued at $12,000. Without the fourth chair, the set is valued at only $6,000, and it will cost $3,000 to restore the ruined chair to its pre-loss condition. The insurer may pay the insured the $6,000—the difference between the set's value before and after the chair was ruined—or the insurer may choose to pay $3,000 for the chair to be restored.

Glass Replacement

Loss for damage by a covered peril to insured building glass is settled on the basis of its replacement with safety glazing materials when required by ordinance or law. This reiterates the coverage provided in the Glass or Safety Glazing Material Additional Coverage. Building codes in many areas require that broken glass doors, storm doors, shower doors, and similar items be replaced only with safety glass or other materials less likely to cause injury. Since safety glazing materials often cost more than ordinary window glass, this condition provides for loss settlement in excess of replacement with like kind and quality, but it does not increase the limits of the policy.

General Policy Conditions

Each homeowners policy includes general conditions that apply to both Sections I and II. These conditions are discussed in the following paragraphs.

The **policy period condition** makes it clear that the policy does not cover any losses that do not take place in the policy period specified in the declarations. For property losses, this means that the property damage occurs within the dates listed on the declarations page. For liability losses, the policy will respond to claims that arise from bodily injury and property damage that have occurred within the policy period.

The **concealment or fraud condition** denies coverage for insureds who intentionally conceal or misrepresent a material fact or circumstance or otherwise fraudulently increase the loss exposure. For Section I coverages, such actions void policy coverage for *all* insureds. For Section II coverages, such actions exclude coverage only for the insured(s) involved in the concealment or fraud. In either case, coverage is denied whether the concealment or fraud is discovered before or after a loss.

Under the **liberalization condition**, the insurer automatically broadens the coverage available through the policy if the insurer has instituted a change that broadens all homeowners policies without charging additional premium. This applies only to changes made to the same edition of the homeowners policy that is owned by the insured. For example, if an individual is insured under a 1991 version of a homeowners policy, a change made to the 1984 version will not affect this insured. Any change to an insured's policy is effective on the date that the insurer makes the change.

The **waiver or change of provision condition**, in order to be valid, requires the insurer to put a change in writing. Also, the insurer is not waiving its rights by asking for an appraisal or an examination. Thus, coverage could be denied, if necessary, even after the insurer examines all the facts of a loss or claim.

The **cancellation condition** specifies the requirements for a valid cancellation of the policy by either the insured or the insurer. The insured may cancel the policy at any time by returning the policy and notifying the insurer in writing when cancellation is to become effective. The insurer, on the other hand, may cancel only for certain stated reasons (determined by state regulation) by delivering a written notice of cancellation to the insured within the stipulated number of days (also determined by state regulation). In the event of cancellation, the premium for the period following the date of cancellation will be calculated on a pro rata basis and refunded to the insured.

The **nonrenewal condition** requires the insurer to provide at least thirty days' written notice (although some states require a longer period for notification) to the insured in the event the policy is not to be renewed. The notice is mailed to the address on the declarations, and even if the insured does not receive it, proof that the notice was mailed is sufficient proof of notice.

The **assignment condition** states that any assignment of the policy without the insurer's written consent is invalid. The policy does not follow the transfer of real or personal property. The new owner must qualify for a homeowners policy, even if it is to cover the same, transferred property.

Under the **subrogation condition**, the insured may waive his or her rights to recovery against any person, if the waiver is in writing and is prior to a loss. Tenants often sign lease agreements that waive their rights against landlords for loss caused by the latter. In the absence of any waiver, an insurer may require the insured to assign his or her rights of recovery against another person to the insurer to the extent of the insurer's payment of a loss. Subrogation does not apply to the goodwill coverages found in Section II—Medical Payments to Others and Damage to Property of Others.

The **death condition** stipulates that if the named insured or spouse should die, the insurer agrees to cover the legal representative as an "insured," but only to the extent that the decedent had an interest in the property covered in the policy. The term "insured" may also include resident relatives and custodians of the deceased's property as identified in the death clause.

Conditions Affecting Section I Only

In addition to the general policy conditions, Section I has its own set of conditions. Among the conditions of Section I are the nuclear hazard clause, the loss settlement clause, the loss to a pair or set clause, and the glass replacement clause, which have already been described. Other conditions are discussed in the following paragraphs.

Insurable Interest and Limit of Liability

When more than one person has an insurable interest, the amount payable for the loss will be no greater than the insured's interest at the time of the loss, subject to the limit of coverage. For example, if the insured has a 30 percent interest in a dwelling, the insurer will pay only 30 percent of a loss to the dwelling but will not pay more than the Coverage A limit.

Insured's Duties After Loss

Among other duties, the insured is required to do the following:

- Notify the insurer of any loss
- Notify the police of any theft
- Notify the credit card or fund transfer card company in case of loss involving such cards
- Protect property from further damage
- Prepare a detailed inventory of damaged property
- File a sworn statement of proof of loss within sixty days of the loss

The insured must perform the following duties as often as the insurer requires on a reasonable basis:

- Show the damaged property
- Provide the insurer with the records and documents it requests
- Submit to examination under oath

Appraisal

Only when an insured and the insurer fail to agree on the *amount of loss*, either can demand an appraisal. Coverage disputes are *not* addressed through appraisal.

In the event an appraisal is demanded, each party chooses an independent appraiser. The appraisers then choose an independent umpire. The appraisers each develop separate estimates of the loss. If the appraisers agree and submit a written report to the insurer, the amount submitted in the report is the amount of settlement. If the two appraisers do not agree, their differences are submitted to the umpire, and if any two of these three parties agree to an amount, that is the amount of settlement. The insured and insurer each pay for their own appraiser and equally pay for any other appraisal costs and the cost for the umpire.

Other Insurance

When other insurance covers a loss, the policy pays its pro rata share. The only exception to this condition occurs when there is insured property subject to special dollar limits. If such property is more specifically covered under other policies, the homeowners policy does not apply to such loss.

Suit Against the Insurer

The insured may sue the insurance company to resolve a coverage dispute. However, no action will be permitted against the insurer unless all policy provisions have been complied with and the action is commenced within one year of the loss.

Insurer Option

If the insurer gives the insured notice within thirty days of receiving the insured's signed, sworn statement of loss, the insurer has the option of repairing or replacing any part of the damaged property with equivalent property rather than paying cash.

Loss Payment

Except as mentioned above, the insurer agrees to make any loss payments to the insured unless some other person is named in the policy to receive such payment. In homeowners policies, a mortgagee is frequently named.

Abandonment of Property

If the insured abandons the property after it is damaged or destroyed, the insurer is not obligated to accept it.

Mortgage Clause

When the mortgagee or trustee of real property is a named insured on the homeowners policy, the insurer may split the payment of any loss settlement under Coverage A or B between the insured and the mortgagee or trustee as their interests appear in the declarations. For example, if the insured and the mortgagee both have 50 percent interest in the property, they equally share the loss, and the insurer may independently pay each of them.

However, in most cases, the declarations page does not indicate the extent of the mortgagee's interest. The insurer issues one check, payable to both the insured and the mortgagee. These two parties then determine the amount each receives for the loss.

In the event that the insured is denied payment, the insurer will still consider the claim of a mortgagee or trustee valid if the mortgagee or trustee fulfills the requirements of a making a claim. If the insurer settles with the mortgagee or trustee and denies the claim of the insured, the insurer becomes the mortgagee or trustee of the property. Furthermore, the mortgagee or trustee will be separately notified in the event of policy cancellation. HO-4 does not include this condition.

No Benefit to Bailee

If the property is possessed by a person or organization (other than the insured), for a fee, at the time of the loss, the insurer will not make any payment that benefits this bailee. The policy covers only the losses of the insured, not the business losses of a bailee for hire. For example, suppose a chair is destroyed by fire while it is being reupholstered at a professional upholstery. The policy will cover damage to the chair, but it will not pay for losses to the upholsterer—such as loss of profit or liability.

Recovered Property

If property is recovered after a claim has been paid, the insured may keep either the payment or the property, but not both.

Volcanic Eruption Period

If a volcano erupts more than once in a seventy-two-hour period, all eruptions in that period are considered one volcanic eruption

Non-ISO Coverages for Homeowners, Tenants, and Condominium Unit Owners

Discussion to this point has considered only the ISO Homeowners Program. Although many companies do use ISO policies, many other companies use their own forms or policies from the American Association of Insurance Services (AAIS).

AAIS Coverages

AAIS is an independent advisory organization that, among other things, provides and files policy forms for its member companies. AAIS has a homeowners policy program that is similar to, and yet different from, the ISO policies discussed in this chapter.

Like ISO homeowners policies, AAIS homeowners policies offer package policies that include both property and personal liability coverage for owner-occupant or tenant-occupants of private residences, including single family homes, apartments, and condominium units. The property coverages provided by the AAIS forms are organized in the same fashion as the ISO forms, with Coverage A applying to dwellings, Coverage B to other structures, Coverage C to personal property, and Coverage D to additional living costs and loss of rent. AAIS forms provide coverage for the dwelling and other structures on a replacement cost basis and coverage for personal property on an actual cash value basis.

AAIS also offers a modular policy option. Under the Personal Monolines Portfolio, insurers are provided with a range of policy form components that can be mixed and matched to provide homeowners coverage to meet the needs of a specific insured. For example, the insured may not desire replacement cost coverage on other structures or may want basic named perils coverage on certain types of property while insuring other types on a broad named perils basis. The modular policy format allows an insurer to meet these individual requests.

There are minor differences between the property coverages offered by ISO homeowners and AAIS homeowners policies. The following items point out some of the differences:

- AAIS homeowners policies cover all property located at a second residence for up to 10 percent of the Coverage C limit, whether or not it is usually kept at the second residence. This means that when Ben, the insured on an AAIS homeowners policy, stays at his vacation home for the summer, the clothes, camera, and other personal belongings he brought with him from his primary residence are covered only to 10 percent of his Coverage C limit, even though this property is usually kept at his primary residence. An ISO homeowners policy would provide full coverage for Ben's personal property while Ben is staying at his vacation home.

- AAIS provides $1,000 in additional coverage for losses involving unauthorized use of credit or fund transfer cards, forgery, or counterfeit currency. ISO sets a limit of $500 for these types of losses.

- AAIS applies a special limit of $1,000 to the loss to grave markers. ISO includes grave markers with other property.

- AAIS explicitly excludes property loss that results from an order of civil authority. ISO explicitly excludes this loss exposure only in HO-3. ISO forms HO-1, HO-2, HO-4, HO-6, and HO-8 exclude this type of loss because it is not a named peril.

Under the AAIS homeowners policy program, Form 1 is the Basic Form, Form 2 is the Broad Form, Form 3 is the Special Form, and Form 4 is the Renters and Condominium Unit-Owners Form. The coverages provided by these forms correspond to the ISO homeowners policies of similar name.

There are minor differences in the perils covered under basic, broad, and special forms of coverage. The AAIS basic and broad policies include coverage for sinkhole collapse. ISO does not cover this peril in either its basic or broad named perils policies. AAIS does not cover loss due to freezing or accidental discharge, but ISO includes these loss exposures in the broad named perils policy.

The AAIS homeowners program includes an additional policy form—Form 5 Special Building and Contents Form. (ISO used to provide similar coverage under a Homeowners 5, but this policy is not currently available.) This form covers the dwelling, other structures, and personal property on an "all-risks" basis. The policy contains additional features, including the following:

- Replacement cost coverage for personal property
- Expanded coverage for watercraft powered by outboard motors (from twenty-five horsepower to fifty horsepower)

Many of the special limits are also increased. For example, $2,500 is available for theft of securities, jewelry, or watercraft.

Independently Filed Forms

Many large insurers develop and file their own policy forms, including homeowners policies. Many of the independent homeowners policy programs are similar to the ISO and AAIS homeowners policies in format, but differ in the specifics of coverage. Although a wide variety of policies is available from independent insurers, the following items list some of the more common features:

- Many insurers include "all-risks" coverage and replacement cost coverage for personal property.
- Higher dollar limits are provided for property such as money (up to $1,000), securities ($5,000 in most cases), and business property on the premises (up to $10,000).
- Coverage for jewelry, furs, and guns is expanded to include misplacement or loss, and the special limits for theft, misplacement, or loss of these items is generally increased.
- Coverage is provided for rebuilding to current building code.

- Coverage is also provided for lock replacement in the event that keys are lost or stolen.

- Reward money is provided for information and the return of stolen property.

Summary

The most common means for treating residential and personal property loss exposures is homeowners insurance. Under the ISO homeowners program, there are six homeowners forms: HO-1, HO-2, HO-3, and HO-8 for owner-occupants of private residences; HO-4 for tenants; and HO-6 for owner-occupants of residential condominium units. Each policy includes property and personal liability coverage. The six forms differ primarily in property coverage on the dwelling, other structures, and personal property of the insured.

The format of a homeowners policy includes a declarations page, a general agreement, a definitions section, a Section I (property coverages), and a Section II (liability coverages). Section I contains four main parts—Property Coverages, Perils Insured Against, Exclusions, and Conditions. There are four primary coverages: A—Dwelling, B—Other Structures, C—Personal Property, and D—Loss of Use. An important part of the property coverages is the Additional Coverages section, which expands the coverage provided by the four primary coverages.

Perils may be insured on a named perils or an "all-risks" basis. A named perils policy covers only those causes of loss listed in the policy, while an "all-risks" policy covers any cause of loss unless the policy specifically excludes it. HO-1 and HO-8 provide basic (or limited) named perils coverage for all types of covered property. HO-2, HO-4, and HO-6 provide broad (basic perils plus several others) named perils coverage for the types of property covered. HO-3, the special form, combines "all-risks" coverage on the dwelling and other structures with broad named perils coverage on personal property.

The property coverages on all policies are subject to general exclusions and general conditions. Losses involving such perils as earth movement and water damage are excluded. The general conditions describe provisions like the loss settlement process and the mortgagee clause.

The ISO homeowners policies are not the only insurance policies that cover the residential loss exposures of individuals and families. AAIS and private insurers have their own homeowners programs that are similar in nature to the ISO program.

Chapter Notes

1. The loss of use coverage provided under the 1991 ISO homeowners policies is modified by a mandatory endorsement to the policies, effective October 1994. The endorsement does not allow recovery for fair rental value unless the residence, or part of it, is actually rented to another individual for residential purposes at the time of loss. Before October 1994, the insured could choose to be reimbursed for additional living expenses or fair rental value.

2. Before October 1994, ordinance or law-related losses were excluded. An insured had to purchase an ordinance or law coverage endorsement to receive coverage for increased construction costs resulting from the enforcement of building codes.

3. Before the October 1994 multistate endorsement was added to the policy, the breakage of glass resulting from earth movement was also excepted, and thus covered, under this exclusion. Such loss, after October 1994, is covered under the glass breakage additional coverage.

4. The application of the deductible to the loss settlement differs, depending on company policy. Some companies reduce the settlement amount (whether it's the modified loss replacement cost or the actual cash value of the loss) by the deductible before making payment to the insured. Other companies consider the deductible as part of the amount not covered and pay the insured the settlement amount determined by the loss settlement clause. However, many companies apply the deductible as described in the text.

Chapter 3

Homeowners Liability Insurance and Homeowners Endorsements

As discussed in Chapter 1, liability can arise from a variety of sources, including premises and personal activities. This chapter focuses on the liability that can result from ownership or use of real and personal property and from the actions of individuals. These sources include premises and personal activities, as well as libel and slander, employment of domestic servants, contracts, recreational vehicles and watercraft, and other incidental activities.

ISO homeowners policies include personal liability insurance as part of their Section II coverages. Also included in Section II are medical payments coverage and some "additional coverages" that cover property damage to the property of others, first aid expenses, and other incidental exposures.

Homeowners policies do not cover all loss exposures faced by individuals and families. These policies are designed to cover the most common loss exposures. Other forms of coverage can be added to the homeowners policies by endorsement to cover less common loss exposures.

This chapter first discusses the coverages provided by Section II of ISO homeowners policies. Following the discussion of Section II coverages, the most common endorsements to the homeowners policies are described.

Homeowners Section II—Liability Coverages

Section II of the ISO homeowners policies insures many of the personal liability exposures faced by individuals and families. Each homeowners policy—HO-1, HO-2, HO-3, HO-4, HO-6, and HO-8—has identical liability coverage. Similar coverage is also available separately in a personal liability policy for people who do not purchase homeowners insurance.

As part of its basic coverage, Section II—Liability Coverages applies to most of an insured's exposures relating to premises, personal activities, contracts, employment of domestic servants, and other incidental exposures such as product liability and host liquor liability. Limited protection is also provided for exposures of boats, snowmobiles, and other vehicles. There are two principal coverages in this section:

- **Coverage E—Personal Liability** protects insureds against the financial consequences of their liability to others for property damage and bodily injury.
- **Coverage F—Medical Payments to Others** pays for, *regardless of whether an insured is liable*, certain medical expenses incurred by persons other than insureds because of injury stemming from insured exposures.

Both personal liability coverage and medical payments coverage are standard parts of the homeowners package.

Section II of a homeowners policy also includes additional coverages that are similar to the additional coverages provided in Section I, which pay for the following:

- Claim expenses
- First aid expenses
- Damage to property of others
- Loss assessment

Coverage E—Personal Liability

Personal liability coverage, as the name suggests, applies to the liability faced by an individual. The insuring agreement for Coverage E states that

> ...if a claim is made or a suit is brought against an "insured" for damages because of "bodily injury" or "property damage" caused by an "occurrence" to which this coverage applies[,]

the insurer will cover not only the damages but also the costs of any defense required by the claim or suit.

Several items included in the insuring agreement are of particular importance. Personal liability coverage applies only to *claims made or suits filed* against *an insured* arising out of *bodily injury or property damage* that result from an *occurrence to which the coverage applies*.

Personal liability coverage is designed to protect an insured from claims or suits alleging the insured's liability, even if the charges are fraudulent. Coverage is triggered by notice to the insurer of potential or actual allegations of the insured's liability. An insurer may be notified of a potential claim by an insured who reports an occurrence for which the insured may be held responsible. Third parties alleging that the insured is liable for injury to them or their property may also notify the insurer by making a claim with the insurer or filing a legal suit. Upon receiving notice, the insurer will begin to investigate and, if the occurrence is not excluded, start to develop a defense for the insured. The insurer will defend the insured even if the charges are fraudulent. If the insured is found liable, the insurer will also cover the damages to the policy limit.

The term "insured" is included in the definitions section of the homeowners policy. For the purposes of liability coverage, an **insured** is the named insured or a resident relative—such as a family member, an in-law of the named insured or spouse, or any person younger than twenty-one who is in the care of any of the preceding persons, including exchange students and foster children who are unrelated wards of the named insured or family member. A neighbor's child who is just visiting the premises is not an insured. The classes of people mentioned above are also insureds in Section I. Section II includes coverage as insureds for three additional categories of entities:

1. Any person or organization that may become legally responsible while using or having custody of any animal or watercraft owned by any insured may be covered. However, another person or organization is not covered for such liability if the use or custody is related to business or is without the permission of the owner. For example, if an insured asks a neighbor to care for the family dog while the insured is on vacation, the neighbor would be covered under the policy if the dog should bite the neighbor's meter reader. But an operator of a dog kennel who has custody of the insured's dog would not be covered by the insured's personal liability coverage.

2. An employee of the named insured, any resident relative, or any unrelated resident younger than twenty-one is considered an insured while using a vehicle to which the homeowners coverage applies. If, for example, a

gardener hired by the named insured injures a passer-by while operating the family's riding lawn mower, the gardener will be "an insured" under the named insured's homeowners Coverage E.

3. Any other person who is using a covered vehicle on an insured location with the permission of the named insured may also be considered an insured. Thus, if Terry, while riding Jamie's dirt bike in Jamie's yard with Jamie's permission, runs into Allison and injures her, Terry will be covered for liability for Allison's injuries under Jamie's HO-2.

The trigger for liability coverage is further limited because it is required that the suit or claim against the insured must allege "bodily injury" or "property damage," and that the "bodily injury" or "property damage" must occur during the policy period. Bodily injury and property damage, as defined, are the only types of injury to which the coverage applies. **Bodily injury** is defined in the policy definitions as bodily harm, sickness, or disease sustained by any person, including required care and loss of services, as well as resulting death. **Property damage**, also defined in the policy definitions, includes physical damage to or destruction of tangible property and any loss of use of tangible property.

If the claim or suit brought by the third party does not allege bodily injury or property damage as defined or if the bodily injury or property damage occurs before or after the policy period, the insurer is not obligated to provide coverage for any damages under Coverage E and the insurer does not have to defend the insured.

For example, damages resulting from such offenses as libel or slander, or involving contractual obligations that do not include property damage or bodily injury, are not covered by the insuring agreement. Endorsements that apply to these types of losses are discussed later in this chapter and in Chapter 6. Likewise, if the policy is in effect from June 1, 1994, to May 30, 1995, it will not cover bodily injury or property damage that occurs prior to June 1, 1994, and after May 30, 1995. The liability policies in force during those periods will cover those claims.

The term "occurrence" is of particular importance in the insuring agreement. The liability coverage applies only to bodily injury and property damage that result from an occurrence. An **occurrence**, as defined by the policy, is "an accident, including continuous or repeated exposure to substantially the same general harmful conditions." This means that one accident is one occurrence even if it involves injury to more than one person or damage to more than one piece of property. It also means that an occurrence may be a sudden event, a gradual series of incidents, or a continuous condition, so long as it is fortuitous. An example of a nonsudden occurrence is the gradual yet accidental seepage of pollutants from a defective septic system into a neighbor's supply of drinking water.

The occurrences to which the coverage applies are qualified by the exclusions contained in Coverage E. Even if an accident satisfies the policy's definition of occurrence, it may not be covered. The situation may be excluded by the policy. For example, an auto accident is generally sudden and fortuitous, but liability arising from an auto accident that results in bodily injury and property damage is not covered by the homeowners Coverage E, because auto liability is specifically excluded. The exclusions to Coverage E are discussed later in the chapter.

If a claim or suit satisfies each of the conditions required by the insuring agreement, the insurer is obligated to defend the insured, with counsel of the insurer's choice, and to pay any damages, including prejudgment interest, resulting from bodily injury or property damage for which an insured is legally responsible. The costs of defense are covered in addition to the Coverage E limit. They do not reduce the amount of insurance that can be used to pay for any damages. However, the insurer is not obligated to provide any further defense after it has paid damages equal to the limit of insurance.

For example, suppose Ned has a $100,000 limit for Coverage E. Ned had a dead tree on the edge of his property that neighbors had repeatedly asked Ned to remove. Ned failed to do so, and, during a windstorm, the tree fell, hitting Ann, a pedestrian, and Walt's home. Ann suffered severe injuries and sued Ned for $125,000. Walt also sued Ned for $35,000 needed to repair his home. Because the suits involve bodily injury and property damage resulting from a covered occurrence, Ned's insurer is obligated to defend him in both cases.

Ann's case is considered first and is decided in her favor. As shown in Exhibit 3-1, the insurer will cover the $100,000 of the $125,000 in damages. Ned is responsible for the remaining $25,000. In addition, the insurer is no longer obligated to defend Ned against Walt's claim involving the same occurrence, since the liability limits on Ned's policy have been exhausted. Ned is now responsible for the costs of his defense against Walt's allegations as well as for any damages that are awarded to Walt.

The insurer covers the costs of defense even if the claim or suit has no merit or is fraudulent. For example, Mark is burning leaves when a neighbor's house catches fire. The neighbor alleges that the fire is caused by a spark from Mark's fire. Suppose the neighbor's house fire is really caused by sparks from the neighbor's own wood stove, which land on the neighbor's roof. Mark's insurer is still obligated to defend Mark against the neighbor's claim that Mark caused the fire because Mark's alleged liability is within the scope of Coverage E.

Whether Mark's insurer will have to pay damages depends on whether the court holds Mark liable.

Exhibit 3-1
Ned's Liability Coverage

Ned's liability coverage limit	$100,000
Ann's Case	
Ann's settlement	$125,000
Ned's coverage	100,000
Ned's responsibility	$ 25,000
Walt's Case	
Walt's settlement	$ 35,000
Ned's coverage	0
Ned's responsibility	$ 35,000 plus defense costs
Ned's total responsibility for liability resulting from the tree's fall =	**$ 60,000 plus defense costs for Walt's suit**

Coverage F—Medical Payments to Others

Coverage F—Medical Payments to Others pays for *necessary* medical expenses incurred by people other than insureds, *for up to three years* from the date of an occurrence that causes bodily injury. **Medical expenses** include "reasonable charges for medical, surgical, x-ray, dental, ambulance, hospital, professional nursing, prosthetic devices, and funeral services."

Note that medical payments are covered for people *other than the insureds*. The definition of insureds is the same as that applicable under Coverage E, with the exception of residence employees. Residence employees can receive medical payments coverage under Coverage F; the named insured, his or her spouse, and resident family members and dependents cannot.

For an individual to receive medical payments coverage from the insurer, the occurrence resulting in bodily injury must meet *one* of the following conditions:

- *The injury occurs to a person who has permission, either expressed or implied, of the insured to be at the insured location.* Coverage F applies to the injuries of invitees and guests but not to the injuries of trespassers.

- *The injured person is away from the insured location, and bodily injury arises out of a condition at the insured location or on property immediately adjoining the insured location*. For example, Jill is walking on the public sidewalk in front of Kim's house when she trips over a garden hose extending from Kim's house to the street, where Kim is washing her car. Jill breaks her wrist. Under Coverage F, Kim's homeowners policy applies to the medical costs of Jill's injury.

- *A person is injured while not at the insured location by an activity performed by an insured.* If Tom receives a broken nose when Sam hits him in the face while tackling him during a football game at the neighborhood picnic, Sam's Coverage F on his homeowners policy would cover Tom's medical costs.

- *The individual is a residence employee who, while off the insured premises yet in the course of his or her employment for an insured, causes bodily injury to another person.* Suppose Rachel is a nanny for April. While hurrying down the lane to the bus stop to meet April, Rachel accidentally bumps into ninety-year-old Mr. Hughes and knocks him down, causing him to bruise his hip. Coverage F of April's parents' homeowners policy will cover the cost of Mr. Hughes' emergency room treatment and x-ray.

- *An individual is injured by an animal owned by or in the care of an insured while off the insured premises.* When Al lets Buster, his twenty-pound dog, out for his morning exercise, Buster nips the heel of the paper boy delivering a paper to the neighbors across the street from Al's home and breaks the paper boy's skin. Al's Coverage F will pay for the paper boy's medical expenses.

Medical payments to others coverage is really a form of health insurance rather than liability insurance, because an insured need not be legally obligated to pay damages to the injured person. Coverage is not based on fault. Thus medical payments coverage—typically written with a $1,000 per person limit—enables the insurer to promptly pay nominal medical expenses of an injured party without admitting liability on the part of the insured. This type of coverage is often referred to as a "goodwill" coverage. If the insured is legally liable for the injuries, Coverage E would respond. Coverage F can help to lessen the financial consequences of an insured's alleged liability, because the medical costs of the injured party are immediately paid without the need to argue over who is at fault and who should bear the financial burden. If the insured is not legally responsible, the insurer is under no obligation to pay damages, but may choose to do so under Coverage F out of goodwill.

Exclusions for Coverages E and F

Coverage E applies to all bodily injury or property damage liability loss exposures that are not otherwise excluded, and Coverage F applies to bodily injury for which an insured *may* be liable unless otherwise excluded. The exclusions are organized into three sections: exclusions that apply to both Coverages E and F, exclusions that apply only to Coverage E, and exclusions that apply only to Coverage F.

Exclusions Common to Both Coverages E and F

The eleven categories of exclusions discussed in the following paragraphs apply to both the personal liability coverage and the coverage for medical expenses of others. The exclusions are summarized in Exhibit 3-2.

Intentional Injury

Bodily injury or property damage that is intended or expected by the insured is not covered. It is against public policy for an insurer to provide coverage for an insured who meant to do harm to another person or to another individual's property.

This exclusion is controversial in some circumstances. It has been invoked by insurers on numerous occasions with mixed results. A majority of court decisions have held for coverage despite the exclusion when the act was intentional but the result was unexpected. In other words, for this exclusion to apply, the insured has to intentionally commit the act *and* mean to injure another person or damage another's property. In one case, for example, a youth and his friends got into an argument with another group of boys while swimming at a lake, and the youth decided to scare the other group by firing a BB gun at a sign near the other group. The youth hit one of the boys in the eye, causing the boy to lose his eye. Since the youth intended only to scare the other boys, not injure them, the court decided that the exclusion did not apply. The court ruled that "the plain language of the policy is in terms of intentional or expected *injury*, not an intentional or expected act."[1]

In addition, the policy probably would protect an insured who inflicts bodily injury to defend himself or herself against an attack or impending attack by another person.

Business Activities and Professional Pursuits

Homeowners Section II coverages are designed to cover personal liability exposures of individuals and families. Accordingly, Section II contains three exclusions that eliminate coverage for most business and professional exposures. These exclusions encourage people to cover their business exposures with commercial or professional liability policies. In some cases, incidental business or professional exposures can be insured by endorsements to the homeowners policy, some of which are described later in this chapter.

Exhibit 3-2
Summary of Exclusions

Common to Coverages E and F[1]

- Intentional injury
- Basic activities and professional pursuits

  - Business engaged in by the insured
  - Rental property
  - Professional services

- Not an insured location
- Motor vehicles
- Watercraft
- Aircraft
- War
- Communicable disease
- Criminal activities

  - Physical, mental, or sexual abuse
  - Controlled substances

- Bodily injury covered by other sources
- Nuclear energy

Coverage E[2]

- Contractual liability
- Owned property
- Property in the insured's care, custody, or control
- Bodily injury to an insured

Coverage F[3]

- Residence employee
- Regular residents

1. The exclusions apply to bodily injury and to liability resulting from bodily injury and property damage.

2. The exclusions apply only to liability resulting from bodily injury and property damage.

3. The exclusions apply only to bodily injury.

Business Engaged in by the Insured The first business-related exclusion eliminates coverage for bodily injury and property damage "arising out of or in connection with a business engaged in by an insured." **Business**, as defined by the policy, includes a trade, profession, or occupation. The exclusion applies to, but is not limited to, "an act or omission, regardless of its nature or circumstance, involving a service or duty rendered, promised, owed, or implied to be provided because of the nature of the business." Thus, if the insured is a carpenter by trade and is sued by a neighbor who alleges that the insured failed to build a porch for the neighbor as promised, the insurer has no obligation to defend the insured or pay damages that result from the suit.

Although the policy defines business to include trade, profession, or occupation, the courts have held that business activities must entail two elements: (1) the expectation of monetary gain and (2) a continuity of the activity. Thus, for example, a hobby such as building bird houses is not a business pursuit if it is not motivated by profit. However, if an individual is building bird houses to sell in flea markets, this hobby may be considered a business activity, and any bodily injury or property damage resulting from the activity will be excluded by a homeowners policy. An endorsement or an insurance policy that covers the insured's business is needed to cover these types of exposures.

Rental Property   The second business-related exclusion applies to bodily injury or property damage arising out of the rental or holding for rental by the insured of any part of any premises. Although the clause appears to mean rental situations in which the insured is either a landlord or a tenant, the exclusion applies only to premises rented by the insured to others—the insured is the landlord.

The exclusion does not apply to three circumstances involving the rental or holding for rental of an insured location:

1. *The occasional rental for use exclusively as a residence.* If an insured, while temporarily away from the residence, rents it out to another person or family for residential purposes, the insured is still covered by the policy. For example, Paul is spending the summer in Europe and rents his house to Liz while he is away. Liz's boyfriend, Tom, is injured when he falls down the basement stairs of Paul's house. Paul's HO-3 policy will cover Tom's injuries—subject to the coverage limit—under Coverage F and will cover Paul for any claim or suit brought by Tom under Coverage E. If Paul always held this residence for rental while he permanently lived elsewhere, he would not be able to insure the rental with a homeowners policy.

2. *The rental of part of an insured location as a residence to no more than two roomers or boarders per single family unit.* The policy continues to cover bodily injury and property damage arising out of those parts of the premises continually held for rental or rented to another individual or family, unless there are more than two roomers or boarders in each unit. For example, Ken owns a two-family house. He lives in one unit and rents the other unit to Rose and her two children. Ken is protected against claims or suits that arise pertaining to Rose's unit of the dwelling. If Ken also rents

out a room in his residence to a college student, he is still covered by his homeowners policy since there is one roomer in his unit and none in Rose's. If Rose sublets the basement of her unit to three college students, then Ken will have to arrange for another form of liability insurance, because his situation is now excluded by his homeowners policy.

3. *The rental, in part, of space on or in the insured location used as an office, school, studio, or private garage.* This exception allows the insured to rent part of the premises to other individuals for business purposes or for private garage usage and to retain coverage under Coverages E and F of his or her homeowners policy. However, the business uses of the tenant are restricted to an office, school, or studio.

These exceptions apply only for the benefit of those who qualify as insureds under the homeowners policy. Coverages E and F do not extend to the liability or goodwill of tenants in these situations.

For example, Ben rents a shed from Charlie for use as a private garage. Ben is responsible for the upkeep of the shed as a condition of the lease. Ben fails to fix a rafter he damaged, and it falls and injures his girlfriend. Charlie's homeowners policy will not make medical payments to Ben's girlfriend on Ben's behalf. However, the insurer may offer medical payments to Ben's girlfriend as a gesture of goodwill to protect *Charlie* from a liability claim brought by Ben's girlfriend.

For situations not excepted from the exclusion, several alternative endorsements are available. These endorsements are discussed at the end of this chapter.

Professional Services The third business-related exclusion eliminates coverage for bodily injury or property damage arising out of the rendering or failure to render professional services. A doctor, lawyer, or accountant with an office at home, for example, will not be covered for his or her liability for professional acts or omissions. Separate professional liability insurance is required for persons with professional liability exposures.

Not an Insured Location

Under this exclusion, no coverage applies to bodily injury or property damage arising out of any premises that are owned by or rented to any insured, or owned and rented to others by an insured, but are not an "insured location."

According to the policy, an **insured location** is one of the following:

1. *The residence premises,* as defined by the policy
2. *Any other premises, structure, and grounds used by the named insured as shown*

in the policy declarations, or acquired by the named insured during the policy period for use as a residence. Coverage here is meant to apply to any secondary residence of the named insured, such as a seasonal dwelling or a city apartment rented by an individual whose primary residence is located elsewhere. Only secondary residence premises of the named insured and spouse are intended to be covered, not those owned or rented by other insureds.

The secondary residence, if owned or used prior to the policy inception, must be declared at the time the policy is issued in order for the coverage to apply. If not declared, no coverage exists. However, if other premises, structures, or grounds are acquired during the policy period, they are automatically covered until the policy expires, at which time they must be reported if protection is to continue.

3. *Any premises used by the named insured in connection with items 1 or 2 above.* This is a catch-all coverage designed to provide the broadest protection available for any additional exposure somehow related to a principal or secondary residence. Coverage, for example, could apply to that part of a storage shed or garage used by an apartment dweller, or to a boat slip used at a campsite.

4. *Any part of a premises not owned by any insured and on which an insured is temporarily residing.* By inference, coverage applies at any temporary residence rented or used by the named insured, spouse, or other insured. Thus coverage could apply to a family member's occupancy in a dormitory as long as that family member is a resident of the household when the dormitory is not in use. Coverage would also apply to the named insured, spouse, or other insured who uses or rents a motel or hotel room, a seasonal dwelling, or a trailer space at a campground.

5. *Vacant land, other than farm land, owned by or rented to any insured.*

6. *Any land owned or rented by any insured, on which a one- or two-family dwelling is being constructed as a residence for an insured.* Construction operations can create bodily injury and liability exposures for which coverage applies, as long as the dwelling otherwise qualifies for coverage and is earmarked for occupancy by an insured. A house being built for sale by an insured would not be covered.

7. *Individual or family cemetery plots or burial vaults of any insured.*

8. *Any part of a premises occasionally rented to an insured for other than business use.* This category serves to catch exposures that are missed by the previous types of property discussed. For example, a hall rented for a party by the named insured is covered in this category.

Once it is determined that the bodily injury or property damage occurred at a location that is not an "insured location," it must be shown that the bodily injury or property damage resulted from a condition of the premises in order for the insurer to deny coverage for liability arising out of the situation. For example, Jake falls down a set of stairs at Luke's summer home and breaks his back. Luke is insured with an HO-3, but he has not declared the summer home (which he purchased prior to the policy period), and, thus, it is considered an uninsured location. If Jake's injury is caused by a condition of the summer home—a step was rotten and gave way when Jake stepped on it—Luke is not covered under Coverage E or Coverage F for Jake's injuries. If Jake's injury is caused by a condition that is independent of the property—Luke accidentally bumped into him—Luke may receive coverage from his HO-3 for liability and medical payments to others.

An exception to this exclusion exists. Coverages E and F apply to bodily injury to a residence employee that arises out of his or her employment by an insured. A **residence employee**, as defined by the policy, is (1) an employee of an insured who is involved with maintaining or using the residence premises, including housekeeping or domestic services, or (2) an employee of an insured who performs similar duties off the residence premises that are not related to a business of an insured. Thus, if an employee of an insured satisfies this definition and his or her injury is caused at an uninsured location, the injury is still covered by the homeowners policies. However, if the employee is or should be covered by workers compensation insurance, his or her bodily injury is still excluded.

Locations that are not insured by the homeowners policies can be covered through endorsements and separate insurance policies. Several of these coverages are discussed at the end of the chapter.

Motor Vehicles

According to the policy, the following sources of bodily injury and property damage are excluded:

1. The ownership, maintenance, use, loading or unloading of motor vehicles or all other motorized land conveyances, including trailers, owned or operated by or rented or loaned to an "insured."

2. The entrustment by an "insured" of a motor vehicle or any other motorized land conveyance to any person.

3. Vicarious liability, whether or not statutorily imposed, for the actions of a child or minor using a conveyance excluded in paragraph (1) or (2) above.

With the above clause, the homeowners policies exclude virtually all bodily injury and property damage arising out of motor vehicles, motorized land conveyances, and trailers. Not only is liability arising out of ownership or use excluded, but also liability resulting from entrustment of vehicles to others and vicarious liability arising from a child's use of a motor vehicle. Furthermore, all types of motor vehicles, from an auto to a riding lawn mower, are excluded (although some types of motor vehicles are excepted from this exclusion, as is discussed below).

The "entrustment" provision of the exclusion has been used by insurers to successfully eliminate coverage for host liquor liability involving auto accidents. For example, in one case,[2] a friend of the insureds became intoxicated at a party hosted by the insureds. While still drunk, the friend borrowed the insureds' car and left the party with another guest. An auto accident left the other guest in the insureds' car injured. The insureds claimed that the motor vehicle exclusion should not apply because their negligence was not vehicle related. An appeals court stated that the homeowners insurance policy was not intended to cover automobile liability, and thus the homeowner's insurer was not responsible for covering the insureds' liability in this situation.

Following the three exclusion provisions is a series of exceptions to the exclusions that provide coverage for some vehicle exposures. If a vehicle, or a situation involving a vehicle, is listed in the exceptions, bodily injury or property damage arising from the vehicle or the situation is covered. The exceptions, and, therefore, the *covered sources* of bodily injury and property damage, include the following.

- *Trailers not towed by or carried on a motorized land conveyance.* Thus liability coverage and medical payments to others coverage would apply to most parked trailers.

- *Motorized land conveyances designed for recreational use off public roads and not subject to motor vehicle registration.* In order to be covered, such vehicles must not be owned by an insured or, if owned by an insured, must be at an insured location. To illustrate, if Nancy operates a go-cart she does not own at an amusement park, she would be covered by her homeowners Coverage E for liability resulting from use of the go-cart. If Nancy owns the go-cart, she is covered for liability only while using it at an insured location.

- *Motorized golf carts when they are being used by people playing golf on a golf course.* Medical expense claims or liability arising out of the use of an owned golf cart for transportation between homes in a retirement community would not be covered.

- *Any motor vehicles or conveyances not subject to motor vehicle registration and*

(1) used to service an insured's residence, (2) designed for assisting the handicapped, or (3) in dead storage on an insured location. With this exception to the vehicle exclusion, liability arising out of lawn and garden equipment or powered and unpowered wheelchairs clearly is covered. Also covered are motor vehicles and conveyances that are in **dead storage**—generally meaning that the vehicle's electrical system is dead or the battery has been removed. A convertible that is not used during the winter is not in dead storage.

There is one additional exception to the motor vehicle exclusion. Bodily injury to a residence employee that arises out of any type of motor vehicle, whether excluded or not, is covered by the homeowners policies if the injury occurs during the course of the residence employee's employment by an insured. The definition of a residence employee is the same as that stated in the "not an insured location" exclusion. However, if the residence employee is covered by or supposed to be covered by workers compensation, such bodily injury is not covered.

The purpose of the liability and medical payments to others coverages in Section II of the homeowners policies is to provide protection against the general loss exposures that are related to the use of the dwelling and the residence premises and to the activities of the insureds. The motor vehicle loss exposures that are *not* covered by the homeowners policies, such as driving a registered auto on the highway, are more appropriately insured under other types of insurance. Most of the motor vehicle exposures that are excepted from the exclusion, and, thus, covered, such as mowing the lawn with a rider mower, are related to the use of the residence premises and are fairly common loss exposures for many homeowners and tenants.

Insurance is available to finance many of the motor vehicle loss exposures not covered by the homeowners policies. Chapters 4 and 5 discuss automobile insurance, and Chapter 6 describes insurance for other types of vehicles such as snowmobiles and motor homes.

Watercraft

The exclusion for watercraft resembles the motor vehicles exclusion. The policy first excludes all coverage for bodily injury and property damage resulting from watercraft with wording that mirrors the first three exclusion provisions in the motor vehicles exclusion—except that "motor vehicles" is replaced with "watercraft." The watercraft exclusion then describes the types of watercraft that are not subject to the exclusion by excepting certain types of vessels.

In most cases, an insured has coverage for bodily injury or property damage arising from borrowed watercraft. However, coverage for bodily injury or property damage resulting from owned or rented vessels is restricted. For example, if an insured injures a swimmer while operating a borrowed jet ski, the insured's liability for the swimmer's injuries would be covered. However, if the insured owned the jet ski, the policy would not pay for the liability loss.

According to the watercraft exclusion, watercraft designed to be "propelled by engine power or electric motor" or sailing vessels, "whether owned by or rented to" an insured, are not covered by the homeowners policies. Thus coverage for bodily injury and property damage arising from virtually all types of watercraft, except rowboats and dinghies, is excluded. However, the following vessels are excepted from the exclusion and, therefore, bodily injury and property damage resulting from their use is covered by homeowners policies:

1. Vessels, other than sailing vessels, powered by inboard or inboard-outdrive engine or motor power
   - Of fifty horsepower or less and not owned by an insured
   - Of more than fifty horsepower and not owned by or rented to an insured

2. Vessels, other than sailing vessels, powered by one or more outboard engines or motors
   - With twenty-five total horsepower or less
   - With more than twenty-five total horsepower if the engines or motors are not owned by an insured
   - With more than twenty-five total horsepower and owned by an insured if the insured (1) declares the vessel at policy inception, (2) owns the motors or engines prior to the policy period and notifies the insurer of his or her intention to insure them within forty-five days of their acquisition, *or* (3) acquires the engines or motors within the policy period. If the engines or motors are acquired during the policy period and are not declared, the coverage applies only for the policy period.

3. Sailing vessels that are less than twenty-six feet in overall length

4. Sailing vessels that are twenty-six feet or more in overall length and not owned by or rented to an insured

5. Vessels that are in storage

Other types of insurance provide coverage for liability exposures arising out of owned or rented watercraft. These coverages are further discussed in Chapter 6.

As with the "motor vehicles" exclusion, the watercraft exclusion does not apply to a residence employee who is injured in a situation involving watercraft while in the course of employment for an insured. If a residence employee is injured on any type of watercraft while carrying out his or her duties for an insured, the bodily injury is covered by the homeowners policy. However, if the residence employee is or is required to be covered by workers compensation insurance, the exception is not effective and the employee's bodily injury is not covered.

Aircraft

For the purposes of the aircraft exclusion, an **aircraft** is "any contrivance used or designed for flight, except a model or hobby aircraft not used or designed to carry people or cargo." Coverages E and F do not apply to bodily injury and property damage arising out of the ownership, maintenance, use, loading, or unloading of aircraft. In addition, just as with motor vehicles and watercraft, the policy does not cover loss resulting from the entrustment of aircraft to any person or from vicarious liability arising from the actions of a child or minor using an aircraft.

Only one exception to this exclusion exists. The exclusion does not apply to the bodily injury of a residence employee who is injured during the course of employment for an insured. However, if the employee is or should be covered by workers compensation insurance, the aircraft exception does not apply and the employee's injury is not covered.

Individuals who face personal aircraft exposures, such as if they own, rent, or borrow and fly a small private plane, may purchase liability insurance specifically designed to cover such exposures.

War

Any bodily injury or property damage arising out of war, as defined in the exclusion, is not covered by either Coverage E or Coverage F. War includes the same situations described in the Section I war exclusion.

Communicable Disease

Coverages E and F do not apply to bodily injury that arises from the transmission of a communicable disease by an insured. Although the exclusion does not specifically refer to sexually transmitted disease, the exclusion was added to the homeowners policies in the mid-1980s following court cases in which plaintiffs were awarded damages from persons who had negligently infected them with genital herpes. As the standard exclusion is worded, however, it could apply to the transmission of any communicable disease that is transmitted by person-to-person contact. The exclusion does not appear to apply to illnesses (such as the flu) involving transmission by airborne particles or to transmission by food and water (such as salmonella).

An individual might be able to obtain coverage for liability arising out of the transmission of communicable diseases through a personal umbrella policy. This form of coverage is discussed in Chapter 6.

Criminal Activities

Two exclusions apply to activities that are primarily criminal in nature. One applies to physical, mental, or sexual abuse. The other concerns the use, sale, manufacture, or trafficking of controlled substances. It is unlikely that an individual will find coverage elsewhere for either of these exposures. Counseling is one way to control exposures to abuse. Avoidance is generally the recommended treatment for activities involving controlled substances.

Physical, Mental, or Sexual Abuse   As the name of the exclusion indicates, the homeowners policies do not cover bodily injury that results from physical, mental, or sexual abuse. Most courts had excluded coverage for these types of situations under the "intentional acts" exclusion, but in at least one jurisdiction courts allowed mental disorder or compulsion of the offender to offset the "intentional acts" exclusion, and insurers were required to provide coverage for physical, mental, and sexual abuse. As a result, the exclusion has been added to specifically address these circumstances and ensure that coverage is not provided for bodily injury arising from abuse.

Controlled Substances   Bodily injury and property damage that arise out of the "use, sale, manufacture, delivery, transfer, or possession" of a controlled substance is not covered by Coverage E or Coverage F. The policy identifies controlled substances, as defined by the Federal Food and Drug Law at 21 U.S.C.A. Sections 811 and 812, to include cocaine, LSD, marijuana, and all narcotics. Legitimate use of prescription drugs, including controlled substances, at the orders of a licensed physician are excepted from the exclusion. Thus, coverage would apply if a visiting child accidentally ingested a host's prescription drug.

Bodily Injury Covered by Other Sources

In some cases, primarily for domestic employees, an insured may voluntarily provide or be required to provide workers compensation insurance or nonoccupational disability insurance. Personal liability coverage will not apply to bodily injury of any individual who is covered by one of these coverages provided by the insured. As noted in descriptions of previous exclusions, this exclusion removes coverage for residence employees subject to workers compensation requirements, who are injured during the course of employment in an occurrence involving uninsured locations, motor vehicles, watercraft, and aircraft.

Medical payments coverage also excludes coverage for bodily injury when the injured person is eligible for workers compensation or nonoccupational disability benefits voluntarily provided or required to be provided by any individual or organization, not just the insured. Thus, if a moving company employee is injured while making a delivery on the insured's property and the employee is eligible for workers compensation benefits, the insured's homeowners policy's Coverage F will not pay for bodily injury to the moving company employee. The exclusion prevents residence employees who are or should be covered by workers compensation insurance from receiving medical expense payments for bodily injury sustained during the course of employment. This exclusion overrides the exceptions to the uninsured locations, motor vehicles, watercraft, and aircraft exclusions. Thus, coverage is eliminated for residence employees' bodily injury resulting from these exposures when the residence employee is or should be covered by workers compensation.

Nuclear Energy

Homeowners liability coverage does not apply to bodily injury or property damage that is covered under a nuclear liability policy, or would have been covered under such a policy if its limits had not been exhausted. The exclusion defines a **nuclear liability policy** as one issued by (1) the American Nuclear Insurers, (2) the Mutual Atomic Energy Liability Underwriters, (3) the Nuclear Insurance Association of Canada, or (4) any of their successors. Such nuclear liability policies are required for operations of nuclear facilities and suppliers and transporters of materials, parts, equipment, and services used by these facilities. An individual's need for such coverage is limited. However, if an individual is an employee of a nuclear facility or its supplier or transporter, and the individual is sued in civil proceedings for damages caused by his or her release of nuclear waste into the water supply, the employer's nuclear liability policy should cover the damages. If the nuclear liability policy is exhausted, the employee's homeowners policy will *not* provide coverage for such a suit.

Medical payments coverage excludes any bodily injury resulting from nuclear reaction, nuclear radiation, or radioactive contamination.

Exclusions Applicable Only to Coverage E

Four exclusions apply only to personal liability coverage. In addition to the exclusions discussed above, which apply to both liability and medical payments coverage, these four exclusions apply only to personal liability coverage:

1. Contractual liability
2. Property owned by an insured
3. Property in an insured's care, custody, or control
4. Bodily injury to an insured

These exclusions are listed in Exhibit 3-2.

Contractual Liability

The homeowners policy excludes liability assumed under any contract or agreement, including agreements or contracts made by members of property-owner organizations, like a condominium association or a homeowners association, to pay loss assessments charged against them. However, the exclusion is stated not to apply to *written* contracts (1) that relate directly to the ownership, maintenance, or use of an insured location *or* (2) in which the liability of others is assumed by the insured prior to an occurrence. In either case, the liability is not covered if it is subject to any other applicable exclusion.

For example, Wes assumes liability for bodily injury and property damage under a written apartment lease. He is responsible for the walkway that connects his front door to the parking lot. Pam slips and falls on ice on the walkway and breaks her leg. Wes's HO-4 will cover any bodily injury liability claims Pam submits, since the lease is a written contract that deals with use of an insured location. Similarly, if Marcy assumes liability under a written rental agreement for a power saw that she will use in church volunteer work away from an insured location, her assumed liability for bodily injury and property damage to others will be covered, because it was assumed before any occurrence for which claim might be made. Marcy's policy will not cover damage to the saw itself because of the care, custody, and control exclusion discussed below.

Owned Property

Personal liability coverage does not apply to damage to property owned by an insured. The coverage is intended to deal with liability exposures. An insured cannot collect under Coverage E for damage caused by that insured to his or her owned property.

Care, Custody, and Control

Property damage to property rented to, occupied or used by, or in the care of an insured is excluded from coverage. Thus if Alex borrows Kyle's riding lawn mower and ruins its engine when he accidentally rides into a pond, Coverage E of Alex's HO-3 policy may not provide defense against, or pay, a claim brought by Kyle arising from the damage to the lawn mower.

When a person rents or uses property belonging to others, he or she has the common law obligation to return the property in essentially the same condition it was in when it was received, barring normal wear and tear. Depending on the value of the nonowned property, the liability exposure can range from minimal to extraordinary. For any substantial exposure, it is generally necessary to obtain some form of property insurance, because liability insurance policies almost always exclude coverage for damage to property in an insured's care, custody, or control.

An exception to this exclusion exists. The exclusion does *not* apply to property damage caused by fire, smoke, or explosion. The coverage provided by this exception commonly is referred to as **fire legal liability** or **fire liability**. This coverage is especially valuable for tenants. If an insured rents an apartment, he or she has liability protection under an HO-4 for damage to that part of the apartment building in the tenant's care, custody, or control caused by fire, smoke, or explosion for which the tenant is responsible. Thus, if the tenant falls asleep in a chair with a lit cigarette in his or her hand and, as a result, a fire destroys the living room and kitchen of the tenant's apartment, the tenant's HO-4 will respond to the damages under Coverage E.

In the homeowners policies, fire legal liability coverage is not limited to real property. It would also apply to, say, property damage to a borrowed kerosene heater that catches fire due to an insured's negligent handling.

Depending on the cause of loss, property damage to personal property used by an insured may be covered under Coverage C. If the peril is covered by Coverage C, the insured may request that the property damage be covered under the policy's personal property coverage. If the peril is not covered under Coverage C or if Coverage C is subject to a deductible, the insured may request coverage under Damage to Property of Others (discussed later in this chapter).

Bodily Injury to an Insured

Coverage E does not apply to bodily injury to the named insured, any resident relatives, or any other residents under the age of twenty-one and in the care of either of the aforementioned.

Exclusions Applicable Only to Coverage F

Two exclusions apply solely to the medical payments to others coverage, in addition to the exclusions common to both the personal liability and the medical payments to others coverages. They are listed in Exhibit 3-2 and are discussed below.

Residence Employee

Bodily injury to a residence employee is covered under Coverage F as long as it (1) occurs on an insured location, or (2) arises out of or in the course of his or her employment by an insured. If the bodily injury arises out of an occurrence off an insured premises and outside the employee's duties, no coverage is available under Coverage F.

The impact of this exclusion along with the residence employee exceptions to the "not an insured location," motor vehicle, watercraft, and aircraft exclusions, is to provide coverage for bodily injury to residence employees in most situations. Coverage F will cover the medical payments to the residence employee, and Coverage E will provide the insured with protection for suits or claims brought by the injured employee, as long as the suit, claim, or employee is not otherwise excluded. In effect, the insured has employers liability coverage under the homeowners policy for bodily injury to residence employees.

Regular Residents

Coverage F does not apply to bodily injury of any person, except a residence employee, who regularly resides at any part of the insured location. Thus, not only are insureds excluded from collecting for bodily injury under Coverage F, but other residents on an insured premises—such as the tenant of a garage apartment—are also not covered.

Additional Coverages

In addition to the personal liability and medical payment to others coverages, four coverages come under the general heading of additional coverages in Section II of homeowners policies: (1) claim expenses, (2) first aid expenses, (3) damage to the property of others, and (4) loss assessment. Although some of these coverages are limited in dollar amount, all apply *in addition to* the other policy limits.

Claim Expenses

Besides any judgment or settlement the insurer pays on behalf of an insured—which is subject to the policy's limits of liability—certain other expenses may be incurred with any claim or suit. The homeowners policy will cover the following claim expenses:

- *Expenses incurred by the insurer and costs taxed against the insured in any suit that the insurer defends.* For example, the insurer pays for the legal representation of the insured.

- *Premiums on any bonds required,* such as an appeal bond. However, the insurer will not pay the premium on bonds that exceed the policy's

Coverage E limit, and the insurer is under no obligation to furnish required bonds.

- *Reasonable expenses*, incurred by an insured at the insurer's request, including actual loss of earnings not to exceed $50 per day, for assisting in a claim or suit.

- *Interest on a court judgment.* Interest may be due a claimant if there is a lapse of time between the point when payment is owed and the time it is actually received by the claimant.

In order to be covered, each of these claim expenses must be associated with a claim or suit that the insurer is investigating or defending for the insured. If the insurer is no longer defending the insured, such as when the Coverage E limits have been exhausted, the insurer is also no longer obligated to cover the additional claim expenses.

First Aid Expenses

Under this additional coverage, the insurer will pay for any expenses incurred by an insured for first aid rendered to others for bodily injury covered by the policy. The first reaction of many people when someone is injured on their premises or when they injure someone while involved in personal activities is to call an ambulance or to take the injured person to a doctor or hospital emergency room. As long as the bodily injury is not otherwise excluded by the policy, the incurred first aid expenses will be covered. First aid to an insured is not covered.

First aid coverage differs from medical payments to others coverage in two ways. First, the expenses incurred for first aid are likely to be less than those incurred for medical payments coverage because first aid includes only expenses for "immediate" medical attention while medical expenses are paid up to three years from the date of injury. Second, an insured is permitted to voluntarily make any payment, assume any obligation, or incur any expense involving first aid to others at the time of the injury. First aid expense is the only coverage under the homeowners policy that permits the insured to do this without invalidating the coverage.

Damage to Property of Others

The personal liability coverage of homeowners policies excludes coverage for damage to property owned by, rented to, or in the care of an insured. Liability for damage to real and personal property occupied or used by the insured is also excluded, with the exception of fire legal liability.

For damage to personal property in an insured's care, custody, or control, coverage is available under Section I of the policy at the insured's option, if the damage is caused by a covered peril. Personal property is covered for actual cash value, less any deductible, up to the policy limits, unless the policy has been endorsed to provide replacement cost coverage.

Coverage for damage to property of others helps to fill the gap between the liability exclusions and the property coverages provided in Section I. It provides replacement cost coverage to $500 per occurrence for property damage not covered by either the liability coverage or Section I. Thus it is available either if the peril is not covered by Section I or to cover any deductible that applies under Section I.

Damage to property of others coverage applies even in the absence of liability. This additional coverage pays for damage to nonowned property caused by an insured who is likely to feel morally obligated to pay such damages, just as he or she feels morally obligated to pay first aid expenses at the time of bodily injury.

Damage to the property of others coverage is subject to its own set of exclusions. No coverage applies for the property damage described below.

Property loss is not covered to the extent that it is recoverable under Section I of the policy. This exclusion dovetails Section II coverage with Section I coverages. Suppose a racing bicycle with a replacement cost of $1,600 and an actual cash value of $1,400 is borrowed by Maureen and is stolen from Maureen's premises. Under Section I of the policy, Maureen's insurer pays the actual cash value of $1,400, less the $250 deductible, or $1,150. Under the damage to property of others, her insurer pays the remaining $450. Between the two coverages, the replacement cost of the loss is paid in full with no deductible.

If property loss is caused intentionally by an insured thirteen years of age or older, it is not covered. This exclusion, unlike the intentional injury exclusion that applies to personal liability and medical payments to others coverages, allows coverage for property damage intentionally caused by insureds younger than thirteen. Although teenagers may be held accountable to the same degree as adults for their acts, young children are not necessarily able to foresee the consequences of their acts. Coverage is not restricted to personal property or to property in an insured's care, custody, or control. Therefore, coverage applies when Donald, age five, damages a neighbor's new sidewalk by walking on it before the concrete dries.

Loss to property owned by an insured, or property owned by or rented to a tenant of any insured or a resident of the named insured's household is excluded. Property owned by any insured, including property rented to a tenant, such as household furnishings contained in a furnished apartment, should be covered under Section I of the homeowners policy or some other form of property insurance. Note that real and personal property rented to an insured is not excluded. Coverage would therefore be available to cover damage to a rented floor scrubber or damage to a rented apartment.

Property loss arising out of the following is also excluded:

- *Business pursuits.* Insurers prefer to cover business exposures under an appropriate form of commercial insurance.

- *An act or omission in connection with premises owned, rented, or controlled by an insured, other than an insured location.* This exclusion, like its counterpart under Coverage E, encourages an insured to obtain property insurance on any exposure—such as long-term rental of property by a family member, or a family member's ownership in a seasonal dwelling—that is not an insured location as defined.

- *The ownership, maintenance, or use of aircraft, watercraft, motor vehicles, or other motorized land conveyances.* This exclusion eliminates coverage for both damage to the aircraft, watercraft, motor vehicle, or conveyance itself and damage to other property resulting from the ownership, maintenance, or use of the aircraft, watercraft, motor vehicle, or conveyance. The purpose is to keep aircraft, watercraft, and auto exposures covered under aircraft, watercraft, and auto insurance policies. Specifically excepted from this exclusion—and therefore covered—are vehicles such as trail bikes designed for recreational use off public roads and not subject to motor vehicle registration.

Loss Assessment

Similar to the $1,000 loss assessment coverage of Section I, this additional coverage of $1,000 applies when a corporation or association of residential property owners makes an assessment against an insured, as a member of the corporation or association, resulting from a liability claim against the association. This additional coverage is not affected by the exclusion applying to loss assessments under Coverage E—thus, while liability coverage will not cover a loss assessment, the additional coverage may, to the $1,000 limit. Coverage applies in *one or the other* of the following cases:

1. The assessment is made as a result of bodily injury or property damage not excluded under Section II of the policy.
2. The claim is based on the association's liability arising out of an act of an unpaid elected director, officer, or trustee of the association. Coverage for

directors and officers liability losses is especially important to members of a condominium unit-owners' association who elect fellow unit owners to manage common property and other affairs of the association as a whole. There is no stipulation that any director's or officer's liability must arise out of bodily injury or property damage.

Like Section II loss assessment coverage, Section II loss assessment coverage applies only to loss assessments charged to the insured during the policy period. This is the case even if the bodily injury or property damage that results in the loss assessment occurs during an earlier policy period.

The conditions that apply to Section I and to the entire homeowners policy were discussed in Chapter 2. The conditions applying to Section II of the policy are described below.

Limit of Liability

The limit designated in the policy declarations for Coverage E—Personal Liability is the total amount applicable for damages resulting from any one occurrence, regardless of the number of insureds covered by the policy, the number of claims made, or the number of persons injured. Furthermore, all bodily injury or property damage that results from any one accident, or from continuous or repeated exposure to substantially the same general harmful conditions, is considered the result of one occurrence. For example, when Hal's deck collapses, twenty of his party guests are injured. Hal's personal liability limit of $300,000 is the most the insurer will pay for the bodily injury resulting from the deck's collapse even though the potential for twenty bodily injury liability suits or claims exists. Once the total claims exceed the $300,000 limit, Hal is responsible for his own defense costs as well as for payment of additional damages.

The limit of liability applicable to Coverage F—Medical Payments to Others is the total amount payable to any one person in any one accident. The standard per person per accident limit under Coverage F of the homeowners policies is $1,000. The insurer in the example involving the collapse of Hal's deck, may pay each of Hal's twenty injured guests up to $1,000 to cover his or her medical expenses resulting from the deck's collapse.

No aggregate limit exists for either Coverage E or Coverage F. Coverage E limits are rejuvenated after each occurrence. Even if one occurrence exhausts the liability limits, the limits are available in full for the next occurrence.

Coverage F limits apply per person per occurrence. Payment to one person does not affect payment to another person injured in the same occurrence, and payment under one occurrence does not affect coverage for the next occurrence.

Severability of Insurance

For some occurrences, it is possible to have a claim involving several insureds. Each insured seeking protection is treated as if each has separate coverage under the policy. However, the limit of liability stated in the policy is not cumulative, regardless of how many claims or suits are brought. Therefore, the insureds may be without adequate coverage, because the policy's limit of liability must be divided among them to pay for resulting damages.

For example, Sharon and Alice are sisters, and both are insured under their parents' HO-3. They fought with Dora, their neighbor. Dora, in the midst of the fight, fell and struck her head on the sidewalk. After lapsing into a coma for four days, Dora awoke with major speech problems and a loss of her short-term memory. Dora's family is suing Sharon for $550,000 and Alice for $100,000. The HO-3 under which Sharon and Alice are insured provides only $500,000 in liability limits. If the court decides against both Sharon and Alice, the most the insurer will pay, in total, is $500,000, even if Sharon is liable for $550,000 and Alice is liable for $100,000.

Consider the three possible outcomes presented in Exhibit 3-3. In Case 1, both Sharon and Alice are liable—Sharon for $250,000 and Alice for $50,000. Their homeowners policy will cover the total $300,000. However, if Sharon is found solely liable for $550,000, as in Case 2, her policy will cover only $500,000. Furthermore, as in Case 3, if Sharon is liable for $500,000 and Alice is liable for $100,000, the policy will only pay $500,000 of the $600,000 total.

Sometimes one insured may make a claim against another insured under the same policy. The insurer will independently represent each insured; however, the total amount of damages paid will not exceed the single liability limit of the policy.

Duties After a Loss

If a loss occurs under Section II coverages, the insured is required to do three things:

1. Notify the insurer

2. Supply information about the claim, including the time, place, circumstances, and witnesses

3. Assist the insurer when requested in any hearings, trials, or settlements

With regard to loss under damage to property of others coverage, the insured is required to submit a sworn statement of loss to the insurer within sixty days of the loss and, if possible, to display the damaged property. Finally, the insured is not permitted, except at his or her own cost, to voluntarily make payment or to assume any obligation or incur any expense other than for first aid to others.

Exhibit 3-3
Possible Outcomes for the Suit Against Sharon and Alice

	Case 1	Case 2	Case 3
Sharon's liability	$250,000	$550,000	$500,000
Alice's liability	50,000	0	100,000
Total liability	$300,000	$550,000	$600,000
Amount covered	$300,000	$500,000	$500,000

Duties of an Injured Person—Coverage F—Medical Payments to Others

The injured person making the claim for medical payments or the person acting on behalf of the injured person is required to give the insurer written proof of claim under oath, to give the insurer authorization to obtain medical records and reports, and to submit to a physical examination as often as requested by a physician selected by the insurer. Notice that it is a third party, not the insurer or the insured, who must perform these duties in order to receive payment under Coverage F.

Payment of Claim—Coverage F—Medical Payments to Others

The fact that an insurer makes payment under Coverage F is not to be considered an admission of liability by an insured or the insurer. The purpose of Coverage F is to prevent litigation by providing payment for an injured party's medical expenses.

Suit Against Insurer

An insurer cannot be sued under this policy until the policy provisions have been met and the insured's obligation has been ascertained by final judgment or agreement by the insurer. This condition also stipulates that no person has the right to join the insurer as a party to action against the insured.

Bankruptcy of an Insured

The bankruptcy or insolvency of an insured does not release the insurer from its responsibility under the policy. Even if an insured has no assets, the insurer is still required to pay any covered claim up to the policy limits because the policy agrees to pay on behalf of the insured rather than to indemnify the insured for payments he or she has made.

Other Insurance—Coverage E—Personal Liability

The personal liability insurance of the policy is excess over any other valid and collectible insurance except insurance written specifically to cover an excess over the limits of liability of the homeowners policy, such as personal umbrella liability insurance, which will be discussed in Chapter 6.

Non-ISO Personal Liability Coverage

Although the ISO homeowners policies are a major source of personal liability coverage, they are not the only source. AAIS homeowners policies and homeowners policies available from independent filers also provide personal liability insurance.

AAIS Coverage

The AAIS homeowners policies include a Section II that provides personal liability and medical payments to others coverages. The overall liability protection provided by the AAIS coverages is similar to that provided by the ISO homeowners policies. The organization and the style of the two policy programs differ.

Coverage L—Personal Liability covers an insured liability for bodily injury and property damage resulting from a covered occurrence. Defense costs and prejudgment interest are not covered under Coverage L. Coverage M— Medical Payments to Others covers the medical expenses of people who are not insured by the policy but who are injured by an accident involving the insured premises or an insured. For the purposes of the AAIS policies, bodily injury is defined *not* to include communicable disease and sexual molestation.

Coverages L and M are subject to several exclusions. The exclusions are not as extensive as those in the ISO policies, because the AAIS coverages provide greater detail in the incidental coverages (additional coverages in ISO policies) for Section II. The exclusions for the AAIS personal liability and medical payments to others coverages include the following:

- War
- Intentional acts of the insureds
- Exposures covered by other policies or coverages, such as (1) watercraft,

aircraft, and vehicles; (2) business and professional pursuits and workers compensation; and (3) nuclear energy.

Three incidental coverages are similar to additional coverage provided by ISO homeowners policies. These include damage to the property of others, claim and defense costs, and first aid expense.

Four incidental coverages clarify several of the exclusions contained in Section II of the AAIS homeowners policies. They are as follows:

- *Contracts and agreements.* Pays for damages resulting from liability assumed by an insured under a written contract in effect prior to the loss and not related to an insured's business activities.

- *Motorized vehicles.* Bodily injury or property damage arising from a motorized vehicle not subject to registration is covered if it (1) occurs on an insured premises or (2) occurs off premises and the vehicle is not owned by an insured. Other situations involving motor vehicles may also be covered.

- *Watercraft.* Bodily injury or property damage arising out of the use, maintenance, loading, or unloading of watercraft, subject to further policy restrictions, is covered.

- *Business.* Coverage applies to that part of an insured premises rented for use as a residence, school, office, or private garage. Also covered are certain incidental activities either performed by minors or related to business—though not business in nature, such as a daughter who mows the neighbor's yard for a small fee.

Independently Filed Forms

The personal liability policies offered by independent filers are similar to the ISO personal liability and medical payments coverages. Some of the more noticeable differences some of these policies have from the ISO coverages follow:

- A $250 per day, rather than a $50 per day, reimbursement for expenses incurred by an insured appearing at a trial at the insurer's request

- $1,000 in coverage for property damage to the property of others, as opposed to $500 available on the ISO policies

- Coverage for personal injury automatically included

Common Endorsements to ISO Homeowners Policies

Throughout Chapter 2 and this chapter, various ISO endorsements have been mentioned that add coverage to or alter coverage provided by the ISO homeowners forms. Some of these endorsements, such as the scheduled personal property endorsement, the inflation guard endorsement, the earthquake endorsement, the business pursuits endorsement, and the permitted incidental occupancies endorsement are commonly used. These and a few other endorsements are discussed in this section.

Special Provisions Endorsement

Many states have different requirements for policy wording and coverage provisions. A standard policy in one state may vary slightly from what is allowed in another state. To overcome the minor differences between the states without having many variations of each homeowners policy, ISO provides **special provisions endorsements** that modify the standard homeowners forms to conform with state requirements on policy coverage and wording. Thus, insurance companies that operate in many states can use the same standard homeowners forms in each state and simply add a state's special provisions endorsement to conform to state requirements.

Scheduled Personal Property Endorsement

Homeowners policies provide protection for the common exposures faced by the typical household. These policies contain exclusions and limitations for some types of personal property that are particularly susceptible to loss, that are difficult to value, or that are not owned or used by many homeowners, and thus are better insured by another coverage that accounts for the special risks associated with the property.

For example, homeowners policies contain special dollar limits on property such as coin and stamp collections that are easily damaged or lost and for which the actual amount of loss may be difficult to determine. Personal property especially attractive to thieves, such as jewelry, furs, silverware, goldware, and guns, is subject to dollar limitations only for loss by theft. Some perils to which certain property is exposed are not covered under Coverage C. For example, Coverage C does not pay for the loss of a gem that falls out of its setting or for a Ming vase that is dropped and breaks. Furthermore, the value of some personal property, such as fine arts, when combined with other personal property, may exceed the amount of insurance automatically provided for personal property under the homeowners policy.

The **scheduled personal property endorsement** can be used to overcome many of these coverage limitations. It is characterized by broad coverage and flexibility. It is available to insureds by endorsement to their homeowners policy or can be purchased separately as a "personal articles floater" policy. A

floater is a policy that covers "floating" property—that is, property that is typically subject to movement from place to place, such as jewelry, musical instruments, and cameras.

Endorsement Provisions

The scheduled personal property endorsement covers property up to a limit that is agreeable to both the insurer and the insured. The endorsement offers "all-risks" coverage with no deductible on specifically identified property, anywhere in the world (except for fine arts). This coverage also applies, in a more limited manner, to property newly acquired during the policy period.

Stated Limit

It is difficult to put a price or value on some property. Antique furniture and fixtures, fine arts, and some jewelry are affected not only by the materials that are used in producing them, but also by the maker and the period in which they were made. Often the value of these items can run into the hundreds or thousands of dollars. Homeowners policies are not designed to handle these situations. They limit items such as jewelry and furs, although antique furniture and fixtures and fine arts are included in the basic coverage limits. The scheduled personal property endorsement allows these special items to be **scheduled**—listed at a limit that is agreed upon by the insurer and the insured as the true economic value of the property—and serves as the coverage limit for the scheduled item. When a loss occurs, the insurer settles the loss on an actual cash value or a replacement cost basis but uses the limit as the maximum amount of coverage available.

An example of the schedule as it appears in the endorsement is provided in Exhibit 3-4. The insured under this schedule has covered two pieces of jewelry and camera equipment up to the stated limits. For example, the most the insured can collect if the diamond necklace is stolen is $7,000.

For items such as antiques, jewelry, and coin collections, the agreed value should reflect the appraised value or market value of the property. For other items, such as camera equipment and golf equipment, the agreed value may reflect the actual cash value or replacement cost. The advantages of the agreed limit are that the insurer and the insured have established a policy limit that is acceptable to both, prior to any loss and that this value reflects the financial worth of the item above its functional or manufacturing cost.

It is important that the limit stated in the schedule be accurate. The homeowners policies do not cover damage to property if the property is "separately described and specifically insured" by another policy. Thus, if property is

Exhibit 3-4

Scheduled Personal Property Endorsement   HO 04 61 04 91

THIS ENDORSEMENT CHANGES THE POLICY. PLEASE READ IT CAREFULLY.

For an additional premium, we cover the classes of personal property indicated by an amount of insurance. This coverage is subject to the DEFINITIONS, SECTION I - CONDITIONS, SECTIONS I AND II - CONDITIONS and all provisions of this endorsement. The Section I deductible as shown on the Declarations does not apply to this coverage.

	Class of Personal Property	Amount of Insurance	Premium
1.	**Jewelry**, as scheduled.	$*10,000	$*50
2.	**Furs** and garments trimmed with fur or consisting principally of fur, as scheduled.		
3.	**Cameras**, projection machines, films and related articles of equipment, as listed.	5,000	30
4.	**Musical instruments** and related articles of equipment, as listed. You agree not to perform with these instruments for pay unless specifically provided under this policy.		
5.	**Silverware**, silver-plated ware, goldware, gold-plated ware and pewterware, but excluding pens, pencils, flasks, smoking implements or jewelry.		
6.	**Golfer's equipment** meaning golf clubs, golf clothing and golf equipment.		
7.a.	**Fine Arts**, as scheduled. This premium is based on your statement that the property insured is located at the following address. at at	Total Fine Arts Amount $	
7.b.	For an additional premium, paragraph 5.b. under Perils Insured Against is deleted only for the articles marked with a double asterisk (**) in the schedule below.	Amount of 7.b. only $	
8.	**Postage Stamps**		
9.	**Rare and Current Coins**		

SCHEDULE*

Article	Description	Amount of Insurance
Diamond bracelet	12 pure 1/3k diamonds, 14k white gold setting	$3,000
Diamond necklace	18" 14k gold chain, pure 2k diamond pendant	$7,000
T-Max 90	35 mm body	$500
300Z lens		$3,000
Hasenbladt	camera body + 2 lens	$1,500

THE AMOUNTS SHOWN FOR EACH ITEM IN THE SCHEDULE ARE LIMITED BY CONDITION 2. LOSS SETTLEMENT ON PAGE 3 OF THIS ENDORSEMENT.

*Entries may be left blank if shown elsewhere in this policy for this coverage.

HO 04 61 04 91   Copyright, Insurance Services Office, Inc., 1990   Page 1 of 3 covered by this endorsement, it will not be covered by the homeowners policy's Coverage C, even if the agreed limit is not high enough to provide full coverage for the damaged property. Thus, if the diamond bracelet listed in the schedule in Exhibit 3-4 is stolen, the most the insured can collect from insurance is $3,000, even if the bracelet is valued at $4,500 at the time of the theft. The homeowners policy insurer will not provide any coverage, and the schedule insurer will not cover more than the limit stated in the schedule.

"All-Risks" Coverage

Personal property, even if it is not subject to a special limit or exclusion of the standard homeowners policies, is covered only for broad named perils. The scheduled personal property endorsement provides "all-risks" coverage for the property listed in the endorsement. As with the "all-risks" coverage available in HO-3, the endorsement covers only direct loss to the covered property. But only four categories of perils are excluded by the endorsement:

1. Wear and tear, gradual deterioration, or inherent vice
2. Insects or vermin
3. War, including undeclared war, civil war, warlike act by a military force, or destruction or seizure for a military purpose
4. Nuclear hazard

Additional provisions applying specifically to fine arts and to stamp or coin collections are discussed later in this section.

No Deductible

The scheduled personal property endorsement provides first-dollar coverage for covered losses to scheduled property. Deductibles are intended to reduce the costs involved with filing and settling small claims on partial losses. For most claims involving scheduled property, the property is a total loss so a deductible is less important than under other forms of insurance.

Worldwide Coverage

The coverage applies to the scheduled items anywhere in the world. One exception exists: the coverage for fine arts applies only in the United States and Canada.

Newly Acquired Property

When an insured acquires property of a class already covered, other than fine arts, the additional property is covered for up to 25 percent of the insurance for that class or $10,000—whichever is the lesser of the two amounts. However, the provision for automatic coverage applies only if the insurer is notified within thirty days of the date the property is acquired and an additional premium is paid for the coverage from the date of acquisition. After the thirty-day period expires, no coverage applies to unreported newly acquired property.

If the newly acquired property is fine arts, and fine arts are already covered under the endorsement, the new property is covered for up to 25 percent of the existing limit of coverage for fine arts. The insured has ninety days to notify the insurer of the acquisition and pay the premium to qualify for the automatic coverage.

General Conditions

The conditions of the homeowners policy, except as modified by the scheduled personal property endorsement provisions, apply to the scheduled personal property. The endorsement itself contains three additional conditions: loss clause; loss settlement; and pair, set or parts other than fine arts.

Loss Clause

The loss clause specifies that the insurance is not reduced by any loss except for total loss of a scheduled item of property. It stands to reason that when specifically described property is totally destroyed, the total amount of insurance on the endorsement should be reduced because the property no longer needs to be insured. In the event that this should happen during the policy period, the insured can either accept a refund of unearned premium, or the insured may apply the unearned premium toward the premium due for insurance on any replacement.

Loss Settlement

With the exception of fine arts, the insurer will determine the value of the property at the time of the loss—the insurer does not have to pay the limit listed on the schedule unless the property is a piece of fine art. While the stated limit serves as the ceiling on what the insurer will pay, the floor is defined by the loss settlement clause. The insurer will pay the *least* of the four following amounts, as determined at the time of loss or damage:

1. Actual cash value of the insured property
2. The amount for which the property could reasonably be expected to be repaired
3. The amount for which the article could reasonably be expected to be replaced with one substantially similar
4. The amount of insurance designated for the property

Fine arts are covered for the amount scheduled.

Thus, for property other than fine arts, the endorsement provides replacement cost coverage subject to the stated limit. For fine arts, the endorsement provides valued coverage.

If stamps or coins in a collection are covered on a **blanket basis**—the value of the collection is listed, not the value of each coin or stamp—the insurer will not pay more than $1,000 for the entire collection and will not pay more than $250 for an individual item or small subset of items, such as a pair of coins or a set of twelve Christmas stamps. Furthermore, if part of the collection subject to blanket coverage is lost, the insurer will not pay more than a portion of the value of the loss. The proportion is determined by the percent of the total collection market value covered by the amount of blanket coverage. In terms of a formula, the amount covered is equal to

$$\frac{\text{The amount of blanket coverage}}{\substack{\text{The market value of the collection} \\ \text{covered by the blanket}}} \quad \times \quad \substack{\text{The market value of} \\ \text{the part of the} \\ \text{collection lost}}$$

For example, suppose Helen has a stamp collection that she insures on a blanket basis for a value of $1,000. One sheet of her stamps, worth $500, is stolen. At the time of the loss, Helen's entire stamp collection had appreciated to a market value of $1,750. The most Helen will receive for her loss is $285.71, determined as follows:

$$\frac{\$1,000 \text{ blanket}}{\$1,750 \text{ market value of collection}} \quad \times \quad \$500 = \$285.71$$

Pair, Set or Parts

Some losses to property insured under the endorsement may involve pairs, such as a pair of earrings; sets, such as a set of drums or golf clubs; or parts, such as parts to a camera or other photographic equipment. In the event of loss involving a pair or set, the insurer may either (1) repair or replace any item to restore the pair or set to its value prior to the loss or (2) pay the difference between the actual cash value of the property before and after the loss. For example, a pair of antique salt and pepper shakers is valued at $1,000. If the salt shaker is broken, the remaining pepper shaker may be valued at only $200 without its mate. In that case, if the insurer could not find a salt shaker to replace the broken one, the insured could recover $800 from the insurer.

When loss is sustained to one part of property consisting of several parts, like a movie projector, the insurer is obliged only to pay for the value of the part of the property that has been lost or damaged.

If the loss to a pair or set involves jewelry or fine arts, the insurer might pay the entire scheduled limit of coverage for the damaged set or pair. The insured, in order to receive the full amount, must surrender the remaining article(s) of the pair or set to the insurer. This approach to pair and set valuation is often referred to as **broad pair and set coverage**.

Types of Property Covered

As shown in Exhibit 3-4, the scheduled personal property endorsement includes coverage for nine classes of property from which insureds may pick and choose to fit their needs. The nine classes of property are jewelry, furs, cameras, musical instruments, silverware, golfer's equipment, fine arts, postage stamps, and rare and current coins.

Jewelry

Jewelry insurable under the endorsement consists of articles of personal adornment composed in whole or in part of silver, gold, platinum, or other precious metals or alloys, whether or not containing pearls, jewels, or precious or semiprecious stones. Other articles eligible for coverage include valuable pens, pencils, cigarette cases, trophies, and similar articles. Articles not eligible for coverage are silver, silverware, pewterware, gold bullion, other precious metals, and unmounted gems. Articles that are insured must be separately described along with the amount of insurance that applies to each described article.

As mentioned above, at the option of the insured, broad pair and set coverage can be purchased. When this coverage is in effect, the full amount shown in the schedule will be paid in the event of loss to a pair or set, provided that the insured surrenders to the insurer the remaining article(s) of the pair or set.

Furs

The class of property for *furs* includes garments trimmed with fur or consisting principally of fur, imitation furs, and fur rugs. Although each item of fur must be described and specifically insured, an ensemble—such as a coat, muff, and hat—can be insured as one item.

Loss caused by insects and vermin is not covered by the endorsement. Since furs are susceptible to this type of damage, proper storage of furs when they are not in use is imperative to control this exposure. Professional furriers are best equipped to provide fur storage services.

Cameras

The *photographic equipment* eligible for coverage includes cameras, projectors,

classes of property eligible for *coin collection* coverage are rare or current coins, medals, paper money, bank notes, tokens of money, and other numismatic property. Also covered are coin albums, containers, frames, cards, and display cabinets containing such collections whether or not owned by the insured.

As noted earlier, stamp and coin collections are subject to additional exclusions. The endorsement does not provide coverage for losses due to the following:

- Fading, creasing, denting, scratching, tearing, or thinning
- Transfer of colors, inherent defect, dampness, extremes of temperature, or depreciation
- Handling

The losses excluded occur to coins or stamps that are commonly handled or worked on and to those that are improperly stored. These types of losses are due to lack of care, and their exclusion parallels the homeowners exclusions of neglect and wear and tear.

The disappearance of stamps or coins that are not separately scheduled or are not mounted on a page that has disappeared from a volume is excluded. This ensures that coins and stamps are not just mislaid or carelessly stored. Items that are specifically scheduled or that are attached or mounted to a page or in a volume are considered more important and more difficult to lose unless by theft. However, if the conditions are met, coverage is provided.

Stamps or coins that are lost while being shipped by mail, other than registered mail, or stolen from an unattended auto during transport are not covered. These exclusions hold the insured to a higher degree of care when transporting or shipping valuable stamps and coins. Registered mail is less likely than other forms of shipment to be lost or stolen. An attended auto is more secure than one that is unattended. If these steps are not taken to protect stamps or coins, loss or theft of such items is not covered.

The endorsement eliminates coverage for articles being transported by a transportation company and for items not considered part of the stamp or coin collection. If under the control and care of an independent transporter, loss of or to coins and stamps is the responsibility of the transporter, not of the owner's insurer. If the property subject to loss is not part of the collection, it should be apparent that it is not covered by the policy unless separately scheduled.

Endorsements That Affect Loss Valuation

Certain homeowners endorsements modify the manner by which the loss is valued. These endorsements are the personal property replacement cost endorsement, the inflation guard endorsement, and the guaranteed replacement cost endorsement.

Personal Property Replacement Cost Endorsement

This endorsement modifies any homeowners policy to provide replacement cost coverage for personal property, and also to dwelling items and other structure items that are otherwise covered on an ACV basis, such as awnings, carpets, and household appliances.

Some items are not eligible for replacement cost coverage under the endorsement. They include the following:

- Antiques, fine arts, paintings, and similar articles of rarity or antiquity that cannot be replaced
- Memorabilia, souvenirs, collectors' items, and similar articles whose age or history contribute to their value
- Articles not maintained in good or workable condition
- Articles that are outdated or obsolete and kept in storage or not in use

When the personal property replacement cost endorsement is added to a homeowners policy that also contains a scheduled personal property endorsement, the replacement cost provisions apply to the scheduled items, except for those otherwise excluded, such as antiques and fine arts (the ACV of antiques is usually their market value, and fine arts are covered for their agreed value).

The endorsement does not increase the coverage limits that apply to these items; it simply alters the method by which the loss is valued. The endorsement does not pay more than the least of the following amounts:

- The replacement cost at the time of the loss
- The actual cost to repair the property at the time of the loss
- The Coverage C limit, if applicable
- Any special limit included in the policy
- The limit applicable to any item described separately in the policy

The term "policy" refers to the homeowners policy and any attached endorsements.

The personal property replacement cost endorsement further states that, if the loss sustained costs more than $500 to replace, the insurer will pay only the ACV of the loss until the property is repaired or replaced. If the insured is not certain that the property will be repaired or replaced, the claim can be made for the ACV of the loss and the insured can file for any increased costs if the property is repaired or replaced within 180 days of the loss.

Inflation Guard Endorsement

During periods of inflation, the replacement cost of a dwelling generally increases. The homeowner desiring full replacement cost coverage must continually verify the adequacy of the policy limits. The **inflation guard endorsement** is a practical procedure to help the insured maintain adequate protection.

The endorsement increases the limits on the dwelling—and thus on the other structures, personal property, and loss of use coverages—by a specified annual percentage. This percentage may be tied to an index such as a construction cost index. The increase is prorated throughout the policy year. For example, if Marge's house is insured for $100,000 with a 4 percent inflation guard, halfway through the year she would have $102,000 coverage on the dwelling.

Guaranteed Replacement Cost Endorsement

Guaranteed replacement cost coverage pays the full cost of replacing a dwelling, even if that cost exceeds the Coverage A limit. To be eligible for this coverage, the insured must typically insure the dwelling for its full replacement cost value at policy inception and agree to periodic adjustments of the Coverage A limit based on an inflation index. (Because Coverage B, C, and D limits are tied to the Coverage A limit, the limits of coverage available for other structures, personal property, and loss of use are also increased based on the inflation index.) The insured must report any alterations to the dwelling that add to its replacement value by 5 percent or more.

When a dwelling is subject to this arrangement, the insurer will pay the smallest of two amounts: (1) the replacement cost of the damaged property or (2) the amount actually spent to make the necessary repairs or replacements.

Endorsements That Cover Business Uses of Residential Property

Some homeowners operate a business out of their homes or rent property to others for residential use. In some instances the property involved in these activities can be covered under homeowners policies by adding an endorsement. Several of these endorsements are discussed in the following paragraphs.

Business Pursuits Endorsement

Section II of the homeowners policies excludes coverage for bodily injury and property damage that arises out of any business activities engaged in by an insured. The **business pursuits endorsement** extends Section II of the homeowners policy to cover bodily injury and property damage arising out of the insured's business activities in connection with a business not owned or controlled by the insured or of which the insured is not a partner. The business pursuits endorsement is available for individuals—such as clerical office employees, sales representatives, bill collectors, and teachers—who may, while at home or otherwise away from the employer's premises after hours, perform some business activities for their employers. However, the endorsement will not cover bodily injury to an insured's fellow employee by the insured during the course of employment.

Teachers may obtain coverage under the endorsement for liability for corporal punishment of pupils. However, liability for teaching activities related to horses, cars, boats, and aircraft is excluded. Driver training teachers or teachers at a riding academy may need special coverage under another type of policy.

Home Day Care Coverage Endorsement

A mandatory ISO endorsement used in most states makes it clear that insureds regularly providing home day care service for compensation to persons other than insureds are considered to be engaged in a business. (Mutual exchange of services and services to relatives of an insured are stated not to be a business.) Thus, home day care operations that qualify as a business are clearly subject to the Section II business operations exclusion. They are also subject to the Coverage B exclusion of other structures used in whole or in part for business purposes and the Coverage C limitations on business personal property ($2,500 for business property on premises and $250 for business property away from the premises).

The **home day care coverage endorsement** can be used to extend the homeowners liability, medical payments to others, and other structures coverages to home day care operations and to make the Coverage C business property limitations inapplicable to such operations. However, the endorsement imposes additional exclusions on liability and medical payments to others coverage. These exclusions apply to the following:

- Corporal punishment or sexual abuse of any person that is inflicted by or at the direction of an insured

- The maintenance, use, loading or unloading, or entrustment by the insured to any person of draft or saddle animals, aircraft, motorized land conveyances, or watercraft for the purpose of instruction in their use

- Injury to any employee of an insured (other than a residence employee) arising out of a day care operation

Incidental Farming Personal Liability Endorsement

Homeowners who sell fruit, produce, poultry, or other agricultural products raised on their residence premises should have their policies endorsed with the **incidental farming personal liability endorsement.** This endorsement protects insureds against any premises and products liability that might arise from the sale of homegrown products. Coverage applies only to farming or gardening operations that are not the principal occupation of the insured—in other words, incidental farming. If farming or gardening operations are a principal occupation, a form of commercial coverage, which is beyond the scope of this text, should be considered.

Structures Rented to Others Endorsement

Coverage B excludes coverage of other structures rented to any person who is not a tenant of the dwelling. Coverage E excludes liability coverage, in certain situations, for property that is rented to others. When the named insured rents out a structure on or off the residence premises to be used as a residence, such as an apartment in a converted detached garage or a rental house, the **structures rented to others endorsement** might be used to provide Section I coverage for a specified amount and to extend Section II liability and medical payments coverages to the structure. Each structure to be covered by the endorsement is identified and listed with the applicable amount of insurance.

Permitted Incidental Occupancies—Residence Premises Endorsement

Coverage B excludes coverage for other structures used in whole or in part for business, and Coverage C limits coverage for business property on premises to $2,500. Section II excludes coverage for business activities or, for some circumstances, the rental of any part of the premises by an insured. If the insurer is willing to cover an incidental business conducted by the insured on the residence premises, coverage for the property involved and liability resulting from its use can be arranged through the **permitted incidental occupancies—residence premises endorsement.**

For business conducted in another structure on the premises, the endorsement provides a separate amount of coverage on the structure, thereby avoiding the Coverage B exclusion. The endorsement also modifies the Coverage C special limit so that it does not apply to property used in the business described in the endorsement.

With regard to Section II, the endorsement modifies the business activities exclusion so that it does not apply to the described business. However, two additional Section II exclusions are added. They apply to bodily injury (1) to any employee of the insured when the injury arises out of the described business (other than to a residence employee while engaged in his or her employment by an insured) and (2) to any pupil when the injury arises out of corporal punishment administered by or at the direction of the insured. Domestic employees are covered under the Section II coverages or through an employer's coverage under its workers compensation insurance policy. Corporal punishment liability coverage may be purchased under the business pursuits endorsement.

In some cases, individuals who operate a small business out of their residence may need more business property and liability insurance than an insurer is willing to cover with a permitted incidental occupancies—residence premises endorsement. For example, a person who builds and sells wood furniture may have valuable machinery located in his or her basement and is exposed to products liability with each piece of furniture he or she sells. An insurance agent operating out of the den in his or her residence may have records of accounts receivable and other valuable papers as well as office furniture and supplies. The agent is exposed to premises liability each time a client visits the office. These individuals may need to consider purchasing a businessowners policy or another form of commercial insurance, as is discussed in CPCU 3 and CPCU 4.

Workers Compensation Insurance

Although it is generally not available as an endorsement to homeowners policies, workers compensation insurance may be necessary for homeowners who hire domestic employees. In an increasing number of jurisdictions, laws require domestic employees to be covered under workers compensation insurance. Some of these state laws mandate benefits for employees working more than a specified number of hours. Even when not required, this insurance can be voluntarily obtained by an employer. A few states require casual employees, such as minors hired to mow lawns, to be covered by workers compensation insurance.

When workers compensation insurance is, or is required to be, purchased, coverage for residence employees under Section II of the homeowners policy does not apply. When workers compensation insurance is not mandatory and an employer does not voluntarily purchase the insurance, protection is available under Coverages E and F of the homeowners policy.

Several other endorsements are important to many homeowners. They include the earthquake endorsement, the personal injury endorsement, the additional insured—residence premises endorsement, and the premises alarm and fire protection system endorsement.

Earthquake Endorsement

No part of the United States is immune from the catastrophic peril of earthquake, yet some areas have a greater probability of loss than others. Earthquake is either not a named peril or is excluded from "all-risks" coverage on the homeowners policies. Coverage against earthquake can be obtained by adding the earthquake endorsement.

The **earthquake endorsement** covers Section I property for physical damage caused by an "earthquake including land shock waves or tremors before, during or after a volcanic eruption." All earthquakes occurring in a seventy-two-hour period are considered a single earthquake for coverage purposes. In addition, the endorsement modifies the Section I earth movement exclusion so that it does not apply to loss caused by earthquake, land shocks, or tremors that occur before, during, or after a volcanic eruption. However, loss caused by flood or tidal wave, even if resulting from the covered earthquake, is not covered. The endorsement also excludes coverage for filling land following a loss and for damage to exterior masonry veneer, with the exception of stucco.

If personal property is covered under an "all-risks" endorsement (such as the scheduled personal property endorsement), the earthquake endorsement only needs to be added for Coverages A and B. "All-risks" coverage available by endorsement includes coverage for loss caused by earthquake.

The earthquake endorsement contains its own deductible provision. The deductible under this endorsement, for damage caused by an earthquake, is typically 5 percent (but can be increased for a premium credit) *of the amount of insurance* that applies to the damaged property and applies separately to each coverage involved in the loss. For example, Jed's house and belongings are insured under an HO-2, with $100,000 coverage on the house and $50,000 on his personal property. He has an earthquake endorsement with a 5 percent deductible clause. An earthquake damages both his dwelling and his personal property. Jed will have to pay a $5,000 deductible (5 percent of $100,000) on the damage to his house and a $2,500 deductible (5 percent of $50,000) for the damage to his personal property—a total deductible of $7,500, regardless of the amount of damage. So, if Jed experienced an earthquake that caused $20,000 in damage to his home and $3,000 in damage to his personal property, he would receive coverage of $15,000 for his home and $500 for his personal property. He would retain the remaining $7,500.

If certain property is insured under an endorsement that increases the limit of coverage for that property, the increased limits are added to the basic limits of the homeowners policy to determine the amount of the deductible. Suppose Jed had insured a painting for $10,000 under a schedule. In the event of earthquake damage to his personal property, Jed would be required to pay a $3,000 deductible—5 percent of $60,000, where $60,000 is the sum of the $50,000 personal property limit under Coverage C and the $10,000 limit for the painting covered by the schedule.

Personal Injury Endorsement

The **personal injury endorsement** amends the homeowners policy definition of bodily injury to include personal injury—injury arising out of the following three groups of offenses:

- False arrest, detention, imprisonment, or malicious prosecution
- Libel, slander, or defamation of character
- Invasion of privacy, wrongful eviction, or wrongful entry

The endorsement is not subject to the exclusions contained in Section II. It has its own exclusions that are more pertinent to personal injury losses. The following items are not covered:

- *Liability assumed by the insured under any contract or agreement.* The assumption of another's liability for personal injury offenses is not common among homeowners.

- *Injury caused in violation of a criminal law committed by or with the knowledge or consent of any insured.* It is against public policy to insure such acts.

- *Injury sustained by any person as a result of an offense directly or indirectly related to the employment of this person by an insured.* This exclusion is directed at personal injury claims of an employer who slanders an employee, for example, or who divulges privileged information about an employee who has been terminated. This excluded exposure could involve a homeowner who hires a resident employee.

- *Injury arising out of the business pursuits of any insured.* Personal injury exposures for business pursuits are insured under commercial general liability policies.

- *Civic or public activities performed for pay by any insured.* Liability for such activities performed for pay can be insured under commercial liability policies. Coverage does apply under the personal injury endorsement for civic or public activities performed without pay.

- *Injury to any insured.* For the purposes of the endorsement, an "insured" is the named insured, any resident relative, and any other persons younger than twenty-one under the care of the named insured or a resident relative. This exclusion eliminates coverage for claims of one insured against another insured.

Conspicuous by its absence is any exclusion for acts committed by or at the insured's direction with intent to cause personal injury. Because this exclusion does not apply under the personal injury endorsement, it appears that an insured would be protected even against malicious acts that cause harm to others.

Additional Insured—Residence Premises Endorsement

When a two-family dwelling or duplex is owned by two individuals and each occupies a separate part, a homeowners policy providing dwelling coverage may be written only for one of the co-owners as a named insured. Because the other co-owner also has an insurable interest in the dwelling and other structures on the premises, that interest can be protected by attaching the **additional insured—residence premises endorsement** to the named insured's homeowners policy, with no extra premium required. This endorsement, in effect, gives the named co-owner protection against loss to the dwelling and other structures. The additional insured can then obtain an HO-4 to cover his or her interest in personal property and to provide coverage for additional living expenses and other coverages.

This endorsement can also be used when an individual sells his or her dwelling on a *land contract basis.* Under this arrangement, the purchaser-occupant of the dwelling enters into a long-term contract to buy the dwelling, with or without a down payment, and agrees to pay the seller installments until the purchase price is fully paid. Until the purchaser's obligation is fulfilled, the title to the property remains with the seller. To protect the seller's interest in the property, the seller can be added without cost to the purchaser's homeowners policy as an additional insured.

Premises Alarm or Fire Protection System Endorsement

When a homeowner has an insurer-approved fire alarm system, smoke detection equipment, or automatic sprinkler system, a *premium credit* is available through the **premises alarm or fire protection system endorsement**. The insured must maintain the system in working order and notify the insurer of any changes in the system or of its removal.

Summary

ISO homeowners policies include coverage for personal liability, medical expenses of others, and related costs that arise out of the ownership or use of real property and personal activities. Section II of the homeowners policies contains the coverages that deal with these exposures.

Coverage E—Personal Liability applies to personal liability exposures that arise out of bodily injury or property damage. The insurer is obligated to defend an insured as well as pay damages on behalf of the insured. The policy limit applies to damages; defense costs are paid in addition to policy limits. Once the limit is exhausted by payment of damages for one occurrence, the insurer is not obligated to defend or pay damages for any remaining claims based on the occurrence. The limit is replenished for the next occurrence. Coverage F—Medical Payments to Others covers medical expenses incurred by people who are not an "insured" under the policy. Payments under this coverage are made without regard to whether an insured is legally liable and are typically limited to $1,000 per person per occurrence. Coverages E and F have several exclusions in common; a smaller number of exclusions apply only to one coverage or the other.

Section II contains additional coverages that pay for such items as claim costs and first aid expenses. These additional coverages are payable in addition to the policy limits for Coverages E and F.

Several endorsements can be added to a homeowners policy. Some endorsements alter the method by which losses are valued; others cover loss exposures excluded or only partially covered by the homeowners policy.

Chapter Notes

1. Physicians Insurance Company of Ohio v. Swanson, 569 N.E.2d OH 906 (1991).
2. Merrimack Mutual Fire Insurance Company v. Sampson, 550 N.E.2d MA 901 (1990).
3. *Personal Inland Marine Manual*, 5th edition (New York, NY: Insurance Services Office, Inc., November 1990).

Chapter 4

Personal Auto Insurance

Americans have come to regard the auto as a necessity. It is used for transportation to and from work, for business and pleasure trips, and for family needs. Because of the high standard of living enjoyed by many Americans, many families own more than one car. Highways carry more cars than they were designed to handle. With a combination of hazards such as unprotected abutments and guardrails, awkward entrance and exit ramps, and other design problems, accidents are difficult for even the careful motorist to prevent.

Critics allege that autos themselves have been inadequately designed, are inferior in quality and workmanship, and are easily damaged. Inflation and energy concerns have caused many Americans to purchase smaller vehicles. The relative light weight of these smaller cars makes them susceptible to extensive damage and serious passenger injury.

All of the foregoing factors have contributed in some way to the frequency and severity of accidents and to their costs to society. Personal auto insurance is one of the primary sources of financing for the costs of auto accidents.

This is the first of two chapters dealing with auto exposures and insurance. The primary focus of this chapter is the coverages provided by the Personal Auto Policy (PAP) and endorsements to the PAP. The ISO PAP is not the only form of personal auto insurance; in fact, many larger companies use their own personal auto policies. However, most personal auto policies offer the same general types of coverages. Therefore, the PAP serves as a focal point for the discussion of personal auto insurance in this text. This chapter mentions the areas in which other personal auto policies differ from the PAP at the end of the chapter.

Chapter 5 continues the discussion of auto insurance by focusing on the problems involved in auto insurance, such as uninsured motorists and no-fault laws. Chapter 5 also describes factors that affect the cost of auto insurance and proposals for making auto insurance fairer and more affordable.

The Personal Auto Policy

Although a variety of auto policies is available for personal auto loss exposures, this section discusses the ISO Personal Auto Policy (PAP). The historical development of the PAP is first described. This is followed by a discussion of (1) the coverages provided by the 1994 PAP, (2) the differences in coverage provided under the 1989 PAP, and (3) several endorsements that may be added to either version of the PAP.

Historical Development

Auto insurance in the United States began in 1898, when Travelers Insurance Company issued the first auto bodily injury liability policy. The coverage was issued to a doctor in Buffalo, New York, at a price of $11.25. Other insurers eventually entered the market offering coverage first on a flat premium basis, followed by premiums that took into consideration such factors as vehicle type and weight, size, territory, and horsepower.

Because lack of uniformity among the first auto policies created much confusion, state legislatures began to require standardization. The first standard basic auto policy became effective January 1, 1936.

The standard "family automobile policy" (FAP) was introduced in 1956 to fill a growing need for broader family protection stemming from the use and ownership of vehicles. The FAP was designed to cover a named insured and spouse for exposure to liability from accidents as well as physical damage to the autos, including loss of use. Particularly noteworthy about the FAP was the protection provided to named insureds against liability arising from the operation or use of the owned auto by other family members. This protection answered a need established by the courts under the **family purpose doctrine**, which held that an owner of an auto was deemed liable for damages arising out of the vehicle's negligent use by a family member.

By the 1970s, many insureds were clamoring for more understandable auto insurance policies. While some insurers introduced their own "plain language" insurance policies, ISO introduced its standard version of a simplified policy, the Personal Auto Policy (PAP) in 1977. The PAP has since been through several revisions and is now the standard policy used in most states, although it may not be used by all companies. The focus of this section is on the 1994 PAP, with references to the 1989 PAP as needed to explain differences between the two editions.

Eligibility for the Personal Auto Policy

The personal auto policy is designed for individuals and families who own private passenger autos. Autos leased for periods longer than six months may also be eligible for coverage as "owned" vehicles under the PAP. The term "private passenger auto" includes the following:[1]

- A four-wheel motor vehicle, other than a truck or van, that is owned or leased for a continuous period equal to or exceeding six months and not used to transport people or belongings and not rented to others

- A pickup or van with a gross vehicle weight not exceeding 10,000 pounds and not used to transport or deliver goods or materials unless the use is incidental to the insured's installation, maintenance, or repair business or if the use is related to farming or ranching

- A vehicle that meets one of the above requisites, is principally garaged on a farm or ranch, and is owned by a farm family partnership or a farm family corporation

Although the purpose of the policy is to cover personal auto losses, coverage may extend to certain losses that result from business uses of an insured vehicle.

Individuals and families who are eligible for coverage under a PAP are limited to the following:[2]

- An individual who owns or leases an acceptable vehicle

- A husband and wife who reside in the same household and own or lease an acceptable vehicle

- Relatives, other than a husband and wife, who jointly own an acceptable vehicle

Individuals and families may purchase a PAP if they satisfy the above requirements. Other types of vehicles and other classes of individuals and families may be insured by the PAP by adding an endorsement to the standard policy. Some of these endorsements are discussed at the end of this chapter and in Chapter 6.

Policy Format

The PAP is a package policy that combines several forms of coverage, including liability and physical damage to an owned auto, into one policy form. The standard unendorsed contract contains three essential preliminary sections:

1. A **declarations page** that contains the policy number, insured's name and address, period of coverage, description of covered autos, limits that apply to the coverage selected, and any deductible amounts.

2. A **general agreement** that states, "In return for payment of the premium and subject to all the terms of this policy, we agree with you as follows." "We" refers to the insurer and "you" refers to the named insured and his or her spouse if a resident of the same household. The phrase serves as a preface to the policy as a whole and makes the insurer's obligations contingent on the insured's payment of premium.

3. The **definitions** section defines certain commonly used terms and their definitions, which are referred to as they appear in the policy provisions. The definitions are discussed as the terms arise in the chapter.

In addition to the declarations, general agreement, and the definitions, the PAP contains six parts:

Part A—Liability Coverage

Part B—Medical Payments Coverage

Part C—Uninsured Motorists Coverage

Part D—Coverage for Damage to Your Auto

Part E—Duties After an Accident or Loss

Part F—General Provisions

With the exception of Parts E and F, each part has its own insuring agreement, exclusions, and special conditions.

All of the parts of the PAP are discussed in this chapter with the exception of Part C—Uninsured Motorists Coverage. As mentioned above, the issue of uninsured motorists is included in Chapter 5, and, therefore, the coverage that helps to deal with the issue is also discussed in Chapter 5.

Your Covered Auto

The definition of "your covered auto" is of importance to the policy coverages. A **"covered auto"** can be any one of the following:

1. Any vehicle described in the policy declarations, which is generally an owned auto, pickup truck, or van. A private passenger-type auto is deemed to be owned if leased for a continuous period of at least six months, and may be named in the policy declarations.

2. A private passenger auto, pickup, or van *acquired* by the named insured *during the policy period* and meeting the eligibility requirements. With respect to vans and trucks, the PAP applies only if no other insurance covers the newly acquired vehicle.

   a. If the newly acquired vehicle *replaces* one described in the declarations, the replacement vehicle is automatically insured without notice to the insurer for all coverages, except physical damage to the vehicle, that applied to the vehicle replaced. If the insured desires to continue or add physical damage coverage, he or she must notify the insurer of that intent within thirty days of the vehicle's acquisition.

   b. If the newly acquired vehicle is *in addition to* those described in the declarations, the vehicle will be provided the broadest coverage applying to the vehicles listed in the declarations. To continue coverage for the remainder of the policy period, the insured must ask the insurance company to insure the additional vehicle within thirty days after the named insured acquires ownership of the vehicle.

3. Any auto or trailer not owned by the named insured while used as a temporary substitute for any other covered auto or trailer that is out of normal use because of its breakdown, repair, servicing, loss, or destruction. However, this part of the definition does not apply to Part D—Coverage for Damage to Your Auto.

4. Any trailer owned by the named insured. A **trailer** is a vehicle, such as a camper, designed to be pulled by a private passenger auto, pickup, or van. Trailer also includes a farm wagon or a farm implement while it is towed by a private passenger auto, pickup, or van.

Part A—Liability Coverage

The first coverage listed in the PAP is auto liability coverage. It provides protection for the named insured and several other classes of people against liability that results from the ownership, maintenance, use, or operation of an auto.

Laws Affecting the Purchase of Auto Liability Coverage

A motorist's choice to obtain personal auto liability coverage is affected by the laws in each state. All states have at least one law that requires a motorist to prove the ability to meet some minimum standard of financial responsibility—whether through insurance or other personal assets—for liability arising out of the operation, use, or ownership of an auto. Two types of laws have evolved: financial responsibility laws and compulsory auto insurance laws. While they are discussed separately below, one or both or a combination of these laws is likely to appear in a state's legal code.

Financial Responsibility Laws

All states have **financial responsibility laws**. The purpose of these laws is to ensure that motorists have the financial ability to pay for any property damage or bodily injury they may cause as a result of their driving. For most people, this entails purchasing auto liability insurance.

Financial responsibility laws establish minimum **financial responsibility limits** that must be met by a motorist to be in compliance with the law. The limits establish the *minimum* amount a motorist must be able to pay for bodily injury and property damage for which a motorist becomes liable due to an auto accident. The limits vary by state. For example, Mississippi has financial responsibility limits of 10/20/5—$10,000 per accident for bodily injury to or death of one person, $20,000 per accident for bodily injury to or death of two or more persons, and $5,000 per accident for damage to the property of others. On the other hand, Alaska has limits of 50/100/25.

Financial responsibility laws require drivers to show proof of financial responsibility *after* an accident, conviction, or judgment. The laws vary considerably, but most often they are triggered by an *auto-related accident* involving bodily injury of any severity or property damage exceeding a specific amount, such as $100, $200, or $350. They may also come into play upon a *conviction*, whether or not accident-related, involving certain specified offenses such as reckless driving or operating a vehicle under the influence of alcohol or drugs; or an *auto-related at-fault accident* if the motorist found to be accountable for the payment of damages fails to pay the judgment within a certain specified period.

The means by which the laws deal with the above offenses vary. With respect to accidents, and possibly for convictions, there are two general types of requirements imposed: security-type laws or security-and-proof-of-future-responsibility laws.

When the **security-type financial responsibility law** applies, any motorist involved in an accident resulting in bodily injury of any amount or property damage over a specified amount is required to *post security* (show proof of ability to pay at least a minimum amount for injury or damage). Security must be in an amount sufficient to satisfy the financial responsibility limit required by the state.

Proof of security can be evidenced in several ways:

- By showing proof of auto liability insurance with bodily injury and property damage limits at least equal to the amounts required by the law

- By posting a bond guaranteeing financial responsibility for those amounts
- By depositing money and/or securities in an amount corresponding to the minimum limits
- By proving that the motorist or the party responsible for the motorist (such as an employer for an employee) is a qualified "self-insured"

Unless proof of security is provided, the motorist forfeits his or her operator's license and vehicle registration. The motorist may also be subject to a fine.

While security-type laws require a motorist who has been in an accident to prove that he or she is financially responsible at the time of the accident, **security-and-proof-of-future-responsibility (security-and-proof) laws** add a requirement: motorists who have been found at fault for an accident are required to show that they will also be financially responsible in the event of future accidents. The future period during which financial responsibility must be shown varies among states.

In practice, proof of financial responsibility for a future period usually is provided to the state by the driver's insurance company. Under the security-and-proof laws, states typically require proof of financial responsibility for three years after the requirement is triggered, that is, from the date of the accident or conviction. For example, if Clark is involved in an auto accident for which he is at fault in a state with a security-and-proof law, he will be required to show proof of financial responsibility for three years from the date of the accident. This period generally coincides with the period during which a chargeable accident or serious conviction is figured into a motorist's premium for auto insurance—a period during which a driver normally finds coverage expensive and difficult to obtain. However, if motorists are insured at the time of an accident or conviction, most security-and-proof laws exempt them from having to show proof of financial responsibility for the future period.

Compulsory Auto Insurance Laws

Compulsory auto insurance laws make it illegal for motorists to operate vehicles without *first* having proof of their ability to pay for judgments resulting from auto accidents. States with compulsory insurance laws require proof of one of the following *when an auto is registered:*

- Auto liability insurance
- A bond guaranteeing a motorist's financial responsibility
- A deposit of money or other valuable certificates as security for satisfying any judgments that may develop from future accidents

In most cases, insurance is used to meet the requirement. Whichever alternative is selected, the amount must correspond to at least the financial responsibility limits specified by the state.

Part A—Liability Coverage Insuring Agreement

In the personal auto policy, Part A—Liability Coverage protects insureds in the event of claim or suit stemming from bodily injury or property damage resulting from an auto accident. The insurer promises to pay (1) damages, including prejudgment interest awarded against an insured only to the limits of liability specified in the declarations and (2) the costs of defending such claims or suits. The insurer bears the full costs of defense—the limits of liability are not reduced by the insurer's cost to defend an insured. The insurer will defend an insured even if the allegations are false. However, the insurer will only defend against those claims or suits alleging damages that (if proven) would be covered by the policy. Furthermore, if some of the alleged damages are covered and some are not, the insurer *will* defend the insureds. The insurer's duty to defend an insured ends only when the limits of liability are exhausted.

With respect to Part A—Liability Coverage, an **"insured"** is any of the following:

- The named insured, his or her spouse, or any family member who owns, maintains, or uses any auto or trailer. A **"family member,"** as defined by the PAP, is a person related to the named insured or his or her spouse by blood, marriage, or adoption and who lives in the same household as the named insured and spouse.

  It must be stressed that only the named insured and eligible family members receive liability coverage for any auto or trailer. Anyone else, such as a friend, must be using a covered auto before he or she is eligible for liability coverage under the named insured's PAP.

- Any person using a covered auto.

- Any person or organization legally responsible for the person using a covered auto. For example, while Nathan is driving his own insured car on a business trip, he causes an auto accident. The other driver sues Nathan's employer. The employer can receive coverage for any damages awarded as well as for defense under Nathan's PAP.

- Any person or organization legally responsible for the actions or omissions of the named insured, spouse, or family members while using an auto or trailer not considered a covered auto and not owned or hired by the person or organization. For example, Joe, the named insured, injures a pedestrian while driving a car donated by a local business for use as a pace car for a foot race organized by Joe's track club. Because neither Joe nor the track club owned or hired the car, Joe's PAP will defend the track club against allegations of liability for the bodily injury to the pedestrian. (Joe will also receive coverage as the named insured in any auto.)

The PAP does not actually define damages, although it does state that damages include prejudgment interest awarded against an insured. **Damages** include compensatory damages that reasonably compensate a person for the loss suffered. A victim may also be awarded punitive damages if they are not otherwise disallowed by state law. Since punitive damages are not specifically excluded from coverage, the policy covers these damages, if state law permits. (State law may allow the awarding of punitive damages but prohibit their being paid by insurers. For states that do not allow the payment of punitive damages with insurance benefits, a state amendatory endorsement, which is discussed at the end of the chapter, will modify the liability insuring agreement to specifically exclude punitive damages.)

The PAP defines **bodily injury** as "bodily harm, sickness or disease, including death that results." Any expenses for which the insured becomes legally liable as a result of bodily injury—such as those for ambulance service, emergency treatment, doctors' fees, hospitalization, physical rehabilitation, prosthetic devices, loss of income or earning capacity, or funeral expenses—caused by an auto accident would all be payable under the PAP liability coverage.

Property damage, as defined by the PAP, is "physical damage to, destruction of or loss of use of tangible property." This definition makes it clear that both physical damage and resulting loss of use of the property is covered. If, for example, Fred's negligent operation of his car causes damage to Sue's car, Fred's PAP will not only pay to repair or replace Sue's car, but will also pay any sums that Fred is legally obligated to pay for obtaining substitute transportation for Sue until her car can be returned to service.

Before an insurance company pays any damages for which an insured is alleged to be legally responsible, the insurer will investigate the claim. If the insurer determines that the insured is likely to be responsible, under conditions where the insurance applies, the insurer generally attempts to negotiate and settle any claim on behalf of the insured. On the other hand, if the investigation indicates that the insured is not likely to be legally responsible for the accident, the insurer may deny the claim or may settle to dispose of a small claim without further costly litigation and potentially increased expenses and damages. Even though the insurer denies the claim, it is still obligated to defend the insured if it becomes necessary to do so. Of course, the damages claimed would have to be covered by the policy.

As an illustration, assume that Karen, an insured, is driving her auto when she collides with Peter as he crosses the street. Peter incurs $75,000 in medical bills as a result of his injuries.

If it appears that Karen was not legally responsible for the accident, as might be the case if Peter had darted out from between two parked cars or was jaywalking, Karen's PAP insurer might choose to deny Karen's liability. If Peter continues to press his claim, Karen's insurer is obligated to defend her because the allegations of Peter's claim, whether founded or not, are not otherwise excluded by the PAP liability coverage. Karen's insurer is also obligated to pay Peter's damages if a court should find Karen legally responsible for the accident.

If the allegations were beyond the scope of the PAP coverage—for example, if Karen were alleged to have been driving a motorcycle when she struck Peter— Karen's PAP insurer may deny that it has any liability. Karen may or may not be liable, but the insurer is under no obligation to provide her defense or pay any claims made against her.

The insurer's promise to provide defense and to pay defense costs is an important part of the liability coverage for at least two reasons. First, defense, being expensive, could result in more costs than the ultimate award for damages. Second, the insurer's assistance and expertise in defense may help prove the insured to be blameless.

Supplementary Payments

In addition to the protection for defense and the payment of damages for which an insured is legally responsible, the PAP also includes a number of other benefits referred to as **supplementary payments**. These payments are covered by the PAP in addition to the limit of coverage for liability and are made only in the cases in which the PAP insurer is involved. The supplementary payments are discussed in the following paragraphs.

Bonds

For the purposes of supplementary payments, "bond" refers to a surety bond that guarantees certain behavior. The policy covers at least part of the costs of three types of bonds: bail bonds, appeal bonds, and release of attachment bonds.

The insurer will pay up to $250 toward the cost of a **bail bond**, which guarantees that the accused insured will appear in court at the time designated for the trial or hearing. The insurer will pay for the bond only if it is needed because of an accident that results in bodily injury or property damage covered by the policy. A bail bond that may be required because of a traffic law violation, such as speeding or driving under the influence when there is no accident, is not within the scope of this coverage. Failure by the insured to appear in court results in the loss of money or security posted by the insurer.

The insurer will also pay the premium for any appeal bond required by the court when the *insurer*, on behalf of the insured, decides to appeal a decision to a higher court. The **appeal bond** guarantees that the insured will pay the judgment, plus interest and costs, if the higher court upholds the decision against the insured and his or her insurer. The bond automatically terminates if the decision is reversed by the appeals court.

The cost of any release of attachment bonds is also covered. These bonds are needed when a claimant asks the court to *attach* (legally take control of) property of the insured. For example, the insured's car might be attached if the insured is a nonresident or is about to leave the state without leaving enough property to satisfy the claim or suit. The insured can release the attachment pending final outcome of the court's decision by providing the court with a **release of attachment bond** which guarantees that the insured will pay any damages and court costs if the court should decide in the claimant's favor. The bond automatically terminates if the court ultimately decides in the insured's favor.

Note that the PAP insurer is not obligated to provide these bonds. The insurer is only obligated to pay the cost of obtaining them. While coverage for the cost of appeal and release of attachment bonds is not limited, the policy only pays to $250 for bail bonds.

Interest

Under the PAP liability coverage, the insurer will pay any interest accruing after a judgment is entered in any suit the insurer defends, for example, when the suit is appealed to a higher court—even if the judgment exceeds the policy's coverage limit. Once the insurer offers to pay any judgment up to its policy limits, plus the accrued interest, its obligation ends. If the insured delays paying the judgment or decides to appeal the suit further, the insured is responsible for the payment of any interest that subsequently accrues. The supplementary coverage does not include prejudgment interest. Prejudgment interest is included in the damages payable and is subject to the limit of liability.

Expenses

The insurer will pay for any loss of earnings by the insured, not to exceed $50 per day for attending any trial or hearing at the insurer's request. The cost of other reasonable expenses incurred by the insured at the insurer's request is also covered. The cost of lodging while testifying at a trial or the expense incurred in traveling to an attorney's office for a consultation are examples of covered expenses.

Exclusions

The liability coverage of the PAP is provided on an "all-risks" basis. Thus the insuring agreement discussed above is limited by exclusions.

Intentional Injury or Damage

No liability coverage is available for a person who causes intentional injury to another person or intentional damage to the property of another. It is against public policy to protect a person against the consequences of injury or damage that he or she intentionally inflicts.

Since the exclusion applies only to the person who causes the injury or damage, it may be possible for the owner of the auto to be protected against vicarious liability for injury or damage caused by another person. For example, if Jon borrows Donald's car and intentionally drives it through Katie's rose garden, Donald's PAP will not protect Jon. However, if Donald should be found liable, perhaps because he entrusted his car to an irresponsible person, Donald's insurer will defend him and pay damages on his behalf.

Damage to Owned or Transported Property

When an otherwise covered person damages his or her own property (such as a garage door), or damages personal property within a covered auto, no liability protection is provided. The purpose for this exclusion is twofold. First, the exclusion reinforces the inescapable fact that a person cannot be held liable to himself or herself for damage that he or she causes to his or her own property. Second, the property, owned or not, is likely to be, or should be, covered by another form of property insurance, such as a homeowners policy or a floater policy.

Damage to Nonowned Property

The liability coverage does not cover a person who causes damage to property rented to or used by, or in the care of, that person, unless the property is a residence or a private garage. For the most part, insurers prefer that this property be covered under another form of insurance (again, a homeowners policy, for example). The rationale for covering auto damage to nonowned residences and private garages is that these structures are not likely to be insured under a property policy by the user or renter who can be held legally responsible for the damage. Thus, if Deb sideswipes the garage attached to the house she is renting, her PAP will cover the damage even though the garage is in her care through her rental agreement.

Injury to an Employee

In most cases, the PAP does not cover bodily injury to an employee of a covered person if the injury occurs during the course of employment. This exposure is typically covered under workers compensation insurance. However, the exclusion does not apply if the employee is a domestic employee and is not covered or required to be covered by workers compensation insurance. For example, Tabitha, the nanny of Isabel's children, is injured in an auto accident while driving Isabel's car home after dropping the children off at school. Tabitha is not covered, and is not required to be covered, by workers compensation. Thus, Isabel's PAP will cover Tabitha's medical expenses resulting from the accident.

Public or Livery Conveyance

The policy does not protect a covered person for liability arising out of ownership or operation of a vehicle used to carry persons or property for a fee. The exclusion does not apply if the vehicle is used in a share-the-expense car pool.

The purpose of the exclusion is to allow the insurer to avoid paying claims for an unacceptable business exposure. People using the auto in a business capacity as a true public or livery conveyance should insure it under a commercial auto liability policy. Courts have repeatedly held a **public or livery conveyance** to be one that is indiscriminately offered to the general public, such as a taxi or a bus. The PAP exclusion is therefore not intended to eliminate coverage when, for example, an insured lends his covered pickup truck to a neighbor for a charge on an incidental basis, such as to move a child's belongings home from his or her college dormitory. However, the exclusion would apply to an insured when operating any auto as a taxi.

Auto Business

The liability coverage generally does not apply to any person legally responsible for damages while employed or engaged in the business of parking, repairing, selling, servicing, or storing vehicles designed for use mainly on public roads, including road testing and delivery. The exclusion prevents coverage for liability exposures that are, or should be, covered under a garage policy or comparable commercial auto liability policy.

However, the exclusion does not apply to any accident arising out of the ownership, maintenance, or use of *the covered auto* by the named insured, spouse, family member, or any partner, agent, or employee of the named insured or family member. Without this exception, Mark—an auto mechanic—would not be covered if he used his own car, insured under a PAP, to provide road service. Meanwhile his wife, Betsy—a visiting nurse—would be covered while using the same car to visit a patient. This exception to the exclusion puts employees engaged in the auto business into the same position as employees engaged in other businesses and using their own cars or any other covered auto. Because of this exception, both Mark and Betsy would be covered.

Other Business Use

In addition to the auto business exclusion, another exclusion deals with all other business uses of vehicles. This exclusion eliminates coverage for any vehicle maintained or used in any business or occupation other than farming or ranching, subject to certain exceptions. Because of these exceptions, liability arising out of the business use of the following vehicles is covered, provided coverage is not elsewhere excluded:

1. Any private passenger auto
2. Any pickup or van owned by the named insured or resident spouse
3. Any pickup or van used as a temporary substitute while the covered auto is broken down, lost, or destroyed or is being repaired or serviced
4. Any trailer while used with a vehicle described in items 1 or 2 above

Examples of what would be covered include private passenger autos of sole proprietorships, partnerships, and corporations, as well as small trucks of individual insureds used in business.

The 1989 PAP does not cover pickups and vans used as temporary substitutes for a covered auto.

The rationale for the other business use exclusion is to prevent covering vehicle exposures that insurers prefer to handle under commercial auto policies. The reasons for the exceptions are twofold. First, individual or family-owned private passenger autos used for business, as well as small trucks used for farming or ranching, are not eligible for commercial auto insurance. Second, an individual who uses his or her owned auto in business is often not protected under an employer's commercial auto policy.

Permission to Use Auto

No coverage applies for use of any vehicle by any person who does not have a "reasonable belief of being entitled to do so" by the vehicle owner. At one time, auto policies required *proof* that permission had been given and that the car had been used within the scope of the permission. This proved difficult, and sometimes impossible, for insurers to determine. Thus the policy exclusion requires that the insurer establish that an individual did not have the "reasonable belief" that he or she was entitled to borrow the auto. The net effect is to exclude any liability coverage for the operator of a stolen car.

Nuclear Energy Liability

The PAP liability coverage is subject to a nuclear energy liability exclusion. This exclusion precludes coverage when any person (1) is covered under a separate nuclear energy liability policy or (2) would have been protected under such a policy if the limits were not exhausted. This exclusion prevents duplicate coverage. The liability insurance carried by nuclear facilities covers any entity, except the U.S. government, that may be held liable for damages in a nuclear accident. If a motorist is or is supposed to be covered by such a policy, the PAP will not pay for nuclear liability losses.

Fewer Than Four Wheels

If any person otherwise covered by liability coverage owns or borrows a motorized vehicle with fewer than four wheels, such as a motor scooter or motorcycle, no protection applies under the PAP. The reasons for this exclusion are to limit coverage to certain types of vehicles and to require that other vehicles be specifically insured for an additional premium. However, this exclusion does not apply in a medical emergency if an insured is operating or using a vehicle with fewer than four wheels. The 1989 version of this exclusion does not make the emergency use exception.

The PAP can be amended by endorsements such as the *snowmobile endorsement* to add coverage for liability exposures of snowmobiles or the *miscellaneous type vehicle endorsement* to add coverage for liability exposures of motorcycles. These two endorsements are discussed in Chapter 6.

Not Designed for Use on Public Roads

The PAP excludes coverage for liability resulting from the use, maintenance, or operation of vehicles not designed for use on public roads. The PAP is not designed to provide coverage for any vehicle having four wheels or more, but only to cover those meant to be operated on public roads. This exclusion eliminates coverage for vehicles such as dune buggies or all-terrain vehicles. However, the exclusion does not apply to liability arising out of the operation or use of such vehicles by an insured in a medical emergency.

The 1989 PAP allows coverage against liability for use by the named insured and resident family members of a nonowned recreational vehicle with four wheels that qualifies as an auto under a state's motor vehicle code, such as a dune buggy.

Vehicles not designed for use on public roads are provided limited coverage under homeowners polices and can be specifically insured by adding a miscellaneous type vehicle endorsement to the policy. This endorsement is discussed in Chapter 6.

Owned or Available for Regular Use

The PAP liability coverage does not apply to any vehicle, other than the covered auto, which an insured owns or to which the insured has regular access. The purpose of this exclusion is to prevent a person from obtaining blanket coverage for liability exposures that should specifically be insured. For example, Alice has a PAP that covers an older auto. She purchases a new auto with the intention of selling the older one, but does not notify her insurer. Two months later, while her older auto is still in use, Alice causes an accident while driving the new auto. Since the new auto is considered an additionally acquired one rather than a replacement, and the thirty-day period for reporting an additionally acquired auto has expired, Alice is without liability protection on her new car. Were it not for this exclusion, Alice would be able to obtain full coverage on both her autos merely by specifically insuring one of them.

This exclusion also applies to nonowned autos furnished or available for the regular use of the named insured or spouse. Generally, the nonowned auto liability coverage of the PAP is designed to provide the named insured with protection for the exceptional occasion when the named insured has to use an auto belonging to another person, including an auto owned by a family member. When a nonowned auto is furnished or readily available to a person, he or she has the chance to use the auto as if it were owned. Without this exclusion, the insurer could unknowingly be insuring the equivalent of an additional owned auto for no additional premium.

In many instances, nonowned autos are furnished for regular use of individuals and families. A common example is a company car furnished to an employee for business and pleasure use. Although this exposure is excluded by the standard PAP, it can be insured for an additional premium with the *extended non-owned coverage for named individual endorsement*, which is discussed at the end of this chapter.

The meaning of "available for regular use" is not always clear-cut. ISO explains that the exclusion is also directed at autos made available through pools, such as those maintained by some businesses and public entities. Because an insured does not use the same pool car on a regular basis, if he or she has access to such a pool any pool car is considered to be available for that employee's regular use. In one case, a court held that "available" requires that the use be to a substantial degree under the control of the insured and under circumstances when the person does not have to obtain keys and permission of the owner each time the auto is used. This exclusion, therefore, could conceivably affect a person who has an open invitation to use another person's auto at any time. Because the meaning of "available for the regular use of" depends upon the circumstances, it may very well be a question of fact for the courts to decide.

Owned or Available for Regular Use of Family Members

Liability coverage does not apply to any vehicle, other than a covered auto, that is owned by or furnished or available for the regular use of any family member. However, coverage is available for the named insured and spouse who are maintaining or occupying any vehicle owned by, or furnished or available for the regular use of, any other family member. The rationale for this exclusion is to eliminate family members' coverage for autos owned by, or furnished, or available for their use since such autos are, or should be, insured under a separate policy. The exception to the exclusion allows the named insured and spouse protection in an accident stemming from their maintenance or use of a family member's auto that may be uninsured or inadequately insured. Since this exception applies only to the named insured and spouse, any other family member would remain without coverage under the named insured's PAP.

To illustrate, Dad and Junior live under the same roof, and each owns a car. Dad insures his car with a PAP, but Junior is uninsured. Although Junior is a family member and therefore an insured under Dad's policy while driving Dad's car, Junior is not insured under Dad's PAP while driving his own car. However, the exception to the exclusion protects Dad if he occasionally drives Junior's car.

Racing or Speed Contests

The PAP does not cover liability arising from the operation, maintenance, or use of any vehicle for prearranged or organized racing or speed contests. The exclusion applies only if the vehicle is located within a facility designed for racing and is maintained, operated, or used in actual competition or in practice or preparation for competition. This exclusion does not appear in the 1989 version of the PAP.

Other Provisions Relating to Liability Coverage

Four other provisions are contained in Part A—Liability Coverage. They are (1) limit of liability, (2) out-of-state coverage, (3) financial responsibility required, and (4) other insurance. These provisions each relate to the liability coverage limits.

Limit of Liability

The limit of liability provision states that (1) the limit shown in the policy declarations is the maximum available for all damages resulting from any one accident and (2) the limit of liability is the maximum that will be paid regardless of the number of covered persons, claims made, vehicles, or premiums shown in the declarations, and vehicles involved in an auto accident.

Part (1) of the limit of liability provision affirms that coverage is provided on a **single-limit basis**. This means that one limit, such as $100,000, applies to all damages because of bodily injury or property damage or both resulting from a single accident. According to ISO, the single limit approach is used because that concept is more easily understood by the consumer than **split limits**. However, split limits can be substituted by adding a *split liability limits endorsement* to the PAP. When this substitution is made, one limit applies to bodily injury to each person; a second limit applies to bodily injury to all persons in each accident; and a third limit applies to all property damage in each accident. An example of the split-limits approach is $100,000 per person for bodily injury, $300,000 per accident for bodily injury, and $50,000 per accident for property damage, commonly shown as 100/300/50.

As noted earlier, in all states, the financial responsibility requirements are stated in split limits. The limit of liability provision provides that if split limits are required by law, the policy automatically adjusts to the required basis. However, when the single limit is replaced by split limits, the total limit of the policy remains unchanged. For example, suppose state law requires liability limits of at least 25/50/10 and the insured has a single liability limit of $50,000. Although the insured does not satisfy the state's law because he or she must be able to cover at least $50,000 in bodily injury claims and $10,000 in property damage claims arising from a single accident—a total of $60,000—the policy will not increase the single limit to satisfy the split limit requirement. The insured will have to purchase additional liability insurance.

The purpose of part (2) of the limit of liability provision is to prevent the stacking of limits. **Stacking** refers to situations in which the insured maintains that, since two or more persons are faced with claims resulting from the same accident, the limit should apply separately to each. Another type of stacking is attempted when the insured maintains that, since the policy covers two (or more) scheduled autos, he or she should be able to have twice the stated limit of liability since a separate premium for each car has been paid. Arguments like these have often been raised by insureds faced with damages exceeding the limit of liability.

The limit of liability provision includes a third subpart that eliminates coverage for the medical expenses that have already been paid by another coverage of the PAP or its endorsements. Part B—Medical Payments Coverage, Part C—Uninsured Motorists Coverage, and endorsements for underinsured motorists cover certain types of medical expenses. The purpose of the additional subpart is to keep an insured from collecting duplicate payments from the same PAP. The 1989 PAP does not include this third provision.

Out-of-State Coverage

Many auto owners or operators could unknowingly violate the financial responsibility laws of other states when traveling away from home. The potential repercussions can be quite severe if the limits of a nonresident's auto policy are lower than the minimum amounts required in other states or if the coverages do not conform to those required. The nonresident could lose his or her license and auto registration, as well as be fined.

The out-of-state coverage provision protects insureds against this loss exposure. If an insured under a PAP is involved in an auto accident in some state or Canadian province where (1) the specified financial responsibility limits are higher than the stated policy limits or (2) compulsory auto insurance is required for all drivers, including nonresidents who may operate vehicles in that state, then the policy automatically provides the minimum required limits or coverages. An insured is *not* required to pay the insurer an additional premium to receive the broader protection, even if a claim is paid that exceeds the specified policy limits.

Financial Responsibility

As mentioned earlier in this chapter, many financial responsibility laws require motorists to show proof of financial responsibility for the future following an accident, conviction, or judgment. The most common proof is an auto policy. The financial responsibility provision of the PAP states that when the policy is certified as proof of financial responsibility, the policy will comply with the law to the extent required. So, for example, if the law requires that the policy cover a certain type of loss that is not covered by the PAP, the policy will be interpreted to cover the loss.

Other Insurance

The purpose of the other insurance provision is to specify how the insurer contributes to the payment of loss when the insured (1) has more than one applicable policy on his or her own covered auto or (2) is legally responsible for loss involving the use of a nonowned auto.

When more than one policy applies to an owned auto, the PAP uses the approach known as **proration by face amounts**. In such a case, the insurer pays only that proportion of the claim or loss that its applicable limit of liability bears to the total applicable limit of liability covering the claim or loss.

This concept is illustrated in the following example. Assume that Everett decided to switch auto insurers and obtained a new policy but did not tell his wife, Debbie, who paid the old insurer's renewal premium. They now have two policies covering their auto. The policy Debbie renewed from Company A has a liability limit of $100,000. The policy Everett purchased from Company B has a $300,000 limit of liability. Thus, the auto is now covered for $400,000 in liability coverage. If their daughter, Sara, is in an accident for which she is deemed to be legally responsible and the damages are $60,000, Company A will pay $15,000 as its share and Company B will pay $45,000, calculated as shown in Exhibit 4-1.

Exhibit 4-1
Loss With Two Policies on a Covered Auto

$$\frac{\$100,000 \text{ (Company A's limit)}}{\$400,000 \text{ (Total limits of both companies)}} \times \$60,000 \text{ loss} = \$15,000$$

$$\frac{\$300,000 \text{ (Company B's limit)}}{\$400,000 \text{ (Total limits of both companies)}} \times \$60,000 \text{ loss} = \underline{\$45,000}$$

Total recovery from both companies $\underline{\$60,000}$

The PAP provides *excess* liability coverage on *nonowned autos*. Generally, a person who uses a nonowned insured auto has primary protection under the insurance applicable to that nonowned auto. In other words, insurance *follows* the auto being used. That being the case, an insured's PAP provides him or her with protection while using nonowned insured autos only when the damages exceed the limit of liability in the policy covering the nonowned auto. When the nonowned auto is uninsured, the PAP provides first dollar liability protection.

As an illustration, assume that Wendy is the named insured on a policy with Company C with a liability limit of $100,000. She borrows an auto from Zeke, who owns the car and insures it with Company D with a limit of liability of $100,000. Wendy is involved in an auto accident while driving Zeke's car and has been found legally responsible for damages amounting to $50,000. Company D, being the primary insurer of Zeke's auto, would pay the $50,000 damages on Wendy's behalf. Suppose, however, that the damages were $125,000. In this case, Company D would pay $100,000 and Company C, being liable for the excess, would pay $25,000. Finally, assume that Zeke did not insure his car, and that the damages caused by Wendy amount to $75,000. Since no other insurance applies to the auto, Wendy is protected under her own policy through Company C for the full $75,000. These three outcomes are summarized in Exhibit 4-2.

Exhibit 4-2
Primary and Excess Coverage Example

	Situation 1	Situation 2	Situation 3
Zeke's Policy Limit Company D	$100,000	$100,000	$ 0
Wendy's Policy Limit Company C	100,000	100,000	100,000
Damages	50,000	125,000	75,000
Amount Paid by Company D*	50,000	100,000	0
Amount Paid by Company C*	0	25,000	75,000

*Zeke's policy pays first because Wendy is driving *his* car at the time of the accident. Wendy's policy pays the excess over Zeke's coverage, subject to her policy limit.

Part B—Medical Payments Coverage

Auto medical payments coverage, Part B of the PAP, is a form of accident insurance limited to land motor vehicle accidents. The medical payments coverage applies without regard to fault. Its purpose is to provide a prompt source of medical expense reimbursement for persons injured while occupying a covered auto or when, as pedestrians, such persons are struck by vehicles. This type of protection may eliminate or reduce the size of bodily injury liability claims that might arise in the absence of prompt reimbursement of medical expenses.

Insuring Agreement

Under the auto medical payments coverage, the insurer agrees to pay reasonable expenses incurred for necessary medical and funeral services because of bodily injury caused by an accident and sustained by an insured. The insurer promises to pay those expenses incurred within three years from the date of the accident.

What is *reasonable* expense may very well be a question of fact. However, the purpose is to prevent payment of expenses that may be considerably higher than those normally incurred for a similar injury in the same locale. Much depends on where expenses are incurred. In a metropolis such as Los Angeles, medical expenses would probably be higher than in a small city like Fort Thomas, Kentucky.

Restricting the expenses or services to those *necessary* is an attempt to preclude costs that may have little to do with the direct treatment of injuries. For example, hiring a private-duty nurse for the convenience of the patient might not be considered a necessary expense.

The phrase "caused by an accident" encompasses not only injury by car crashes regardless of fault, but also injury sustained by accidental means, such as closing a door on one's hand or finger. However, "caused by an accident" would preclude recovery for any injury or death intentionally caused.

The persons whose injuries are covered by Part B are those who meet the definition of **"insured"** that appears in the medical payments section of the PAP. This definition includes two groups: (1) the named insured and family members and (2) other persons. The named insured and family members receive broader coverage than the latter group.

Subject to other policy provisions and exclusions, the named insured and family members have coverage for medical expenses and other services incurred for injury or death under the following circumstances:

- While occupying a motor vehicle. **Occupying** is taken to mean "in, upon, or getting in, on, out of or off." Thus, coverage applies, unless otherwise excluded or limited, to the named insured and family members when (1) using or operating a motor vehicle, (2) occupying a vehicle as a passenger, (3) upon a vehicle while, for example, performing repairs or maintenance, (4) departing a vehicle, or (5) entering a vehicle. Injuries sustained when under a vehicle for maintenance or repair appear not to be covered, but a factual situation would have to be resolved by the courts.

- As pedestrians, when struck by a motor vehicle designed for use mainly on public roads or a trailer of any type. Thus, the named insured and family members are covered if, as pedestrians, they are struck by such vehicles as motorcycles or tractor trailer trucks, but they are not covered if they are struck by dirt bikes or farm tractors.

Persons other than the named insured and family members are covered only while occupying a *covered* auto. Thus, no other coverage is available under Part B for such persons while pedestrians, even if they are struck by the named insured's car. Furthermore, given the definition of "your covered auto" discussed above, coverage is precluded while persons other than the named insured and his or her family members are occupying a nonowned auto—other than a substitute auto—being used by the named insured or family members. The reason for this restriction is that these other persons would likely have medical payments coverage under the policy covering the nonowned auto.

Perhaps the most troublesome question concerns *when* expenses and services are *incurred*. That is, do services have to be rendered within three years, or is it sufficient that the services be deemed necessary, even if not performed until after the three years? Although "incurred" is expected to encompass only services rendered, there have been cases in which the courts allowed coverage because services could not be performed within the specified period. For example, in one case,[3] a child sustained jaw injuries that could not be treated until the child's permanent teeth were fully grown. The father paid the estimated costs in full prior to the expiration of the time limit, but the services did not take place until the time limit had expired. The court decided in favor of the father and child.

The PAP addresses the problem of expenses incurred versus services rendered by replacing the term "expenses incurred" with "services rendered" in the insuring agreement. This establishes that the insurer intends to cover only those expenses associated with services rendered within the three-year period. Prepaid expenses will not be covered unless the services are received in the required time. However, the 1989 PAP does not include this stipulation.

Exclusions

The medical payments insuring agreement is subject to several exclusions, many of which resemble the PAP liability exclusions and exist for essentially the same reasons.

Fewer Than Four Wheels

No coverage applies to accidents that occur while a person is occupying a vehicle having fewer than four wheels. For example, medical payments coverage does not extend to a person occupying a motor scooter. Medical payments coverage on these vehicles can be obtained along with the purchase of separate motorcycle or motorbike liability insurance when the exposure arises. Note that the exclusion applies only to persons *occupying* such vehicles. If the named insured or a family member was struck as a pedestrian by a motor scooter, he or she would be covered as long as the scooter qualified as a motor vehicle designed for use mainly on public roads.

Public or Livery Use

When the covered auto is being used to carry persons or property for money, there is no coverage for persons occupying the vehicle. The public or livery exclusion is clearly stated not to apply to shared-expense car pools. Moreover, the exclusion applies only to *occupancy of the covered auto.* Thus, if the named insured or a family member is injured while occupying a taxi cab that is not a covered auto, he or she will qualify for medical payments coverage under his or her PAP.

Use as a Residence or Premises

No coverage is available for persons occupying any vehicle located for use as a residence or premises. This exclusion is directed at camping vehicles or motor homes that have been driven or pulled to a site for use as a permanent or temporary residence and present a different type of risk to the insurer. Other forms of insurance can be obtained for these exposures, some of which will be discussed in Chapter 6.

Workers Compensation

If a person is injured while in the course of employment, no coverage is available under the medical payments coverage of the PAP if workers compensation benefits are required to be, or are voluntarily, provided for the injuries. This exposure, like that under the liability coverage, is ordinarily covered under workers compensation insurance. If such insurance is not required (such as for domestic or casual employees in some jurisdictions) and not voluntarily provided by the employer, and the employee is injured while occupying the named insured's covered auto during the course of employment, medical payments coverage is available. The PAP medical payments coverage also applies in the event the named insured or a family member is struck as a pedestrian in the course of employment and workers compensation insurance is not required or available.

Owned or Available for Regular Use

No coverage applies while a person is occupying or is struck by any vehicle owned by the named insured or a family member, or furnished or available for the named insured's or a family member's regular use, other than a covered auto. However, the named insured and his or her resident spouse are provided medical benefits when they are injured while occupying a family member's auto. Like the corresponding exclusion in the PAP liability coverage section, this exclusion eliminates coverage for an "owned but not insured" auto, with the exception of the named insured and spouse occupying a family member's auto.

For example, Allison is the named insured on a PAP. Hugh is her husband, and Bob and Emily are their resident teenage children. Emily has her own car, which is uninsured. If Hugh is injured while driving Emily's car, Allison's PAP will cover Hugh's injuries. However, if Bob is injured while riding in Emily's car, he would not be covered by his mother's PAP.

Unpermitted Use

When a person occupies a vehicle without a reasonable belief of being entitled to do so, medical benefits are not provided for resulting injuries. Just as with the liability coverage exclusion, the exclusion eliminates coverage for operators and passengers of stolen vehicles.

Business Use

In most cases, Part B does not cover injury to people occupying a vehicle when it is being used in the business or occupation of an insured. However, coverage does apply to injury sustained while occupying (1) a private passenger auto that is a covered auto, (2) a pickup or van owned by the named insured, or (3) a trailer, as defined, while used with one of these vehicles. Thus, coverage for fellow employees is not provided unless they are injured while occupying the named insured's truck for farming or ranching, and workers compensation does not apply. A spouse or friend who accompanies the named insured on business would be covered only if he or she is traveling in a car, truck, or van owned by the named insured, or in a trailer being towed by one of these vehicles. The purpose of the exclusion is to allow the insurer to deny coverage for business exposures that should be covered by commercial insurance.

War and Nuclear Hazard

No coverage is provided for injury caused by or resulting from (1) the discharge of a nuclear weapon, whether accidental or not; (2) war, whether declared or not; (3) civil war; (4) insurrection; (5) rebellion or revolution; or (6) nuclear reaction, radiation, or radioactive contamination, whether controlled or uncontrolled, and however caused. The rationale for excluding these exposures is that they are deemed catastrophic and basically uninsurable.

Racing or Speed Contests

Medical payments coverage contains an exclusion for bodily injury

> Sustained while occupying any vehicle located inside a facility designed for racing, for the purpose of:

a.   Competing in; or

b.   Practicing or preparing for;

Any prearranged or organized racing or speed contest.

Thus, if an insured is injured while racing at the local speedway—even if driving his or her covered auto—the medical expenses will not be covered by the PAP. However, because the exclusion applies only to bodily injury sustained while *occupying* a vehicle, the insured is covered if injured as a pedestrian or bystander.

The 1989 PAP does not contain this exclusion.

Other Provisions Relating to Medical Payments Coverage

In addition to the insuring agreement and exclusions that apply to Part B, several other provisions further clarify the coverage. Two of the major provisions are discussed below.

Limit of Liability

The medical payments coverage limit shown in the declarations is the *maximum payable to each injured person*, regardless of the number of persons covered, claims made, vehicles or premiums shown, and vehicles involved in an accident. To avoid paying more than once for the same medical benefits, the provision simply states that an insured may not receive coverage for a loss that has been or will be covered by Part A, Part C, or an underinsured motorists endorsement.

The 1989 PAP achieves the same offsetting effect with different policy wording. The 1989 policy stipulates that any expenses paid under the medical payments coverage will be reduced by any amounts paid or payable for the same expenses under the PAP liability coverage or uninsured motorists coverage.

Many states do not permit this offset and, therefore, allow duplicate payments. Where the offset is allowed, payment for medical expenses is contingent upon an agreement in writing by the injured person or that person's legal representative to the effect that any payment received under the coverage will be applied toward any settlement or judgment the injured party is awarded under the liability or uninsured motorists coverages.

Other Insurance

The "other insurance" provision for medical payments coverage is the same as the corresponding provision under the liability coverage. Thus, if other auto medical payments insurance is available for an owned covered auto or a pedestrian, the insurer pays only its proportionate share. However, for injuries associated with an event involving a nonowned auto, coverage of the PAP applying to an injured individual is excess over any other collectible auto insurance coverage providing payments for medical and funeral expenses. If no other insurance is available, the PAP applying to the injured individual will apply as if its coverage were primary.

Note that this "other insurance" provision pertains only to other auto medical payments insurance. No coordination of benefits provision exists that would reduce recovery under the PAP if the covered person also recovers his or her medical expenses under a health insurance policy.

Part D—Coverage for Damage to Your Auto

The physical damage coverage of the PAP, referred to as Part D—Coverage for Damage to Your Auto, provides two optional forms of coverage: (1) collision and (2) other than collision (traditionally called comprehensive). Both coverages pay the insured for the actual cash value of direct and accidental damage to the covered auto or any nonowned auto (as defined) less any deductible that applies.

Insuring Agreement

The insuring agreement for Part D is divided into three subparts. The first section contains the actual promise to pay. The second section defines the terms "collision" and "other than collision." The third section defines the term "non-owned auto."

Definition of Collision and Other than Collision

Two types of physical damage coverage are available under the standard PAP: (1) collision and (2) other than collision. It is important to differentiate between the two types of coverages for two reasons. First, coverage is provided only for those causes of loss that fall within the types of coverage selected and paid for by the insured. If a loss is caused by fire and the policy covers only collision loss, the insured will not be able to recover from his or her auto insurer. Second, a different deductible amount may apply to each of the coverages. The other than collision deductible is often less than the collision deductible.

Collision is defined as the upset of a covered auto or a nonowned auto or its impact with another vehicle or object. **Other than collision** (OTC) is not really defined by the policy because it is an "all-risks" coverage that covers all perils, *other than collision*, that are not otherwise excluded. However, the insuring agreement names several causes of loss that are deemed to be other than collision:

- Missiles or falling objects
- Fire, explosion, or earthquake
- Theft, larceny, vandalism, malicious mischief, riot, or civil commotion
- Windstorm, hail, water, or flood
- Contact with a bird or animal
- Breakage of glass

This list of perils does not mean that other than collision covers only those perils. It merely makes clear that any loss by those perils is not considered to be collision. For example, if a covered auto is damaged by explosion or riot, any resulting loss will be paid under OTC coverage even though the loss may have been caused by actions that could otherwise be called collision, such as rioters overturning a vehicle.

The last part of the definition of collision states that breakage of glass, if it accompanies a collision, is considered a collision loss. This eliminates the need for the insured to pay two deductibles, one for the collision damage under the collision coverage and one for glass breakage under the OTC coverage.

Despite the clarity of the collision definition and the perils specifically identified as other than collision exposures, problems can still arise, especially when an insured purchases only OTC coverage or when the latter coverage applies with a lower deductible than the collision deductible. For example, suppose Ginger has OTC coverage with no deductible and collision coverage with a $250 deductible. While she is driving the covered auto, a wheel cover flies off and dents the underside of a body panel. Repairs are estimated at $200. Ginger maintains that the damage is covered under the other than collision coverage, reasoning that the loss was caused by a missile or a falling object. Her insurer, on the other hand, argues that the damage is a collision loss because the auto collided with the wheel cover.

Questions of coverage can be a problem unless both of the physical damage coverages are purchased and both have the same deductible. When a question does arise, the answer will be heavily influenced by the circumstances causing the loss. It is important to remember that the covered auto does not have to be in actual operation to have a collision loss—it can be parked. Also, collision is not limited to collision with other vehicles. A vehicle can collide with any other object.

Definition of "Non-Owned Auto"

The definition of "non-owned auto" is unique to Part D of the PAP. A **"non-**

owned auto" is any private passenger auto, pickup or van, or trailer (as defined by the policy) that meets both of the following conditions:

- The auto is not owned by or furnished or available for the regular use of the named insured or any family member
- The auto is in the custody of or being operated by the named insured or any family member

This definition is broad enough to include a short-term rental car in most circumstances and may therefore be an alternative to purchasing the collision damage waivers sold by car rental companies.

A "non-owned auto" also includes any auto or trailer used as a temporary substitute for a covered auto owned by the named insured that is out of normal use because of its breakdown, repair, servicing, loss, or destruction. Vehicles used as temporary substitutes for a covered auto are included in the definition of a covered auto for all other coverages in the PAP, but in Part D they are considered nonowned autos. A temporary substitute for a vehicle owned by the named insured but not qualifying as a covered auto—for example, an owned car the insured has chosen not to insure—does not qualify as a nonowned auto.

The Promise

The insurer promises to pay for direct and accidental loss to a covered auto or any nonowned auto, including its equipment. A deductible, if any applies, will be deducted prior to payment of the loss. The insured may purchase collision coverage, OTC coverage, or both coverages. However, many insurers will not provide coverage only for collision; they require OTC coverage to be purchased with collision coverage or by itself. The declarations will reflect the insured's decision with a premium charge and the applicable deductible for each coverage selected. For example, Val insured her car for both collision and other than collision. Her collision deductible is $500, and her other than collision deductible is $250. The excerpt from her declarations page, shown in Exhibit 4-3, shows this information. On the other hand, Luke has insured his car only for OTC damage with a deductible of $250. The excerpt from his declarations page, also shown in Exhibit 4-3, indicates his choice. Coverage will apply to those causes of loss chosen by the insured. Thus Luke will not have coverage for collision, whereas Val will. Both Luke and Val will have coverage for other than collision loss such as theft or vandalism.

The physical damage coverage clarifies that the deductible is a per occurrence deductible. If more than one covered or nonowned auto to which the PAP applies is involved in the same accident, the insureds are responsible for only the highest applicable deductible. For example, suppose Ian and his resident

Exhibit 4-3
PAP Declarations Page Excerpts

Val's Coverages

4 Coverages, Limits of liability and Premiums. Coverage is provided only where a premium or limit of liability is shown for the coverage.

Auto	A-Liability—in thousands	B-Medical payments each person	C-Uninsured motorists in thousands	D-Damage to your auto Actual cash value minus deductible		Towing and labor per disablement
				1-Collision loss	2-Other than collision loss	
	$ 300	$ 10,000	300	$ 500	$ 250	$ 100

Auto	Cov. A	Cov. B	Cov. C	Cov. D-1	Cov. D-2	Towing	Supp. Cov.*	Auto Total
	$ 180	$ 93	$ 100	$ 90	$ 45	$ 7		$ 515
	$							
	$							
	$							

Luke's Coverages

4 Coverages, Limits of liability and Premiums. Coverage is provided only where a premium or limit of liability is shown for the coverage.

Auto	A-Liability—in thousands	B-Medical payments each person	C-Uninsured motorists in thousands	D-Damage to your auto Actual cash value minus deductible		Towing and labor per disablement
				1-Collision loss	2-Other than collision loss	
	$ 100	$ 5,000	50	$	$ 250	$ 25

Auto	Cov. A	Cov. B	Cov. C	Cov. D-1	Cov. D-2	Towing	Supp. Cov.*	Auto Total
	$ 175	$ 62	$ 75	$ 0	$ 63	$ 3		$ 378
	$							
	$							
	$							

son Scott both own cars insured under the same PAP. Ian's car is subject to a $500 collision deductible, and Scott's car is insured with a $250 collision deductible. If Ian and Scott collide, the total deductible that will apply to their losses will be $500—the amount of the largest applicable deductible.

If damage results to a nonowned auto, the broadest coverage applicable will be provided to that loss. For example, suppose Justin insures two autos under his PAP—one for OTC coverage only and the other for both OTC and collision coverages. If Justin borrows a friend's car and drives into a tree, the loss will be covered for the broadest coverage available on Justin's PAP—both other than collision and collision coverages.

The meaning of *direct and accidental loss* is key to the coverage yet is not always clear. Generally, a **direct loss** is one in which the covered peril is the direct and proximate cause of loss.

Accidental loss typically means loss that is unintentional, unexpected, and unforeseen. In at least one court case, **accidental** was determined to mean unintentional and unexpected *from the insured's point of view.* In this case, a husband had intentionally run into his wife's car with another vehicle. The court decided that, since the wife had no control over her husband's actions and did not foresee his colliding with her car, the collision was accidental from her point of view and therefore covered by her collision coverage.[4]

Exclusions

Part D of the PAP contains its own set of exclusions that further define the coverage provided by the physical damage coverages. The exclusions are discussed below.

Public or Livery Use

Like other coverages of the PAP, Part D contains an exclusion of loss while the auto is being used to carry persons or property for a fee unless it is being used as a share-the-expense car pool. The rationale of this exclusion is discussed earlier in the context of Parts A and B of the PAP.

Wear and Tear, and so on

No coverage applies for damage due and confined to (1) wear and tear, (2) freezing, (3) mechanical or electrical breakdown or failure, or (4) road damage to tires. The rationale for excluding these losses is that they are events foreseeable with prolonged use of an auto even when it is properly maintained.

Note that the losses are excluded only when they are *due and confined* to those events. There are two schools of thought as to what **due and confined** means.

On the one hand, many people interpret this to mean that the exclusion applies only to initial damage, while ensuing damage is covered. For example, in one case,[5] a vehicle's hood latch broke, allowing the hood to fly up and damage the vehicle. The court ruled that the damage resulting from the hood's flying up would be covered, although the damage to the broken latch would not. On the other hand, especially with respect to mechanical breakdown or failure, some people believe that the actual breakdown or failure is the cause, and that any ensuing loss is excluded. In a case representing this school of thought,[6] a vehicle's thermostat failed, allowing the engine to overheat unnoticed, which resulted in damage to the engine. The court ruled that the engine damage was due and confined to the mechanical breakdown of the thermostat.

Specifically excepted from this exclusion is damage by wear and tear, freezing, mechanical or electrical breakdown or failure, or road damage to tires, all resulting from *total theft* of a covered auto. In these situations, theft is the proximate cause of loss. For example, if a covered auto is stolen and abandoned and found only after a freezing spell damages the engine block and radiator because of lack of antifreeze, the resulting damage would be covered under OTC coverage because the theft was the cause of the loss. Coverage would also apply under OTC coverage if the stolen auto were driven recklessly, causing damage to the engine and tires and excessive wear and tear on the auto.

War and Other Catastrophic Losses

Loss resulting from radioactive contamination; the discharge of a nuclear weapon, accidental or not; war, declared or not; civil war; insurrection; and rebellion or revolution are excluded because of their catastrophic nature.

Campers or Trailers

This exclusion eliminates coverage for any trailer or camper body owned by the named insured and not described in the declarations. However, the exclusion states that a camper body or trailer acquired by the named insured during the policy period will be covered if the named insured asks the insurer to insure it within thirty days after it is acquired.

Governmental Action

The physical damage coverage will not apply to loss to any covered vehicle that is destroyed or confiscated by governmental or civil authorities. The PAP clarifies that the purpose of the exclusion is to eliminate coverage for total loss of a vehicle because it is confiscated or destroyed by governmental or civil authority. Partial losses that occur while a covered auto is in the custody of the government or civil authorities are covered if caused by a covered peril.

If a finance company or other creditor is listed in the declarations as a loss payee, its interest in the destroyed or confiscated auto is excepted from the exclusion and would be covered in the event of such a loss. This exception is provided by the **loss payable clause**, which, when endorsed to the policy, states that the insurer will indemnify the loss payee even if the insured is denied coverage because of fraudulent or illegal activities.

The 1989 version of the PAP identifies specific governmental actions that are excluded. It states that coverage is not available for a vehicle that is confis-cated or destroyed because the named insured or family members (1) took part in illegal activities, such as transporting controlled substances, or (2) did not meet the standards of the Environmental Protection Agency or the Depart-ment of Transportation, such as when a car is impounded if the registration has expired. The 1994 provision deletes reference to illegal activities or failure to meet standards since, in most cases, these are the only causes for confiscation by governmental or civil authority.

Equipment-Related Exclusions

Although the physical damage coverages of the PAP apply to the covered auto *and its equipment*, the policy does not define the term "equipment." What is considered equipment must be inferred from what is not. To this end, Part D of the PAP contains four separate exclusions that apply to the following types of equipment:

- *Electronic equipment designed for the reproduction of sound or the reception and transmission of audio visual or data signals, including media and accessories.* These items include, but are not limited to, radios and stereos; tape decks and tapes; compact disc players and compact discs; telephones, citizens' band radios, and two-way mobile radios; video and audio cassette record-ers and tapes; and personal computers and tapes or disks. The exclusion does not apply to (1) equipment designed solely for the reproduction of sound and its accessories if it is *permanently installed* in the covered auto (media such as tapes and compact discs are still excluded), (2) equipment needed for normal operation of a covered auto or monitoring its systems, or (3) electronic equipment that is "removable from a housing unit which is permanently installed in the auto" and that operates only from the power of the auto's electrical system, while the equipment is in or on the covered auto at the time of the loss.

The items described in (3) include pull-out compact disc players. While such items are in the auto, they are covered by the PAP but when they have been removed from the auto for protection against theft they are insured by a personal property coverage such as that available on a homeowners policy. The 1989 PAP excludes coverage for items described in (3).

- *Awnings, cabanas, and equipment used to create additional living facilities.*

- *Equipment designed or used for locating or detecting radar or laser beams.* The 1989 version excludes coverage only for radar location and detection equipment.

- *Customizing equipment and furnishings.* This exclusion is directed at pickups and vans that may come equipped with furnishings and homelike facilities, such as special carpeting or cooking facilities, worth thousands of dollars more than standard factory equipment. This exclusion also eliminates coverage for custom paint jobs and murals, on any auto, that increase the potential severity of a loss.

These classes of equipment are extremely popular and have potentially high value, making the equipment especially vulnerable to loss by theft. So, apart from the exceptions relating to some permanently installed items, the exposure is considered too great for the basic premiums charged for the physical damage coverages. Furthermore, although these items are popular, many individuals do not have a need for coverage of these classes of equipment and are unwilling to pay a higher premium that includes the costs of the unnecessary coverage. However, most excluded equipment can be covered by separate buy-back endorsements (which are discussed later in this chapter) or other forms of insurance such as floater policies.

Nonowned Auto Exclusions

Three exclusions are applicable to autos not owned by the named insured. The first of these eliminates coverage for loss to any nonowned auto when the auto is used by the named insured or family member without having the reasonable belief that he or she is entitled to do so.

Another exclusion applies to loss to any nonowned auto being maintained or used by any person while employed or otherwise engaged in the business of selling, repairing, servicing, storing, or parking vehicles designed for use on public highways, including road testing and delivery. For example, if a parking garage attendant dents the front fender of a temporary substitute while parking it for the named insured, the named insured's PAP will not cover the physical damage to the car.

The third exclusion eliminates coverage for loss to any nonowned auto being maintained or used by any person while employed or otherwise engaged in a business other than the auto businesses listed in the above exclusion. However, this exclusion does not apply to the maintenance or use by the named insured or any family member of a nonowned auto that is a private passenger auto or trailer as defined in the policy.

Racing and Speed Contests

The racing and speed contests exclusion eliminates coverage for otherwise covered autos if they are damaged while involved in racing or speed contests. The exclusion applies only while the auto is inside a facility designed for racing and involved in actual competition or in the preparation for competition. The 1989 PAP does not contain this exclusion.

Rental Vehicles

Physical damage coverage qualifies coverage for damage to rental vehicles otherwise covered as nonowned autos. The coverage provided by the insuring agreement is fairly broad and has allowed car rental companies to collect from an insured's PAP even when the insured is not legally responsible for the damage to the rental car. Some states have addressed this problem by passing laws that prohibit rental car companies from holding a renter liable for damage to rental vehicles. The exclusion denies physical damage and loss of use coverage for rental vehicles rented to an insured in states that have a such a law. The 1989 PAP does not contain this exclusion.

Transportation Expenses

Transportation expenses is a supplementary coverage that applies only in the event of *total theft* of a covered auto, not partial theft such as stealing a battery or other equipment or another peril that leaves the vehicle inoperable. The insurer agrees to pay the insured up to $15 a day, subject to a maximum of $450 for transportation expenses incurred by an insured because of the covered auto's total theft or destruction by covered perils. The insurer also agrees to pay the insured up to the same limits for loss of use expenses for which an insured becomes liable because of total theft or destruction by a covered peril of a nonowned auto.

For example, suppose an insured borrows a friend's car and it is stolen. The insured's policy will pay up to $15 per day for the friend to rent a car until his or her stolen car is found or permanently replaced. The payment is subject to the $450 maximum limit.

No deductible applies to transportation expenses. However, when transportation expenses coverage is triggered, the policy does not cover expense actually incurred until forty-eight hours after the theft. Coverage ends when the covered auto is returned for use or the insurer pays for the loss of the vehicle.

The 1989 PAP covers transportation expenses only for total theft of the covered auto or a nonowned auto. For example, if the policy applies to collision damage and to other than collision loss, transportation expenses resulting from collision damage will not be covered by the 1989 PAP but will be covered by the 1994 policy. Extended coverage can be added to the 1989 PAP with an *extended transportation expenses coverage endorsement* to the PAP. This endorsement is discussed at the end of the chapter.

Limit of Liability

The amount ultimately paid by the insurer is limited to (1) the actual cash value of the damaged or stolen property or (2) the amount required to repair or replace it—whichever is *less*. As a practical matter, when the vehicle is deemed a partial loss, the insurer pays the cost to repair it. If the vehicle is a total loss, the insurer pays the actual cash value of the vehicle immediately before the loss

Actual cash value and cost to replace are important concepts both in determining whether damage is repairable and in settling total losses and **constructive total losses** (the cost to repair is greater than the actual cash value). Actual cash value is not expressly defined by the PAP but is commonly held to mean the replacement cost of the auto and its equipment, less depreciation. The limit of liability provision notes that an adjustment will be made for depreciation and physical condition in determining the actual cash value at the time of the loss. However, since a fairly regular trade in used cars exists, it is generally easier to establish a value on a **market value basis** (what amount similar cars are currently selling for). Accordingly, most total losses are adjusted on the basis of market value as established in a number of publications that report on current used-car sales prices.

Consider, for example, an auto that was purchased new two years ago for $14,000 and is now totally destroyed by collision. Today a comparable new auto is worth $20,000. However, the insurer is not liable for either the $14,000 or the $20,000. Instead, the insurer is liable only for an amount sufficient to replace the auto with a similar one *of like age and condition at the time of the loss*. Thus, the insured receives an amount comparable to the value of a $14,000 auto that is two years old, less the applicable deductible. This amount may be easily determined by referring to a publication that lists the current market value of the same year, make, and model as that destroyed in the collision.

The PAP qualifies the amount to repair or replace the property. Only the amount needed to repair or replace property with property *of like kind and quality* is covered. Furthermore, the insurer will not pay for any amount of betterment that results from the repair or replacement. For example, suppose Fran's car is vandalized. The seats are torn, and the tires are sliced. Because

Fran has OTC coverage, her insurer will pay to repair or replace the seats and tires, but only with seats and tires of like kind and quality. Suppose Fran had vinyl seats and low-grade tires. If she were to repair her seats with leather and replace her tires with high performance radials, the insurer will still pay only to the amount necessary to repair her seats with vinyl and purchase low-grade tires. The 1989 PAP does not make a distinction with respect to kind and quality of replacement materials.

Payment of Loss

When a covered physical damage loss occurs, the insurer has the option to pay the loss in money, or to repair or replace the property. If the covered auto or its equipment is stolen and recovered, the insurer may exercise an option to return it to the insured at its own expense and to pay for any damage to the property resulting from the theft. However, the insurer also reserves the right to keep all or part of the damaged or stolen property at an agreed or appraised value.

The payment of loss provision specifies that if the loss is paid with money, sales tax on the damaged or stolen property is included in the payment. The 1989 PAP does not specify that sales tax will be included in payment. This caused confusion in determining the amount of loss payment and is one of the reasons for including the provision in the 1994 PAP.

No Benefit to Bailee

The no benefit to bailee clause states that the insurance will not benefit, directly or indirectly, any person who assumes control of a covered auto for business purposes. For instance, a parking garage or auto repair shop may specify on the parking ticket or service order that any insurance carried by the insured will be for the benefit of such business as a bailee. If Eugene's auto is damaged while in the custody or control of an auto shop, the shop may try to absolve itself from any liability if damage is payable under Eugene's auto physical damage insurance. The no benefit to bailee provision invalidates such attempts and preserves the right of the insurer to subrogate against a negligent bailee for hire following payment of loss to the insured.

Other Sources of Recovery

When other sources of recovery, such as coverage under a travel or accident policy or a benefit provided by a credit card company, are also available to cover a loss to a covered owned auto or its equipment, it is a condition of the other sources of recovery provision that the insurer pay only its share. The insurer's share is the proportion that the insurer's limit of liability bears to the total of all limits on the sources of recovery. Since most physical damage insurance is written on an actual cash value basis rather than as a stated amount, it could be difficult for two or more insurers to agree on the limit to be apportioned to determine the loss. Usually, one insurer will pay the entire loss and will then submit the settlement to a committee on interinsurance arbitration to determine the proper apportionment between the insurers. Disputes of this nature are seldom of concern to insureds.

A separate clause applies to other sources of recovery covering a nonowned auto, such as a rental company's self-insurance or an insurance policy purchased by the owner of the car. This clause states that the insurance under this PAP is excess over any other source of recovery on the nonowned auto. Generally if the owner of the auto borrowed or used by the insured has physical damage insurance, the only part of the loss not covered by that insurance will be a deductible. If the deductible on the insured's PAP is less than that on the owner's policy, the insured's coverage will pay for the remaining loss above the insured's deductible.

Appraisal

If the insurer and the insured agree that there is coverage, but disagree on the amount of physical damage loss, either may demand an appraisal. The routine to settle the matter is specified in the appraisal clause, and is similar to the procedure used in the homeowners policies. Each party must select a competent appraiser, and the two appraisers must select an umpire. The appraisers are required to determine separately the actual cash value and the amount of loss. If they fail to agree, they must submit their differences to the umpire. An agreement by any two of the three persons involved is considered to be binding.

Part E—Duties After an Accident or Loss

Part E of the PAP lists certain duties the insured must perform after an accident or loss. In order to receive payment for loss under the policy, the insured has certain general duties after an accident or loss, as well as certain specific duties for losses involving uninsured motorists coverage and coverage for damage to your auto. These duties are discussed below with the exception of duties for loss involving uninsured motorists coverage, which will be described in Chapter 5 with the discussion of Part C of the PAP.

General Duties

In general, following any loss, the insured is obligated to notify the insurance company promptly of all the particulars concerning a loss and submit proof of loss when required. The insured is also expected to cooperate with the insurer in the investigation, defense, or settlement of any claim or suit.

Duties for Physical Damage Claims

In addition to the general duties, an insured who makes a claim for a physical damage loss must take the necessary steps after the loss to protect the auto from further damage. Any reasonable expenses incurred in doing so will be paid by the insurer. Storage charges for a damaged auto, if necessary, might be such a covered expense. The insured also is required to notify the police promptly if the covered auto is stolen. Finally, the insured is expected to cooperate in permitting the insurer to inspect and appraise the damaged property before the loss is settled.

Part F—General Provisions

Some of the more important conditions expressed in the general provisions section of the PAP are discussed below.

Bankruptcy

The insurer must fulfill its obligations under the policy even if the *insured* declares bankruptcy or insolvency.

Fraud

The insurer will not cover any insured who makes fraudulent statements or engages in fraudulent conduct in connection with any accident or loss for which a claim is made. For example, if an insured deliberately abandons a covered auto and reports the car as stolen, the insurer will not cover the loss if it becomes aware of the insured's fraudulent conduct.

Legal Action Against the Insurer

Sometimes an insured may wish to bring legal action against his or her own insurer. According to the policy terms, the insured must fully satisfy all the terms of the policy before he or she can bring legal action against the insurer. Furthermore, under the liability coverage, legal action cannot be taken against the insurer until the insurer agrees (in writing) that the insured is liable for damages or the amount of the obligation has been determined by a court. Any action to determine an insured's liability is not allowed by the policy.

The Insurer's Right To Recover Payment

If any payment is made by the insurer, the insurer may, to the extent of payment, take over the rights of the person to whom payment was made against the negligent third party. The person to whom such payment is made by the insurer must do whatever is necessary to preserve those rights of subrogation. A number of states prohibit subrogation to recover payments made under medical payments coverage.

For example, suppose Cindy and Les are involved in an auto accident for which Les is found at fault. Each is injured. To expedite the payment of their medical expenses, each makes a claim and receives payment from his and her own insurance company. Cindy tells Les and his insurer that, because she has been covered by her policy, she does not need to collect any damages from Les or his insurer. Cindy has violated the insurer's right to recovery if the state allows the insurer to subrogate.

The subrogation rights of the insurer do not apply under the physical damage coverages against any person using the covered auto with the reasonable belief that he or she is entitled to do so. For example, assume that Sue and Kim each have a PAP with liability and physical damage coverage. If Sue borrows Kim's car with permission and is involved in an accident, Kim's PAP will pay for the damage to Kim's car. Kim's insurer cannot subrogate against Sue.

Policy Period and Territory

Coverage under the PAP applies only to accidents and losses that occur during the policy period and within the United States, its territories or possessions, Puerto Rico, or Canada. Coverage also applies to accidents involving the covered auto while being conveyed between ports within the above territory.

The coverage territory does not include Mexico. Although a PAP endorsement, usually referred to as **Mexico coverage**, provides a limited degree of coverage in Mexico, the endorsement is not a substitute for purchasing auto liability insurance from a licensed Mexican insurance company when a United States resident drives his or her car into Mexico. Mexican authorities do not recognize an insurance policy issued by other than a licensed Mexican insurer as evidence of financial responsibility. Thus, following an accident in Mexico, a United States resident without liability insurance from a Mexican insurer could be detained, have his or her car impounded, or be subject to other penalties until he or she can prove financial responsibility. The necessary insurance is frequently obtained from insurance agents located in states bordering Mexico.

Termination

The termination provision specifies the rights and obligations of the insured and the insurer concerning cancellation and nonrenewal of the policy. An insured may cancel the policy at any time by notifying the insurance company. However, an insurer may cancel only under the following circumstances:

1. The named insured fails to pay the premium due
2. Any insured's drivers license is suspended or revoked
3. The named insured lied on the application for insurance

With respect to nonrenewal, the insurer has the right to renew or not renew every six months if the policy has a six-month (or shorter) period, and every year if the policy has an annual period.

The insurer must provide a ten- or twenty-day (depending on the reason) notice of cancellation or nonrenewal to the insured.

Despite the agreement concerning when notice may be given and how it is to be mailed, along with the number of days and the permissible reasons for doing so by the insurer, most states have laws that deal with cancellations and nonrenewals of policies. Any adjustments to policy wording that must be made for various states will be noted in the state amendatory endorsement (discussed later in this chapter) for the states in question.

The 1989 PAP termination provision differs in two respects. First, it allows only for annual nonrenewal decisions even if the policy has less than a one-year term. Second, the provision states that if the law of the state in question requires a longer period of notice, requires a special procedure for giving notice, or modifies any of the reasons stated in this provision when the policy can be canceled or nonrenewed, the insurer will comply with those requirements. In many states, the termination provision is modified by a state amendatory endorsement.

Important Endorsements for the Personal Auto Policy

Although the PAP is designed to meet the auto insurance needs of many individuals and families, many exposures are not adequately covered by an unendorsed PAP. Several endorsements can be added to the basic PAP to meet the special needs of insureds.

Liability Coverage Exclusion Endorsement

In some cases, when more than one insured is involved in an auto accident that is caused by an insured and results in bodily injury to at least one other insured, the injured insured may allege liability against the at-fault insured. When the insureds involved include the named insured and family members, an **intrafamily suit** may arise, with one family member suing another family member to receive coverage for bodily injury under the PAP's liability coverage. An unendorsed PAP does not exclude this type of situation. However, a **liability coverage exclusion endorsement**, mandatory in many states, excludes coverage for claims involving bodily injury to a named insured or family member. The purpose of the exclusion is to prevent collusion among family members who can profit by being both insureds and claimants under the same policy. For example, Sally is driving her husband, Brian, to work when she negligently collides with another car and causes serious bodily injury to Brian. If the PAP is endorsed with the liability coverage exclusion, it will not cover Sally's liability for Brian's injury. The rationale is that it would be difficult to prevent Brian and Sally from colluding to produce an exaggerated claim when both stand to benefit from any payments received from the liability insurer.

The liability coverage exclusion endorsement is worded so as to exclude a broader range of suits than the intrafamily suit. To illustrate, Erin's car is covered by a PAP with the liability coverage exclusion endorsement. While Erin and her friend Zack are traveling in Erin's car, she allows him to drive while she rests in the passenger seat. Zack causes an accident, and Erin is injured. Because the exclusion eliminates coverage for bodily injury to the named insured or family member, Zack's liability for Erin's injuries will not be covered under Erin's PAP—even though Zack and Erin are not members of the same family and even though Zack was an insured under Erin's policy when the accident occurred.

Use of Nonowned Vehicles

In many cases, individuals have regular access to and general use of vehicles they do not own. The PAP does not provide coverage for liability, medical expenses, and damage to the vehicle arising out of the use of such autos, with several exceptions. Two endorsements that allow coverage for certain exposures involving nonowned vehicles are (1) extended non-owned coverage for named individual and (2) named non-owner coverage.

Extended Non-Owned Coverage for Named Individual

The PAP eliminates coverage for nonowned vehicles that are available for the regular use of its insureds. However, the **extended non-owned coverage for named individual endorsement** extends the liability and the medical payments coverages of the PAP to cover the individual(s) *named in the endorsement* while using or occupying a nonowned auto, which is furnished and available for an insured's regular use, for any type of business purposes except any auto business. To effect coverage, an individual must be named to the endorsement; the proper coverage(s)—liability, medical payments, uninsured motorists (discussed in Chapter 5), or a combination of these coverages—must be selected; and a premium must be paid for the protection. A spouse or family member is *not* automatically covered by the endorsement—he or she must be specifically named to the endorsement.

As its name suggests, the endorsement is designed to cover exposures arising from nonowned autos. The following are examples of individuals who might purchase an extended non-owned coverage endorsement:

- An employee who is furnished a vehicle for his or her regular use, or a volunteer fire fighter who is assigned to regularly operate an emergency vehicle

- An employee who has regular access to the company's fleet of vehicles for business use

- An employee who is furnished with a company vehicle of any type for his or her regular use for business or pleasure

These types of situations are not uncommon.

Liability Coverage

Regarding the liability coverage, the extended non-owned coverage endorsement deletes or replaces four PAP Part A exclusions and, thus, broadens coverage. The first exclusion to be deleted is that relating to liability arising out of the ownership or operation of a vehicle while it is being used to carry persons or property for a fee. So, for example, if Mel is named in the endorsement and is employed as a limousine driver, Mel will be covered for liability and medical payments under his own PAP while driving his employer's limousine. However, because of the Part A "other insurance" clause, the applicable PAP liability coverage will be excess over any liability insurance carried on the limousine by its owner. Because the public or livery exclusion is deleted, the endorsed PAP would cover the named individual while using a covered auto to carry persons or property for a fee.

The second exclusion considered eliminates coverage for nonowned pickups and vans used in any business other than (1) farming or ranching or (2) the business of selling, repairing, servicing, storing, or parking automobiles. This exclusion is replaced by an exclusion that eliminates coverage only while any type of auto is used in a business described in (2). By replacing the PAP exclusion with the endorsement exclusion, coverage is provided for nonowned autos of any type that the named individual might use in any business other than one of the auto businesses listed in (2) above.

The third and fourth PAP exclusions eliminate PAP liability coverage for nonowned vehicles that are furnished or available for the regular use of the named insured or any family members. The endorsement deletes these exclusions from the PAP, and, thus, the endorsement provides coverage for liability resulting from the use, for example, of an auto owned by the business but used by an insured for making sales calls.

Fellow-Employee Suits

The extended non-owned coverage endorsement provides important protection against **fellow-employee suits**. Neither business auto nor commercial general liability policies protect an employee against any claim or suit brought by a fellow employee who sustains injuries during the course of business because of the employee's acts or omissions. Sometimes, although infrequently, insurers delete the exclusion. Some states do not allow such fellow-employee suits and require bodily injury claims to be covered by workers compensation programs. However, a number of states do not have this restriction, or the restriction has been limited by judicial interpretation. Thus, when suits are permitted and commercial auto policies contain a fellow-employee exclusion, the personal assets of an allegedly negligent employee could be at stake.

Although the PAP protects an insured against fellow-employee suits, the coverage is limited to the use of a covered auto. The insured is not protected under the PAP for a fellow-employee suit resulting from the negligent, or allegedly negligent, operation of a public conveyance such as a taxi or bus, a pool car furnished and available for the regular use of the employee, or a nonowned pickup or van used in business. With the extended nonowned liability coverage, the named individual is protected against a fellow-employee suit involving the above exposures.

Medical Payments Coverage

If the extended non-owned medical payments coverage is purchased, the endorsement deletes, with respect to the *individual named on the endorsement only*, the PAP Part B exclusions pertaining to owned autos not insured under the policy and nonowned autos furnished or available for the regular use of the named insured or any family member. The deletion of these Part B exclusions in conjunction with the endorsement's denial of coverage for owned autos that are not insured by the PAP allows coverage only for autos, pickups, and vans that are nonowned and furnished or available for the regular use of the named individuals. In addition, the endorsement modifies the medical payments exclusion of bodily injury to except, and thus provide coverage for, any person who sustains an injury while occupying a vehicle being used in the business of an insured.

Auto Business Endorsement

The extended non-owned coverage endorsement does not delete the PAP Part A exclusion that pertains to vehicles used in the auto business. The exclusion can be deleted, *for the named individuals only*, by a different endorsement—the **extended non-owned coverage for named individual (auto business) endorsement**.

The auto business endorsement does not eliminate the other four liability exclusions deleted by the regular extended non-owned endorsement. Thus, with respect to liability insurance, the auto business endorsement *alone* covers the named individual only for the use of a nonowned auto *in the auto business*, provided the auto is not furnished or available for the regular use of the named individual and his or her family members. In order to have the broader scope of coverage for autos being used to carry persons or property for a fee, for autos furnished or available for the regular use of the named individual or family members, and for autos used in other than an auto business, an employee of an auto business should be named in both the regular extended non-owned coverage endorsement and the auto business endorsement.

To illustrate, assume Jenny is a car salesperson. The dealership allows her to drive home any one of several dealership cars on the lot each night and return it the next morning. Any car Jenny takes home on a particular night could be said to be "available" for her regular use and, therefore, is excluded under Jenny's PAP on her own car. If the regular extended non-owned endorsement is attached to Jenny's PAP with Jenny shown as a named individual, Jenny's PAP will cover her while using any car made available by the dealer, as long as she does not use the car in the dealer's auto business. If Jenny wants to be covered under her PAP when driving nonowned autos while actually on the job, she also needs to be a named individual on the auto business endorsement attached to her policy. Furthermore, if Jenny's husband wants coverage for use of a nonowned car that Jenny drives home from the dealership after work, he must be named to the regular extended non-owner endorsement; he is not automatically covered by this endorsement.

Named Non-Owner Coverage

The **named non-owner coverage endorsement** enables people who do not own an auto to insure some of their auto loss exposures. Even in today's mobile society, many people do not own an auto. This group includes young adults who cannot afford to purchase and maintain an auto, people who live in metropolitan areas where parking or garaging is a problem, those for whom public transportation or a van pool is a satisfactory substitute, and some people who no longer wish to drive on congested streets. Although these persons do not own an auto, they still have an exposure if they use an auto belonging to someone else. Even persons who do not drive might be held liable for an auto accident if, as passengers, they distract the driver or fail to warn the driver of some hazard.

Named non-owner coverage is provided at a lower premium than would be charged for coverage for an individual who owns an auto. For example, the liability and medical payments premium typically may be 50 percent of the premium to obtain the same coverage on an owned auto. Since other coverage generally "follows the car" rather than the driver, the named nonowner *usually* will be covered by any insurance purchased by the owner of the auto in question, and the named non-owner coverage is excess over other such coverage. However, it is not always enough to rely on the insurance that "follows the car." In some cases, coverage on the car may be inadequate or nonexistent. Even if the nonowned auto usually used is well insured, a person without coverage of his or her own may still face severe exposure by borrowing another auto.

The named non-owner coverage endorsement provides coverage only to the individual named in the endorsement. If a spouse intends to drive other autos, he or she also must be named on the endorsement. A schedule in the endorsement designates the single or split limits to apply for liability coverage, as well as limits for medical payments and uninsured motorists coverage, if the latter two are desired.

When the endorsement is attached to the PAP, all the provisions of the PAP apply except as noted on the endorsement. Thus, for liability coverage, the named individual is protected for maintenance or use of any covered auto as defined by the policy. If medical payments and uninsured motorists coverages are selected, the named individual is covered while using or occupying a covered auto. Coverage is provided on an excess basis.

The named non-owner coverage endorsement does not include an option for physical damage insurance. While the liability coverage does apply to property damage, it does not cover property damage to property in the care, custody, or control of the insured or to autos available for regular use by the insured. The only source of coverage that nonowners have for damage to the cars they borrow is the physical damage insurance, if any, carried by the auto's owner.

If the named individual under the endorsement does purchase an auto, he or she has insurance on that auto for thirty days from the purchase date. If the individual also purchases a policy for the newly acquired auto during the thirty-day period, coverage under the named non-owner coverage endorsement is automatically terminated. During the thirty-day period, unless a policy on the auto has been purchased, coverage for medical payments and uninsured motorists extends to all occupants of the new auto, not just the individual named on the endorsement.

Additional Property

The PAP does not cover certain types of property that include, but are not limited to, cellular telephones, compact disc players, refrigerators, and stoves that may be installed in vehicles. Endorsements to the PAP are available to cover each of these types of property. The endorsements dealing with property contained within covered autos are described below. Coverage for other vehicles is discussed in Chapter 6.

Coverage for Media

Many autos have cellular telephones, citizens' band radios, mobile radios, upgraded stereo systems, or scanners. This equipment is expensive and especially susceptible to loss by theft. Under the physical damage coverage provisions of the PAP, equipment of this type is covered only if it is permanently installed in the opening in the dashboard or console normally used by the auto's manufacturer for installation of a radio. Also excluded by the PAP are tapes, compact discs, records, and other devices used with the equipment.

Broader coverage is available under the **coverage for audio, visual and data electronic equipment and tapes, records, discs and other media endorsement**. With this endorsement, the exclusions pertaining to these types of property as well as any deductible that normally applies to these items are deleted. First-dollar coverage then applies for loss to electronic equipment like cellular telephones and upgraded stereo systems and their accessories, but only when the equipment is permanently installed in the covered auto at the time of the loss. The requirement that the equipment be *permanently installed in the auto* is less stringent than the deleted exclusion. The meaning of *permanently installed* is subject to interpretation, but is commonly held to mean that the equipment is bolted in place somewhere in the car. Coverage also applies to equipment that can be removed from an auto although the equipment's housing unit must be permanently attached and the equipment must operate solely from the auto's electrical system. Equipment that can be removed, such as a pull-out compact disc player, must be in the vehicle at the time of the loss for coverage to apply.

Although theft is undoubtedly the major peril, coverage applies against any loss for which the covered auto is otherwise insured. Thus, if the vehicle is covered for other than collision loss, and an engine fire damages the equipment, the loss will be covered by the endorsement.

With respect to tapes, records, discs, and other media, the insurer agrees to pay for direct and accidental loss to these items only when (1) the equipment is owned by the named insured or a family member, and (2) the equipment is in the covered auto at the time of loss.

The limit of liability for equipment is scheduled for a stated amount, whereas the limit for tapes and other media is set at $200 per loss. At no time will the insurer pay more than the actual cash value or the amount to repair or replace the items with property of like kind and quality, subject to the limits of liability on the insured property.

In some states, equivalent coverage must be purchased through two endorsements—the **coverage for sound receiving and transmitting equipment endorsement** and the **coverage for tapes, records or other devices endorsement**.

The 1989 version of the coverage for audio, visual and data electronic equipment and tapes, records, discs and other media endorsement contains two modifications:

1. It does not cover electronic equipment, or its accessories, that can be removed from the auto even if it is housed in a permanently attached housing unit and operates solely from the auto's electrical system, such as a pull-out compact disc player.

2. Repair or replacement cost is not expressly constrained to the amount necessary to repair or replace the stolen or damaged property with property of like kind and quality.

Customizing Equipment Coverage

The PAP excludes coverage for items included in some vans such as special carpeting, custom painting and murals, and facilities for cooking and sleeping. In order to cover this property, a **customizing equipment endorsement** must be added to the PAP. The endorsement deletes the PAP exclusion and, thus, provides coverage for these types of property. However, the endorsement does not cover electronic items otherwise excluded by the PAP—the endorsement discussed above is required to cover these electronic items.

The limits of liability for property covered by the endorsement are scheduled. The type of property damage to be covered—collision or other than collision—and a deductible *for each item listed* must also be selected. The endorsement will pay no more than (1) the actual cash value, (2) the cost to repair or replace, or (3) the policy limit for an item that is damaged or destroyed by an insured peril. In the event that more than one item is damaged or stolen in a single accident, the deductible applies only once.

Miscellaneous Endorsements

Several other endorsements are also important. These are discussed below.

Extended Transportation Expenses Coverage

Loss of use can create major expense for the car owner who has to rent a substitute auto until his or her owned auto is repaired or replaced, regardless of the cause of loss. In the 1989 version of the PAP, only the transportation expenses following the total theft of a covered auto are covered. Loss of use of an auto often follows its damage or destruction by perils other than total theft, such as fire or collision. Some families can control this exposure by having more than one car, but many families find it difficult to get along without all owned autos being operable.

Broader coverage for loss of use is available under the **extended transportation expenses coverage endorsement**. When this endorsement is attached to the 1989 PAP, the insurer will reimburse the insured for expenses incurred to rent a substitute auto, but only when *all* of the following conditions are met.

1. The owned auto is named in the policy *and* in the endorsement, and a premium is paid for the coverage.
2. The covered auto is withdrawn from use for longer than twenty-four hours.
3. The withdrawal is caused by loss due to collision or another peril otherwise covered by the PAP. For example, if the PAP does not cover collision loss, the endorsement will not cover loss of use due to collision.

When these conditions are met, the insured will be reimbursed for up to $15 a day for rental charges, subject to a maximum of $450, for the period reasonably required to repair or replace the auto.

The extended transportation expenses coverage endorsement also allows the insured to increase the limits of liability for loss of use. For autos covered by the policy (including nonowned autos), the insured can increase coverage to $30 per day, subject to a maximum of $900, for the period reasonably required to repair or replace the auto.

The 1994 PAP includes coverage for loss of use arising from perils other than total theft of the covered auto. Therefore, the 1994 version of the extended transportation expenses endorsement, to avoid duplicate coverage, provides only for the increased limits of liability.

Towing and Labor Costs Coverage

Available in limits of $25, $50, or $75, the **towing and labor costs coverage**

endorsement pays the costs of towing the covered auto when it is disabled. The cost of labor performed at the place of disablement is also covered up to the limit, which applies to each disablement. Thus, if the vehicle breaks down five times during the policy period, the insurer may pay up to the limit five times.

Amendment of Policy Provisions

Each state has its own laws that specify policy content and policy wording with respect to auto insurance. The PAP does not satisfy some of the requirements in several states. In order to avoid developing many different versions of the PAP, **amendment of policy provisions endorsements** are designed to alter the standard PAP's wording to conform with each state's requirements. In this manner, the standard PAP can be used in every state, and an endorsement can be attached in those states that require different wording.

Amendatory Endorsement

During the transition from the 1989 to the 1994 PAP, some companies may have a large supply of 1989 policies that they wish to use before ordering the new policies. In order to allow companies to exhaust their supplies of 1989 policies and provide the most current auto insurance coverage, the **amenda-tory endorsement** is available. This endorsement contains all of the revisions made in the 1994 PAP. When it is attached to the 1989 PAP, the coverage becomes equivalent to the 1994 PAP.

Common Variations in Auto Insurance Coverage

The ISO PAP is not the only form of personal auto insurance. In some states, different policy forms are used because of state insurance regulations. More importantly, many insurance companies market their own, independently filed policy forms. In fact, most of the larger auto insurers do not use the PAP.

In some respects, an independently filed form may provide broader coverage than the PAP, perhaps to make the insurer's private passenger program more desirable to customers; or, an independently filed form may provide narrower coverage than the PAP, perhaps to reduce the losses that the insurer would otherwise have to pay. However, the protection is of the same general nature.

While other auto insurance policies provide the same general coverage as the PAP, certain coverage specifics often vary. These variations in coverage can be important when a claim is involved. For example, the PAP liability coverage applies to trailers designed to be pulled by a private passenger auto, pickup truck, or van. Some policies may exclude liability coverage for such trailers used as an office, a store, a display, or a passenger trailer. This is important to an insured whose personal office trailer is destroyed in a collision with another vehicle. Persons with exposures affected by these variations in coverage should consider them carefully when selecting among several insurance policies. Moreover, producers, underwriters, and adjusters should be aware of some significant coverage differences they can expect to find when examining different policies.

Examples of variations that result in more restrictive coverage under an independently filed policy than under the PAP are as follows:

- Some policies exclude liability and medical payments coverage for the named insured and spouse while using or occupying an auto owned by or furnished or available for the regular use of a family member. The PAP does not.

- Some policies require a person seeking coverage to have had actual permission to use the auto and to have operated the auto within the scope of the permission granted. The PAP requires only that a person have the reasonable belief that he or she is entitled to use the car.

- Some policies exclude liability assumed by an insured under contract or liability for the injury to a fellow employee of any insured. The PAP does not have any comparable exclusions.

Variations in policy provisions that broaden the coverage of the PAP typically take the form of incidental or supplementary coverages not included in the PAP. These coverages usually are subject to nominal limits, or cover loss exposures of low potential severity, and include the following:

- Some personal auto policies supplement liability coverage with explicit coverage for expenses incurred by an insured for immediate medical or surgical relief at the time of an accident involving an insured auto, regardless of the insured's liability. First aid expenses might be incurred, for example, when an insured's auto collides with another auto and the insured calls for an ambulance to transport the injured occupants of the other car to a hospital. The highest priority is to get prompt medical treatment for those who require it, and this supplementary coverage reimburses an insured, even an insured who has no liability for the accident, who pays for the first aid expenses so that the accident victim(s) can be treated.

- Some policies cover damage by specified perils to personal effects, such as clothing and luggage, contained in a covered auto. Coverage is usually subject to a $100 or $200 per occurrence limit that cannot be increased.

- A policy may provide that, if the auto is disabled because of a covered loss that occurs beyond a certain distance (such as fifty miles) from the insured's residence, the insurer will pay (1) the commercial transportation fees for the occupants of the auto to return home or to reach their destination and (2) the cost of extra meals and lodging needed when the loss results in delays.

- Some policies contain a provision that waives the collision deductible when the covered auto collides with another auto insured by the same insurance company. Sometimes such a clause also states that the deductible will be waived if the covered auto collides with any other auto, provided that the other driver is solely at fault and has valid property damage liability insurance.

- Some insurers provide an optional coverage that applies when a newly manufactured auto is insured. For specified perils, the insurer agrees to pay the full repair cost of the vehicle or replace it with an equivalent *new* car if the covered auto is totaled. This is especially useful to individuals who lease new autos or buy an auto with a minimal down payment. If the auto is severely damaged or destroyed during the early part of the lease or loan agreement, the insured may owe more than the insurer will cover. This optional coverage addresses this problem by simply paying for a comparable new car, not paying the actual cash value of the damaged auto.

Summary

The PAP has six parts, four of which are coverages and two of which are conditions. Five of the parts (Part A—Liability Coverage, Part B—Medical Payments Coverage, Part D—Coverage for Damage to Your Auto, Part E—Duties After an Accident or Loss, and Part F—General Provisions) are described in this chapter. The liability coverage applies to liability of an insured arising out of bodily injury or property damage caused by an auto accident. The medical payments coverage applies to the costs to treat bodily injury of the insured and occupants of a covered auto arising out of an auto accident. The physical damage coverage provides protection against collision, other than collision loss, or both, to the covered auto or eligible nonowned autos. Each of the coverages contains its own insuring agreement, exclusions, and provisions that further define the coverage. Part E specifies the insured's duties after a loss, and Part F spells out the general conditions of the policy.

Several endorsements are available to cover exposures not treated by the unendorsed PAP. Other personal auto policies are also available from insurers that independently file their policies.

Chapter Notes

1. *Personal Vehicle Manual*, 3d ed. (New York, NY: Insurance Services Office, Inc., September 1990), p. G-1.
2. *Personal Vehicle Manual*, p. G-1.
3. Maryland Casualty Company v. Thomas, 289 S.W. (2d) 652 (1956).
4. Central National Insurance Company v. Adams, 319 S.E. (2nd) 486 (1982).
5. Lunn v. Indiana Lumbermens Mutual Insurance Company, 201 S.W. (2nd) 978.
6. Fireman's Fund Insurance Company v. Cramer, 178 So. 2d 581 (1964).

Chapter 5

Auto Insurance Issues

Although the purpose of insurance is to protect insurance buyers, society is always challenged to provide compensation for auto accident victims. Many motorists who cannot afford insurance, or who have few assets to lose, operate vehicles without the means to pay for damages for which they are liable after an auto accident. Accident victims and their families might be left without compensation.

A related problem involves those drivers who have some ability to pay for the damages they cause but do not have enough assets or insurance to fully compensate the victim of a serious accident.

One of the principal reasons that many individuals do not purchase any, or an adequate amount of, auto insurance is its cost. Many people who drive simply cannot afford to pay the increasing premiums for auto insurance. Yet, insurance companies must charge fair and adequate premiums that allow each insured motorist to pay his or her share of the insurer's costs. These costs are influenced not only by a driver's personal driving record and characteristics, but also by general trends in American society, such as more drivers on congested highways, more litigation, and rising medical treatment costs. All of these factors combine to create high-cost auto insurance.

These issues are the focus of this chapter. The first part of the chapter deals with the financial responsibility of motorists. The second part considers the factors that influence the cost of auto insurance.

Financial Responsibility of Motorists

Motorists, by law, are supposed to be able to pay at least some minimum amount toward bodily injury and property damage resulting from their negligent operation of a vehicle. Many drivers are not able to meet this requirement. Many other motorists, while able to satisfy the minimum financial responsibility standards, still leave their victims undercompensated. Despite many attempted solutions, these problems have never been entirely resolved. Today at least five types of legislation relate to these problems:

1. Financial responsibility laws
2. Compulsory auto insurance
3. Laws establishing unsatisfied judgment funds
4. Uninsured and underinsured motorist statutes
5. No-fault auto insurance laws

In different ways, each of these laws addresses the problem of providing compensation for accident victims, yet each has its weaknesses.

Financial Responsibility Laws and Compulsory Auto Insurance Laws

The operation of financial responsibility laws and compulsory auto insurance laws is discussed in Chapter 4. These laws affect an individual's decision of whether to buy auto liability insurance and, if so, the amount of liability insurance to purchase. The purpose of these laws is to ensure that all motorists have the ability to pay at least a minimum amount for bodily injury and property damage resulting from auto accidents for which they are held financially responsible. Unfortunately, financial responsibility laws and compulsory auto insurance laws do not completely solve the problem of inadequate compensation for auto accident victims.

Weaknesses of Financial Responsibility Laws

While both security-type financial responsibility laws and security-and-proof-of-future-responsibility laws may be effective in reducing the number of motorists unable to meet some minimum standard of financial responsibility (for the most part, uninsured motorists), major drawbacks exist. First, even if the motorist's license and registration are revoked, there is no guarantee that the financially irresponsible driver will not continue to drive. Second, the requirements of most financial responsibility laws do not become effective until after an accident, conviction, or judgment. Innocent victims of an accident may still not be compensated. Third, many motorists still go uninsured and are otherwise unable to meet the financial responsibility limits. Fourth, most of the financial responsibility limits are too low to fully compensate victims of serious, or even fairly minor, injuries.

Weaknesses of Compulsory Auto Insurance Laws

Compulsory auto liability insurance laws are opposed by many entities, including insurance companies. The following criticisms may be raised concerning compulsory auto insurance laws[1]:

- Uninsured motorists who have avoided the system continue to drive and cause accidents that leave innocent victims unprotected.

- Enforcing compulsory auto insurance laws can be difficult, expensive, and ineffective.

- The cost to administer and enforce compulsory auto insurance laws is borne by all taxpayers, not just those who drive.

- Innocent drivers and passengers are still not protected from drivers of stolen vehicles and unregistered vehicles or hit-and-run drivers.

- Compulsory auto insurance laws do not address drivers from other states.

The high cost of auto insurance provides significant economic incentives to those who are willing to evade laws. Moreover, law enforcement personnel—at least in some communities—tend to place a low priority on policing uninsured motorists.

Unsatisfied Judgment Funds

An **unsatisfied judgment fund** is designed to provide a source of recovery for victims of motor vehicle accidents when a wrongdoer is unable to pay any judgment. At present, the few states that have these funds also have compulsory insurance laws. In some instances, such funds preclude recovery when a claimant is occupying or operating an uninsured vehicle, or operating a vehicle while the claimant's license or the auto's registration has been suspended or revoked.

Unsatisfied judgment funds also provide for recovery, with some limitations, when injury or, in some states, property damage is caused by an unknown or hit-and-run motorist. One limitation is that the scope of these funds is commonly restricted to accidents that occur within the state. Some funds require proof of physical contact between the unknown vehicle and the claimant or the claimant's vehicle. This requirement prevents recovery of damages when an injury or property damage is actually the result of the claimant's negligence. Without the condition, a claimant could, for example, fall asleep at the wheel, collide with a tree, and then falsely claim that this one-car accident was caused by an unidentified motorist who left the scene. On the other hand, the condition can cause severe hardship to a motorist who is actually run off the road by an unidentified motorist.

Before benefits can be collected from an unsatisfied judgment fund, certain procedures must be followed. For example, if a person has a legitimate claim against an uninsured motorist, the claimant is required to proceed against such motorist as if no fund were in existence. Thus, the claimant must prove that the other motorist was negligent by obtaining a judgment against him or her. Only after the judgment has been rendered and goes unpaid can the claimant seek indemnification from the fund.

The benefits paid by unsatisfied judgment funds vary. None provides complete indemnification for all losses. Generally, the maximum amount payable corresponds to the states' financial responsibility limits. Some funds also consider collateral sources of recovery. That is, the amount of any judgment payable by the fund may be reduced by any amount received or likely to be received by the claimant from insurance, including benefits from workers compensation and similar laws.

The methods for financing unsatisfied judgment funds vary. Generally, money to operate them comes from one or more of the following sources:

- An additional fee assessed to persons who register an auto
- A penalty assessed to uninsured motorists
- A surcharge assessed to motorists charged with a moving violation
- An amount assessed on insurance companies that write auto insurance in the state, depending primarily upon a pro rata formula relating each insurer's net written premiums to the total auto insurance premiums written by all the insurers in the state

Unsatisfied judgment fund laws do not attempt, at least directly, to reduce the number of uninsured motorists. These funds, instead, give some auto accident victims the opportunity for compensation when the obligations of others cannot be fulfilled. The major weakness of these funds is that they do not become operative until a judgment goes unsatisfied or the victim proves that his or her injuries were caused by an unidentified motorist. Some legal actions against motorists may be so time-consuming that even those who have a legitimate cause of action are discouraged from pursuing the appropriate legal remedy. In such instances, the unsatisfied judgment funds are of no value.

Uninsured and Underinsured Motorists Coverages

Many motorists do not purchase, or do not purchase enough, auto liability insurance, even if it is required under a compulsory auto liability insurance law. Others purchase auto liability insurance from an insurance company that becomes insolvent. In these cases, it is the victims of the uninsured or underinsured motorist who suffer. Like unsatisfied judgment funds, uninsured and underinsured motorists coverages are designed to indemnify the innocent victims for their losses caused by an uninsured or underinsured negligent motorist.

Uninsured motorists coverage provides compensation to insureds who have suffered bodily injury in an accident with an *at-fault motorist* (1) who has no bodily injury liability insurance, (2) who is the owner or operator of a hit-and-run vehicle, or (3) whose insurance company denies coverage or is or becomes insolvent.

Uninsured motorists insurance also compensates victims of insured at-fault motorists whose bodily injury liability limit is less than the minimum limit required by the financial responsibility law in the insured's state. This is rarely needed, because insurers will not, or are not allowed to, sell amounts of auto liability insurance below a state's financial responsibility requirements.

The insurance puts the insureds in the same position as if the motorist responsible for the accident had bodily injury liability insurance and is legally liable for the injury. However, the coverage does not require that a judgment first be assessed against the negligent motorist as is necessary for payment under an unsatisfied judgment fund.

Underinsured motorists coverage is also available in many cases to protect an insured against an accident caused by another motorist who is insured to or above the extent required by law, but whose limits are not adequate to pay all damages in a serious accident. It also potentially provides the insured victim with a source of recovery that does not depend on the operation of an unsatisfied judgment fund.

Uninsured Motorists Coverage

The majority of states require auto insurers to offer uninsured motorists coverage to all insured motorists who are their policyholders. The offer may be rejected by the insured, usually in writing. The writing requirement presumably ensures that insureds understand the possible effect of rejecting the coverage.

A few states (Maryland, New Jersey, New York, and North Dakota) with unsatisfied judgment funds also require that uninsured motorists insurance be purchased. The unsatisfied judgment fund is unnecessary for those who have uninsured motorists insurance but is available to persons who may not be covered by uninsured motorists insurance (such as out-of-state drivers and pedestrians).

Uninsured motorists coverage can be controversial. Regardless of the policy provisions used by an insurer, it is the **uninsured motorists statute** that governs who is protected and under what circumstances. Generally, the statute is not consulted until an insurer denies coverage. Insurers have been required to pay claims outside the scope of the policy because of the way uninsured motorists statutes were interpreted by the courts.

The discussion that follows describes the uninsured motorists provisions that appear in Part C of the ISO personal auto policy (PAP). In many states, these provisions are either modified or replaced by uninsured motorists endorsements. While there are many variations from the uninsured motorists provision found in Part C of the PAP, a discussion of the basic provisions provides a general understanding of the coverage applications.

Insuring Agreement

Under Part C of the PAP, the insurer agrees to pay those *compensatory damages* that an *insured* is *legally entitled* to recover from the owner or operator of an *uninsured motor vehicle* for *bodily injury* suffered by the insured and caused by an accident. The italicized phrases are explained below.

Compensatory Damages   The policy specifies that it will provide coverage only for compensatory damages. Coverage is not intended for punitive damages. The coverage is designed to pay for losses that arise out of bodily injury, such as medical expenses and lost wages. Punitive damages are awarded against a negligent party as punishment for performing the actions resulting in negligence. These damages do not reimburse the victim for losses, and thus are generally not covered by uninsured motorists coverage (although they may be in some states).

Insured   The policy pays compensatory damages only for those persons insured under the policy. The following are considered to be **insureds** under the uninsured motorists coverage:

1. *The named insured and any family members.* Coverage applies to them while using a covered auto, whether owned or not, and while not occupying a vehicle. This means that insureds are covered if involved in an accident caused by an uninsured motorist while the insureds are pedestrians, occupants of another's auto, or occupants of an owned and covered auto.

   The vehicle that the named insured or family member is occupying must be one that is not otherwise excluded. For example, assume that Rhonda is struck by an uninsured motorist while occupying a motor vehicle owned by Rhonda's husband, which is not insured for uninsured motorists coverage under their personal auto policy. She will *not* receive coverage under the uninsured motorists coverage that applies to her auto that is named on the same PAP. This prevents a named insured from having uninsured motorists coverage on two or more owned vehicles by paying the premium for coverage on only one vehicle.

2. *Persons other than the named insured and family members while occupying a covered auto.* Generally, these people have protection only while occupying an auto covered by the named insured's policy, including nonowned autos that qualify for coverage, such as a temporary substitute for the auto named in the policy declarations. While occupying nonowned autos not covered by the policy yet being used by the named insured or family members, others have, or should have, coverage under their own uninsured motorists coverage.

3. *Persons entitled to recover for damages because of bodily injury to persons described in (1) and (2).* Included in this group could be parents, legal guardians, spouses, and legal representatives of the insureds' estates. A husband, for example, might be entitled to recover for the loss of consortium if his wife is disabled in an accident caused by an uninsured motorist.

Legally Entitled   The insuring agreement further stipulates that the insurer does not cover losses to which the insured is not legally entitled. Uninsured motorists coverage is designed to cover those injuries suffered by an innocent insured at the fault of another motorist who does not have auto liability insurance. In other words, the insured's uninsured motorists coverage acts in place of the negligent motorist's auto liability insurance. Thus, the compensatory damages covered by the insured's policy are only those for which the other motorist would have been legally and financially responsible and to which the insured is legally entitled. If the insured is not legally entitled to reimbursement or indemnification from another motorist, PAP medical payments coverage and the insured's health insurance would be alternative sources of recovery.

The insuring agreement further qualifies legal entitlement by stating that the insurer is not bound by any judgment stemming from a suit brought without the insurer's consent. This is an extremely important provision. If any insured were to file suit against the negligent motorist and obtain a judgment without the written consent of the insurer, any damages awarded may not be payable under the coverage. The provision reduces the chance of collusion between the insured and an uninsured motorist. It also prevents the insured from giving the negligent uninsured motorist a release that could negate the insurer's rights of subrogation (if allowed for uninsured motorists claims in the state) as assigned to the insurer by the insured, and the insurer would be unable to proceed against the negligent driver for reimbursement of the damages paid. The insurer may simply not pay the damages and allow the burden of recovery to fall upon the insured.

Uninsured Motor Vehicle   An **uninsured motor vehicle** is defined as one of the following:

- *A land motor vehicle or trailer, the owner of which does not have a bodily injury liability policy or a bond filed with his or her state of residency.* An auto liability policy is the usual method of establishing evidence of financial responsibility. Additionally, in those states that have compulsory insurance, auto liability coverage or a bond filed with state authorities is normally a condition to using a motor vehicle on the highways.

- *A land motor vehicle or trailer to which an insurance policy (or a bond) for bodily injury applies at the time of an accident, but with a limit of liability less than the minimum specified for bodily injury under the financial responsibility or compulsory auto insurance law of the state in which the insured's covered auto is principally garaged.* For example, if the minimum financial responsibility limit in the victim insured's state is 25/50 bodily injury, and a motorist from another state has an auto policy with limits of 15/30 bodily injury, the auto covered by the latter policy is considered to be an uninsured motor vehicle. Persons who are insured by a PAP are not likely to be uninsured motorists if their limits are lower than those specified in other states where they may go; as noted earlier, the PAP automatically adjusts the liability limits to the minimum financial responsibility limits specified in the statutes of the other states or the Canadian provinces. However, some policies other than the PAP might not provide this automatic protection.

- *A hit-and-run land motor vehicle or trailer, whose owner or operator cannot be identified, that hits (1) the named insured or a family member, (2) the covered auto, or (3) a vehicle that the named insured or any family member is occupying.* The word **hit** means that, insofar as injuries resulting from the occupancy of a vehicle or the use of a covered auto are concerned, evidence of actual physical contact with the hit-and-run vehicle must exist. In other words, the injuries sustained by so-called "phantom vehicles" are not covered. If they were covered, an insured could run off the road because of his or her own carelessness and then file a claim under the uninsured motorists coverage, where in all likelihood the benefits will be higher than those provided under Part B—Medical Payments. However, the courts of some states have interpreted "hit-and-run vehicle" to include a vehicle that forces the insured off the road without actual contact between the two vehicles.

- *A land motor vehicle or trailer to which an auto policy (or bond) applies, but the insurer or the surety (the entity that guarantees the bond) of which denies coverage or becomes insolvent.*

Although *any type* of land motor vehicle or trailer may qualify as an uninsured motor vehicle, the uninsured motorists coverage lists six exceptions. The following are not uninsured motor vehicles:

- *Any vehicle or equipment owned by or furnished or available for the regular use of the named insured or family member.* This exception prevents an insured from collecting uninsured motorists coverage for injuries involving a vehicle he or she owns or regularly uses but does not insure for *liability* coverage. An insured cannot substitute the uninsured motorists coverage on one auto for liability coverage on an owned but not insured auto.

- *Any vehicle or equipment that may be owned or operated by a self-insurer under any motor vehicle law, unless the self-insurer is or becomes insolvent.* A self-insurer may not have insurance, but it must meet the financial responsibility requirements of the state having jurisdiction. Assuming a self-insurer is qualified, recovery must be sought directly against the self-insurer, just as if it had auto liability insurance. If the self-insurer is shown to be insolvent, the exception does not apply and the insured may receive coverage under his or her uninsured motorists coverage.

- *Any vehicle or equipment that is owned by any government agency.* Government agencies sometimes have sovereign immunity, meaning that, even if a government branch or agency is at fault, it cannot legally be held liable. An insured is not entitled to recover for damages under uninsured motorists coverage when the government agency is not legally responsible for its acts and omissions. Although federal agencies still enjoy some sovereign immunity, the trend among the states and other levels of government is toward abrogation of those immunities. Thus, it may be possible for a victim to sue and collect from the government agency responsible for damages.

- *Any vehicle or equipment operated on rails or crawler treads.* Trains and mobile equipment are not uninsured motor vehicles, because they are not the types of vehicles for which coverage is designed. A person who is injured when hit by a train will have to make a claim directly against the railroad. Equipment operated on crawler treads, such as bulldozers, power shovels, graders, and other types of contractor's equipment, are usually considered to be "mobile equipment," and as such are automatically covered under general liability policies for their liability exposures both on and off public roads. An injured party should seek to recover damages from the contractor or other owner of that equipment and its liability insurer.

- *Any vehicle or equipment designed for use off public roads while not on public roads.* The off-road exposures of vehicles and equipment designed for use off public roads can be covered by other forms of insurance. Nevertheless, circumstances arise when vehicles designed for use off public roads are considered uninsured motor vehicles while used on public roads. For example, a person operating a farm tractor, a dirt bike, or a dune buggy that cannot be registered for road use might cause an accident on public roads by hitting a vehicle occupied by an insured. If vehicles designed for use off public roads are not covered by insurance and their operators are at fault for resulting injuries, such vehicles may qualify as uninsured motor vehicles—assuming they are not otherwise subject to any exclusions (such as operated on crawler treads or owned by a government agency).

- *Any vehicle or equipment located for use as a residence or premises.* A trailer, such as a mobile home or camping unit, while being pulled by a motor vehicle that qualifies as uninsured, is considered to be an uninsured motor vehicle. Such a vehicle is not affected by this exception. But a trailer, while situated at a mobile home park, camp, or other land site for use as a residence, is not within the scope of coverage. This liability exposure should be insured under another form of personal liability or property insurance.

Bodily Injury   The insuring agreement states that the coverage is designed to cover only losses due to bodily injury. However, the uninsured motorists coverage can be endorsed to include coverage for property damage caused by an uninsured motorist (discussed in more detail later in this chapter). In some states, the uninsured motorists coverage is replaced by an endorsement to the PAP that contains coverage for bodily injury and property damage caused by uninsured motorists.

Exclusions

In addition to the qualifications placed on land motor vehicles and trailers, the uninsured motorists coverage contains several specific exclusions, as described below.

Owned But Not Insured   The PAP excludes coverage for any insured while occupying or when struck by a vehicle, including a trailer, *owned by the insured seeking coverage*, if the vehicle is not covered for uninsured motorists coverage under the PAP. The PAP also excludes coverage for any family member injured while occupying or when struck by a vehicle owned by the named insured but covered by uninsured motorists coverage on a primary basis on another policy. However, the PAP does allow coverage under it's uninsured motorists coverage for insureds occupying or struck by a car owned by another insured but not insured with uninsured motorists coverage.

For example, Jenny and Oscar are insureds under their father's auto policy. Oscar owns an auto, but it is not covered by his father's policy or any other uninsured motorists coverage. Jenny is riding in her brother Oscar's car when it is hit by an uninsured motorist and Jenny suffers bodily injury. Jenny receives coverage under her father's policy because she is riding in another insured's auto, not her own. However, Oscar does not receive coverage under his father's uninsured motorists coverage because he is occupying his owned auto that is not covered by uninsured motorists coverage.

The 1989 PAP eliminates coverage for any insured injured while occupying or upon being struck by a vehicle, including a trailer, *owned by the named insured or any family member*, which is not insured for uninsured motorist coverage under the policy. Thus, under the 1989 policy, Jenny would not be covered under the 1989 version of the PAP, because she is riding in another insured's auto that is not insured by her father's PAP.

This exclusion prevents the insured from insuring one vehicle and seeking coverage for other owned vehicles as uninsured motor vehicles under the uninsured motorist coverage.

Without Insurer's Consent   While the insuring agreement excludes coverage for damages resulting out of suits brought without the insurer's written consent, this exclusion prohibits coverage for an unauthorized settlement— even if the suit was approved by the insurer. This precludes an attempt by the insured or his or her legal representative to seek damages under the uninsured motorists coverage after settling with the negligent party. In other words, the injured person cannot seek coverage under his or her uninsured motorists insurance and also settle directly with the negligent motorist.

As a Public or Livery Conveyance   Accidents caused by uninsured motorists are not covered by the policy when the insured is occupying or using a covered auto to transport people or property for a fee. Share-the-expense car pools are excepted from the exclusion and are therefore not excluded from coverage.

Without Reasonable Belief or Permission   If an insured is injured by an uninsured motorist while operating or using a nonowned auto without having reasonable belief that the owner has granted permission, the insured's injuries will not be covered under his or her uninsured motorists coverage.

Workers Compensation or Disability Benefits Laws   The exclusion states that coverage does not apply to bodily injury that is or should be covered under workers compensation or disability benefits laws. This provision is for the sole protection of the insurer. If an insured is injured by an uninsured motorist during the course of employment and the injury is compensable under workers compensation, the workers compensation insurer can often proceed against a third party to recover amounts paid. The insurer, as a third-party indemnitor, could otherwise be confronted with such suit by the workers compensation insurer.

Punitive or Exemplary Damages   This exclusion clarifies ISO's intent that uninsured motorists insurance should cover only compensatory damages.

Limit of Liability

The limit of liability is a single limit that applies to each accident. Split limits are available by endorsement. The single limit is stated to be the maximum for all damages, regardless of the number of covered persons, claims made, vehicles or premiums shown in the declarations, or vehicles involved in the accident. The purpose of this provision is to prevent, to the extent permitted by courts or other PAP provisions, the stacking of limits.

Stacking occurs when one coverage limit is added to another for the maximum amount of coverage available or when the coverage limit is multiplied by the number of covered autos or insureds involved in an accident. For example, if Beth and Todd are both insureds under the same PAP with $100,000 of coverage for Part C and the limit is allowed to apply separately to each, the limit could be stacked and allow actual coverage to $200,000. The policy, however, only allows to $100,000 in coverage based on the limit of liability clause. As another example, Kirk has two autos insured under the same PAP, which provides uninsured motorists coverage of $100,000. Although the policy applies separately to each auto, the limit of liability for injuries caused to Kirk by an uninsured motorist is $100,000; it is not $200,000.

Some states do not allow the limit of uninsured motorists coverage to exceed the amount of bodily injury liability coverage purchased by an insured. For example, if an insured purchases $100,000 of bodily injury liability coverage under Part A of a PAP, the insured may purchase $100,000 *or less* in coverage under Part C of the PAP.

Any amounts otherwise payable as damages under this coverage are subject to reduction by payments received from the person responsible for the operation of an uninsured motor vehicle and by sums paid or payable under workers compensation or disability benefits laws. This prevents duplication of benefits.

The last provision of this section states that any payments received under Part A or Part B of the PAP or under any underinsured motorists coverage endorsed onto the PAP are not covered by Part C—Uninsured Motorists Coverage if allowed by state law. This provision is designed to prevent duplication of benefits.

The 1989 PAP provides that any payment made to an insured under uninsured motorists coverage will reduce any amount that person is entitled to recover for the same damages under Part A—Liability coverage. It does not go as far as the 1994 provision in preventing the duplication of benefits.

Other Insurance

The "other insurance" provision of this coverage is identical to that applying under Part A—Liability. Coverage for a vehicle not owned by the named insured or spouse is considered to be excess over any other collectible insurance. For example, if Michael and Bud each have a PAP and Michael is driving Bud's car, Michael will be covered by Bud's PAP if injured in an accident caused by an uninsured motorist. If Bud has no insurance, then Michael's own PAP will cover him. Similarly, if Michael's damages exceed the limit of Bud's PAP, Michael's policy will pay in excess of Bud's policy limit.

The PAP caps the amount available from all applicable uninsured motorists coverages at the highest single policy limit to prevent stacking of uninsured motorists coverages. Returning to the above example, suppose the uninsured motorists coverage limit on Michael's PAP is $300,000 and the limit on Bud's coverage is $100,000. According to the uninsured motorists coverage other insurance clause, the most Michael can collect for his injuries is $300,000— the amount of his coverage, which is the highest limit available. He *cannot* add his limit to Bud's for $400,000 in coverage. Furthermore, because Michael is driving Bud's car, if Michael's medical expenses exceed $100,000, Bud's policy will cover the first $100,000 and Michael's policy will cover the expenses exceeding $100,000. However, the portion paid by Michael's policy will not exceed $200,000, because Michael cannot collect more than $300,000 in total from both policies.

The PAP also stipulates that any coverage will be provided on a pro rata basis when more than one coverage applies to the same expenses. Thus, if the PAP and other coverages apply to a loss on a primary basis, the PAP will pay only its share of the loss. If the PAP and other coverages apply on an excess basis, the PAP will pay only its share of the loss. The insurer's share is equal to the proportion the limit on the uninsured motorists coverage bears to the total available under the applicable coverages. However, the total amount collected from the coverages cannot exceed the highest limit of all the applicable coverages.

Continuing with the above example, suppose Michael is also an insured under his parents' PAP, which provides $100,000 worth of uninsured motorists coverage. When Michael is injured while driving Bud's car, Bud's policy remains primary and both Michael's and Michael's parents' coverages are excess. If Michael's medical expenses amount to $200,000, Bud's PAP pays the first $100,000. The next $100,000 is shared by Michael's insurer and his parents' insurer according to the proportion their coverage limits bear to the total excess coverage. Michael's insurer covers $75,000, and his parents' insurer covers $25,000, as calculated in Exhibit 5-1.

Exhibit 5-1
Payment for Michael's Medical Expenses

Michael's medical expenses	$200,000	
Bud's coverage limit (primary)	$100,000	
Amount to be covered by excess coverages	$100,000	
Michael's coverage limit (excess)		$300,000
Michael's parents' coverage limit (excess)	$100,000	
Total excess coverage		$400,000
Michael's insurer's share	$300,000/$400,000 = 75%	
	75% of $100,000 = $75,000	
Parent's insurer's share	$100,000/$400,000 = 25%	
	25% of $100,000 = $25,000	

The 1989 PAP differs from the 1994 PAP in two respects. First, it does not limit the amount of recovery to the highest limit of all applicable policies. Thus, if Michael, Michael's parents, and Bud each had 1989 PAPs, Michael would be covered to $500,000 for his injuries under the three uninsured motorist coverages. Second, although the clause is designed to achieve the same effect, the 1989 PAP other insurance clause does not describe the pro rata provision in terms as explicit as those used in the 1994 policy.

Arbitration

The final provision of the uninsured motorists coverage deals with arbitration. As noted earlier, uninsured motorists coverage is controversial. Unlike liability coverage, in which damages are paid on the insured's behalf to others, uninsured motorists coverage directly benefits the insured by paying the insured on behalf of others. An insured will want not only to obtain recovery, but also to recover as much as possible. A problem sometimes arises, however, because the insurer will not pay damages as if the coverage were a form of accident insurance. Instead, the insurer will pay only when the insured is legally entitled to damages—the uninsured motorist is at fault or the accident was caused by a hit-and-run motorist. Questions of fact may arise regarding these coverage prerequisites. Sometimes, disputes also arise concerning the amount of recovery. Such disputes are subject to binding arbitration when permitted by state law. The ground rules are specified under the arbitration provision.

The PAP restricts the use of arbitration. Under the arbitration clause, arbitration must be consented to by both parties—one party cannot force the other into arbitration. Furthermore, only disputes concerning the amount of coverage may be considered—questions about whether coverage applies are not allowed to be arbitrated. Thus only if both parties agree to arbitration concerning the amount of settlement may the arbitration proceed. The arbitration provision in the 1989 PAP states that when the insurer and the insured cannot agree on (1) whether the insured is legally entitled to recover or (2) the amount of damages, either party may make written demand for arbitration.

Under either version, once arbitration is set to begin, each party is obligated to select an arbitrator to represent it, and the two arbitrators select a third arbitrator. If the first two arbitrators fail to agree on a third arbitrator within thirty days, a request for selection can be made of a judge of a court that has jurisdiction. It is further agreed that each of the parties pays for its own expenses and that both share the expense of the third arbitrator.

A decision is binding in most states if agreed to by at least two of the three arbitrators. Arbitrators may decide whether the insured is legally entitled to damages and the amount of the insured's recovery. If the amount of damages exceeds the state's minimum financial responsibility limit, the arbitrator's decision is not binding, and either the insured or the insurer may demand a trial within sixty days of the arbitration decision. If this demand is not made within the time limit, the decision becomes binding—subject to the limit of the uninsured motorists coverage.

Duties After an Accident or Loss

Part E of the PAP stipulates that an insured seeking coverage under Part C— Uninsured Motorists Coverage must satisfy the general duties after an accident or loss. In addition, the insured must, as soon as possible, notify police if a hit-and-run motorist is involved, promptly notify the insurer, and send copies of all legal papers if a suit is filed following any accident.

Uninsured Motorists Property Damage Coverage

As originally conceived, uninsured motorists statutes addressed only bodily injury resulting from accidents caused by uninsured motorists. Over the years, an increasing number of uninsured motorists statutes have been expanded to include both bodily injury and property damage. Consequently, ISO has developed endorsements for adding **uninsured motorists property damage** (UMPD) **coverage** to the PAP only in those states where such coverage must be either purchased or offered. Because a different endorsement is used in each state requiring UMPD, the coverage is described here in terms of its general characteristics.

Typically, UMPD is provided by amending the usual uninsured motorists insuring agreement to include both bodily injury and property damage caused by an accident. In some states, property damage is defined to mean only injury to or destruction of the covered auto. In several states, however, the definition also includes any property owned by the named insured, any family member, or any other occupant of the covered auto while such property is contained in "your covered auto." In other states, property damage may simply be defined as injury to or destruction of the property of an insured — it is neither restricted to a covered auto, nor must it be contained in the covered auto.

Some state endorsements define property damage to include loss of use of the damaged property, others specifically exclude loss of use, and still others are silent on the matter. When an endorsement is silent regarding loss of use, the insurance department of that state may be able to provide an interpretation. This issue is particularly relevant to claim settlement. If the definition of property damage includes loss of use, the insured may be able to recover not only the cost of repairing or replacing the covered auto (or other property) but also the cost of renting a substitute auto until the covered auto is returned to service (assuming, of course, that the uninsured motorist would be held liable for such costs). If loss of use is excluded, the cost of renting a temporary substitute auto or obtaining other transportation will not be covered.

Recall that the auto owner already has rental reimbursement coverage provided (1) in the 1994 PAP if the covered auto is damaged due to covered perils and (2) under Part D of the 1989 PAP in the event that the covered auto is stolen and must be replaced. The auto owner may also purchase an extended transportation expense endorsement for the 1989 PAP that pays the cost of renting a substitute auto if the covered auto must be removed from use because it is damaged by an insured peril, other than total theft. If the applicable UMPD coverage does not cover loss of use, the named insured may have such coverage in a 1994 PAP if the peril is covered or loss of use insurance can be provided under a 1989 PAP by endorsing such coverage to the PAP.

A common feature of UMPD endorsements is an exclusion stating that the coverage does not apply to the first $200 or $300 (or other stipulated amount) of property damage sustained by each insured in an accident. This exclusion has the same effect as a deductible.

Relation to Physical Damage Coverage

UMPD is duplicated to a large degree by any collision physical damage insurance the named insured has purchased on the covered auto. The physical damage coverage against collision is applicable whether the collision is caused by an uninsured motorist, an insured motorist, or even the named insured. When an uninsured motorist is responsible for collision damage to the covered auto and the named insured has both UMPD and collision coverage on the auto, the insurer will pay the insured's damages in full under the physical damage coverage, less the collision deductible and subject to coverage provisions. Any remaining unpaid damages will be paid under UMPD, less the UMPD deductible. Essentially, UMPD covers the difference in deductibles.

For example, assume that Sam's PAP provides UMPD coverage with a $200 "deductible" and collision coverage with a $500 deductible. If Sam's covered auto is struck by an uninsured motorist causing $2,000 damage, Sam will be able to collect coverage for the damages to his car for which the uninsured motorist is legally liable under his physical damage coverage, less $500. However, Sam can then collect an additional $300 under his UMPD coverage, representing the difference between the two "deductibles."

Limit of Liability

UMPD coverage is also subject to a dollar limit of liability. Thus, the named insured cannot collect more than the applicable limit for damage to the covered auto or any other property in one accident. It is possible, of course, that the limit could be less than the amount of property damage done by the uninsured motorist. Assume that Mae's sedan sustained damages amounting to $6,000 and that her UMPD is limited to $5,000 with a $250 "deductible." Mae previously discontinued collision coverage on her sedan, so only the UMPD applies to the damages. The most Mae will recover is $5,000. (In most states the $250 would be deducted from the total loss. However, some states may allow the $250 deductible to be applied to the coverage limit, resulting in a payment of $4,750.)

Underinsured Motorists Coverage

Another coverage that is an outgrowth of uninsured motorists coverage is underinsured motorists coverage. It comes into play when an at-fault driver has auto liability insurance that meets or exceeds the minimum financial responsibility requirements, but the limit of insurance is inadequate to pay the insured's damages.

Need for Coverage

In a growing number of instances, persons with high limits for uninsured motorists coverage are involved in accidents in which the other at-fault motorists are insured for at least the minimum state required limits. The at-fault motorists therefore cannot be considered uninsured motorists within the coverage definitions. While these injured motorists are able to seek recovery from the negligent motorists' auto liability insurance, an insured motorist may recover an amount that represents less than his or her full damages. For example, a victim who obtains a $75,000 judgment may find that the party against whom judgment is made has insurance for only $25,000 and no other assets to make up the difference.

How Underinsured Motorists Coverage Is Provided

In some states, the applicable uninsured motorists statute requires either that the motorist purchase or the insurer offer coverage against the underinsured motorists exposure. In other states, no requirement to purchase or offer such coverage may exist, but an insurer may voluntarily offer it. The major advantage of underinsured motorists coverage is that an injured person can collect under his or her own underinsured motorists coverage when the limits of the other party's auto liability insurance are exhausted. This is true even though the other party's limits may exceed those of the applicable financial responsibility or compulsory insurance law.

How the policy provisions for underinsured motorists coverage are expressed varies from state to state. An underinsured motorists endorsement can be added to the PAP form to provide the coverage as a supplement to the uninsured motorists coverage already in the PAP form. In several states, however, a single endorsement providing both uninsured and underinsured motorists coverage replaces the uninsured motorists coverage of the standard PAP. These endorsements may contain separate definitions of "uninsured motor vehicle" and "underinsured motor vehicle," or they may simply define "uninsured motor vehicle" to include both types of vehicles. Any other state variations from the standard uninsured motorists provision of the PAP are built into the endorsement.

Underinsured Motorists Coverage Endorsement

To illustrate the characteristics of underinsured motorists coverage, this text examines the standard ISO underinsured motorists coverage endorsement by which the coverage can be added as a supplement to the uninsured motorists coverage of the PAP. Important variations from this standard endorsement are also discussed.

The underinsured motorists coverage endorsement specifies that the insurer will pay only the compensatory damages the covered person is legally entitled to recover because of bodily injury caused by an accident with an owner or operator of an underinsured motor vehicle. An **underinsured motor vehicle** is defined as one to which bodily injury liability insurance or a financial responsibility bond applies for a limit that is equal to or greater than the minimum amount required by the state, but less than the limit of a person's underinsured motorists coverage. This definition is based on a **limits trigger**; that is, the underinsured motorists coverage comes into play when the insured's underinsured motorists coverage limit is greater than the at-fault motorist's liability limit. Consider the following three examples that are illustrated in Exhibit 5-2.

Exhibit 5-2
Limits Trigger Example

	Situation 1	Situation 2	Situation 3
Tom's Underinsured Motorist's Limit	$100,000	$100,000	$ 50,000
Lynn's Liability Limit	12.5/25	50,000	75,000
Tom's Damages (Lynn's Fault)	75,000	60,000	100,000
Is Tom's Underinsured Motorists Coverage Triggered?	Yes	Yes	No

For example, Tom purchases underinsured motorists coverage with a limit of $100,000. Lynn purchases an auto liability policy with the minimum required limits of 12.5/25 bodily injury liability. Both are involved in an auto accident caused by Lynn. Tom's damages amount to $75,000. Because Lynn's liability coverage is not great enough to cover Tom's injuries *and* her liability limit is less than Tom's underinsured motorists limit, Tom's coverage will be triggered.

As another example, suppose Tom has a $100,000 underinsured motorists limit and Lynn buys an auto liability policy with a limit of $50,000—more than enough to meet the minimum required limits. If Tom's damages are $60,000, he will collect from Lynn's insurer *and* his underinsured motorists coverage. Thus, the latter protection applies even if the limits of the offending driver's policy are greater than the required minimum. The criterion for underinsured motorists protection is only that the *liability limits of the other party's policy be less than the insured's underinsured motorists limits.*

A third example demonstrates this key point. Suppose Tom has a $50,000 limit on his underinsured motorists coverage and Lynn has a $75,000 limit on her liability coverage. If Lynn causes an auto accident that results in $100,000 in injuries to Tom, Tom will receive payment from Lynn's insurer and nothing from his underinsured motorists coverage. Lynn's liability limit exceeds Tom's underinsured motorist's coverage, thus he cannot collect additional funds from his underinsured motorists coverage.

Some states have enacted underinsured motorists statutes that require coverage broader than that described in the preceding paragraphs. This broader coverage comes into play when the liability limits of the at-fault party's policy are less than the insured's actual damages, rather than less than the limits of the insured's underinsured motorists coverage and is referred to as a **damages trigger**. In these states, an insured would be entitled to underinsured motorists coverage even when his or her underinsured motorists coverage limits are less than or equal to the at-fault party's liability limits. For example, assume Anne has purchased underinsured motorists coverage with a $50,000 limit. Randy has purchased auto liability coverage with a $100,000 limit. Randy causes an accident resulting in bodily injury to Anne. If Anne's damages are $150,000, Anne's underinsured motorists coverage will be triggered, since Randy's limit is less than Anne's damages. However, if Anne's damages are $75,000, her underinsured motorists coverage will not be triggered. The key criterion under the damages trigger is that the *insured's injuries are greater than the liability limits of the at-fault driver.*

As implied in the above examples, underinsured motorists protection only applies after the limits of liability of the other motorist's policy or bond have been exhausted by the payment of any judgment or settlement. Thus, underinsured motorists insurance is treated as *excess* over the collectible insurance covering the loss. The amount payable as excess, however, can be determined by two different methods.

The ISO standard underinsured motorists endorsement reduces the limit of liability for the insured's underinsured motorists coverage by the amount paid by the at-fault motorist. For example, Ted has $100,000 of underinsured motorists coverage. He is involved in an auto accident with Don. Ted receives injuries amounting to $100,000. Don's liability limit is $12,500 (which meets the minimum requirements), and it is exhausted in partial payment of Ted's damages. Ted's insurer will pay the remaining $87,500. However, suppose that Ted's damages are $150,000. Ted's insurer will still pay only $87,500—the limit of Ted's underinsured motorists coverage ($100,000) reduced by the amount paid by Don's insurer ($12,500). Under the endorsement, the total amount recoverable from both the negligent driver and the insured's policy is the limit on the underinsured motorists coverage, *not* the limit plus what the at-fault motorist pays. To collect the full amount of damages, Ted would have needed to carry limits of at least $150,000.

In some states, the amount payable under the underinsured motorists coverage is the difference between the actual damages and the at-fault motorist's liability limits, subject to the underinsured motorists coverage limit of liability. For example, if Ted were insured in one of these states and suffered $150,000 in damages due to an auto accident caused by Don, Don's insurer would pay $12,500. That leaves $137,500 of Ted's injuries uncovered by Don's liability insurance. Ted has a $100,000 underinsured motorist coverage limit, which will be paid in full to him, so he will receive a total of $112,500. In these states, the total amount of coverage available for an accident involving an underinsured motorist is the sum of the liability limit of the at-fault motorist and the underinsured coverage limit of the victim.[2] These three examples are illustrated in Exhibit 5-3.

Exhibit 5-3
Amount Paid by Underinsured Motorists Coverage as Excess Coverage

	Underinsured Motorists Coverage Limit Reduced by Liability Payment Received		Underinsured Motorists Limit Added to Liability Limit
	Situation 1	Situation 2	Situation 3
Ted's Underinsured Motorist's Limit	$100,000	$100,000	$100,000
Don's Liability Limit	12,500	12,500	12,500
Ted's Damages (Don's Fault)	100,000	150,000	150,000
Amount Paid by Don's Policy	12,500	12,500	12,500
Amount Paid by Ted's Policy	87,500	87,500	100,000
Total Paid for Ted's Injuries	100,000	100,000	112,500

Aside from the above coverage concerns, the provisions of the underinsured motorists endorsement are similar to the provisions of the uninsured motorists coverage offered by the PAP. The general rules of the ISO *Personal Auto*

Manual state that (1) underinsured motorists coverage can be written only when it applies to all covered autos and (2) underinsured and uninsured motorists coverage must be written for the same limits.

Weaknesses of Uninsured and Underinsured Motorists Coverages

In some respects, uninsured and underinsured motorists coverages and unsatisfied judgment fund laws serve the same purposes. Both provide a source from which persons may recover for their injuries caused by financially irresponsible motorists. The injured persons may still sue the negligent driver, although that driver might not have enough assets with which to pay for the victim's injuries. The coverages and funds give the injured persons an opportunity to secure financial recovery that would not otherwise exist. However, none of these reduces the number of uninsured motorists. Furthermore, uninsured and underinsured motorists coverages are paid for by the insured, not by the at-fault motorist. This transfers the cost of the negligent driver's losses to the responsible insured.

No-Fault Insurance

While unsatisfied judgment funds, compulsory insurance, and uninsured and underinsured motorists coverage reduce the number of uncompensated and undercompensated accident victims, they do not entirely eliminate the problem. Before the development of no-fault insurance, proponents of auto insurance reform charged that insurance costs were rising at an alarming rate; yet, those injured in auto accidents still faced serious problems collecting needed compensation for their injuries. Employer-provided health care plans were not widespread, and, although more people are currently covered by health insurance, many people still do not have adequate protection for injuries arising in auto accidents.

In the past, when and if injured persons did recover, the recovery process was slow and costly, often requiring lengthy investigations to accumulate enough evidence to support recovery to the satisfaction of a trial court. In addition, attorneys' fees and other costs of trial preparation were paid from the amount recovered. This frequently left the victim with little more than reimbursement for legal expenses, if that. It was further observed that, while many seriously injured victims were inadequately compensated, smaller claims often were overpaid by insurers to avoid costly litigation.

Advocates of no-fault insurance contended that the inadequacies of the tort liability system rendered it incapable of fairly and comprehensively meeting the needs of auto accident victims in contemporary society. To strengthen their position, they pointed to the apparent success of workers compensation laws, which operate on a no-fault basis. Theoretically, workers compensation laws guarantee compensation to employees injured in work-related accidents for their medical expenses and for a portion of their lost wages, regardless of how the accident is caused. Rehabilitation services are also available in an effort to return an injured individual to gainful employment and a meaningful life. In return, employees forfeit their right to sue the employer for damages. This is considered by many to be a fair exchange, and perhaps the only solution to an otherwise insurmountable problem. With such parallels between the problems of industrial accidents and auto accidents, reformers asked the question, "Why couldn't a workers compensation type of approach be applied to the auto compensation problem?" By the early 1970s, the stage was set for a different auto compensation system, and public pressure was such that legislators were finally ready to act.

No-Fault Laws

No-fault laws have affected more than half of the American population. A large portion of that public perceived a no-fault mechanism that provided some form of comprehensive first-party benefits that were payable promptly, without delays and obstacles inherent in a tort liability system, as an improvement over existing fault systems. **No-fault laws** might be simply described as an attempt to distribute needed funds promptly to injured auto accident victims.

More than twenty states and the District of Columbia now have laws providing that policyholders obtain compensation for auto accidents from their own insurers. Just over half of these states place restrictions on the right to sue—referred to as modified plans—and the other half has added first-party insurance benefits to the traditional liability system—referred to as add-on plans.[3] No state has enacted a "pure" no-fault law that would completely eliminate the right to sue. However, at least two states have repealed their no-fault laws and others have passed optional no-fault laws.

Modified Plans

A **modified plan**, the most common form of no-fault legislation, partially restricts the right to sue, but does not completely eliminate it. To offset this limitation on the right to sue, a comprehensive personal injury protection (PIP) package is provided to the injured auto accident victim—without regard to fault. Most states place a ceiling or maximum on the PIP benefits, although one state (Michigan) provides medical and rehabilitation benefits that are unlimited both in time and amount, as long as they are reasonable and the charges are no greater than the usual and customary cost for such services.

The unique element of a modified plan is called a threshold. This element distinguishes it from both pure and add-on plans. A **threshold** may be defined as a boundary that must be crossed before an injured person can make a tort liability claim. Bodily injury claims that do not cross the threshold are limited to payment of actual **economic loss**—that is, medical expenses, a percentage of lost income, and substitute services expenses—*from their own insurer.* When the threshold limit is exceeded, the injured person, in addition to his or her claim for actual economic loss, can make claim for **noneconomic loss factors**—losses not easily measurable in dollars, such as pain and suffering, inconvenience, and mental anguish—*against the at-fault motorist.*

A threshold can be either monetary (also referred to as dollar) or verbal.

- With a **monetary** or **dollar threshold**, the injured victim can sue if resulting medical bills exceed a certain dollar amount. Most modified plans contain monetary thresholds that permit suits or tort claims only when medical expenses exceed the threshold amount *or* when the injury is serious or permanent, as defined by law.

- With a **verbal threshold**, no dollar boundary applies. Instead, the right to sue is determined by the seriousness of the injury as expressed in words such as "permanent disfigurement." Few states have verbal thresholds.

The following examples illustrate these distinct concepts. Massachusetts' no-fault law contains a monetary threshold. The law prohibits tort liability claims unless the injured person incurs medical expenses in excess of $2,000 (the dollar threshold), or suffers death, permanent injury, fracture of any bone, permanent disfigurement, permanent loss of any bodily function, or loss of a body member (the injury threshold). Michigan's verbal threshold provision stipulates that an injured person or heirs cannot sue or make a liability claim unless that injured person has suffered death, serious impairment of body function, or permanent serious disfigurement. A Massachusetts resident who is injured in an auto accident and incurs $2,001 or more in medical expenses without sustaining a serious injury can sue the other motorist for noneconomic loss, such as pain and suffering, and can also collect medical expenses from his or her own insurer. A Michigan resident, however, who incurs sizable medical expense without sustaining serious injury cannot sue, even for noneconomic loss. The monetary threshold approach focuses on the amount of medical bills in order to determine when the injured party can sue, whereas the verbal threshold approach focuses solely on the nature and extent of injury.

A modified plan, then, partially restricts the right to sue, but simultaneously provides PIP benefits that are payable promptly without regard to fault. The distinguishing feature of the modified plans is the threshold.

Add-On Plans

An **add-on plan** is essentially an expanded version of medical payments and disability benefits coverages. Benefits provided are similar to the PIP benefits available in modified no-fault plans, but there is *no restriction on the right to sue*. Consequently, the tort liability system is unaffected in states with add-on plans. The injured person is simply allowed to receive coverage in a timely manner for actual economic loss resulting from bodily injury. In addition, many add-on plans contain offset provisions that entitle a no-fault insurer to reimbursement for no-fault benefits paid to the injured person. The insurer is allowed to subrogate against the negligent motorist and his or her insurer or, if the injured person receives a liability settlement from the at-fault motorist, the insurer may be reimbursed from the settlement proceeds.

Voluntary No-Fault Plans

A **voluntary no-fault plan** offers first-party coverage comparable to modified and add-on plans on a strictly voluntary basis. These voluntary plans are not imposed by law. Insurers are not required to offer such coverage, and insureds are not required to accept such coverage if it is offered. While no limitation exists on an injured person's right to sue, an insurer may have the right to subrogate against any negligent party to the extent of the benefits it pays to its insured.

Choice No-Fault Plans

Choice no-fault plans are an alternative to the preceding types of no-fault plans. Some insureds prefer to retain their right to sue and do not want to restrict their right of recovery under tort, especially for such noneconomic damages as pain and suffering. Proponents of choice no-fault argue that those who choose to be compensated by the tort liability system should be allowed to do so. Insureds should also be allowed to opt out of the tort liability compensation system for auto injuries. Choice no-fault plans are supported as a means of meeting the needs of all insureds.

As with voluntary plans, an insured has the option, at the time the auto insurance policy is purchased or renewed, of choosing to be covered under no-fault insurance. The major difference between choice no-fault plans and voluntary no-fault plans is the restriction on the insured's right to sue under choice no-fault. Premium reductions are offered in return for limitations on the right of tort recovery for certain types of automobile injuries. Variations in coverages as well as in the rules for compensating damages are possible. After electing a no-fault option, the consumer chooses coverages and limits to fit his or her individual needs.[4]

Other Characteristics of No-Fault Laws

Other distinguishing characteristics of no-fault laws involve type of vehicles covered; extraterritorial (out-of-state) coverage; offsets, coordination of benefits, and deductibles; coverage following auto or individual; and subrogation. The following comments are general. No effort is made here to provide a detailed state-by-state analysis.

Vehicles Covered   The majority of no-fault laws apply to all autos, both private passenger and commercial, subject to registration. Most states specifically exclude motorcycles, although a few states include them in the plan or at least make coverage optional.

Out-of-State Protection   No-fault laws are designed to provide broad territorial coverage. Insured residents of a no-fault state typically are covered while using the vehicle anywhere in the United States, its territories, possessions, or Canada. Many state laws provide no-fault benefits for nonresidents driving in the no-fault state. Ordinarily, all insurers licensed to write auto insurance in the no-fault state must stipulate that every policy written, regardless of where the policy is issued, will provide the coverage required by the no-fault state when the nonresident is in that state. Usually, nonadmitted insurers also are requested to stipulate the same proviso, so that no-fault coverage can be as all-encompassing as possible.

Offsets, Coordination of Benefits, and Deductibles   Most health insurance provides coverage for many of the same losses insured by no-fault insurance. In an effort to minimize situations in which an injured person may recover from several collateral sources for the same loss, no-fault laws contain built-in **offset provisions** that make other insurance primary. In calculating the recovery under no-fault insurance, benefits received from federal or state insurance plans—such as social security, workers compensation, and disability benefits laws—are ordinarily deducted. Thus, PIP benefits are secondary, or excess, to these plans.

Generally, no deduction applies to private health insurance. An injured person can recover from both the health and PIP insurers. This obviously results in some duplicate recovery. Some no-fault states, however, have attempted to reduce the overall cost of auto insurance by introducing **coordination of benefits provisions**. Considering collateral sources of recovery, these provisions make either the health or auto insurance primary and require that the premium for the excess insurance source be reduced accordingly. Optional deductibles or PIP benefits represent another means of reducing the cost of no-fault insurance and are another way of coordinating benefits from more than one source.

Primary Coverage Following Auto or Individual No-fault laws vary as to whether primary PIP "follows" the auto or the individual. When coverage *follows the auto*, injured occupants of an auto collect no-fault benefits under the vehicle owner's policy. If an insured is injured as a pedestrian, he or she will receive benefits from the insurer of the vehicle involved in the accident. When coverage *follows the individual*, an injured person receives benefits from his or her insurer, even if injured as an occupant of another vehicle or as a pedestrian.

Ordinarily, when more than one source of personal injury protection benefits are available to an injured person on a primary basis, benefits are prorated among the various coverages so that payment in excess of the actual loss is not received.

When the primary insurance source is unavailable, secondary sources become available. For example, in states where coverage follows the auto and the owner is uninsured, the driver's policy becomes primary. If the driver, too, is uninsured, the injured person can resort to his or her own personal injury protection. When no insurance is available from any other source, many no-fault laws provide for an assigned claims plan, which is designed to compensate the victim of an uninsured accident. An **assigned claims plan** is similar in concept to an unsatisfied judgment fund. Although the plan is managed by the state, it is funded by insurers that are assigned claims and required to pay the benefits deemed necessary to compensate victims of uninsured accidents. The number of claims assigned to a given insurer depends on the volume of auto insurance the insurer writes in that state. Once the assigned claims are settled, the insurer has a right of subrogation against the owner and the driver of the uninsured auto. Furthermore, an uninsured motorist who fails to reimburse the insurer within a certain period can lose his or her driver's license and vehicle registration.

Subrogation The majority of no-fault states permit some form of subrogation against a negligent motorist's insurer to the extent of PIP benefits paid, or at least provide for reimbursement to the PIP insurer in the event that its insured receives a liability recovery from a third party. Like other no-fault provisions discussed here, subrogation provisions vary from state to state.

Personal Injury Protection (PIP) Endorsements

Insurers operating in states with a no-fault law must offer coverage to fulfill the requirements of the law. ISO provides a **personal injury protection (PIP) endorsement** that may be attached to the personal auto policy insuring a vehicle subject to a no-fault law. Separate endorsements, which reflect the differences in the no-fault laws across the states, are available for each state.

Coverage Under Modified No-Fault Laws

In states with modified no-fault laws, personal injury protection is statutory. That is, state laws specify the provisions of the PIP endorsements—including benefits, amounts, and thresholds. The format of the various PIP endorsements is fairly consistent among the states, despite variations to adjust for differing statutes. Each endorsement includes:

- An insuring agreement listing the benefits
- Exclusions
- A definitions section for the terms used in the endorsement
- A limits of liability provision stating the amount of benefits available for each of the coverages itemized in the insuring agreement
- Conditions by which the insured and insurer must abide

It is beyond the scope of this text to analyze in detail the specific provisions of the PIP endorsement used in each state that has adopted a no-fault statute. The following sections describe the types of coverage provided by PIP endorsements and some of the common variations in coverage, specifically (1) the benefits provided, (2) the persons to whom coverage applies, (3) losses or accidents outside the scope of PIP, and (4) the constitutionality clause.

Benefits   Most of the personal injury protection endorsements of states that have modified no-fault laws provide coverage for the following:

- *Medical Expenses.* The medical expenses coverage of the PIP endorsements resembles the medical payments coverage provided by the PAP—including the prerequisite that the expenses covered must be reasonable and necessary. However, the PIP endorsements do not limit the time within which the expenses must be incurred. In most cases, PIP medical expenses are subject to a maximum dollar limit for each accident.

  The medical expense benefits of the PIP endorsements may include rehabilitation services (although some states have a separate benefit for those services). They also specifically permit nonmedical remedial treatment by religious methods or by spiritual healing, provided the practice is permitted or licensed by the law of the state in question. Thus, although the medical payments coverage of the PAP does not specifically mention that coverage applies, some expenses related to Christian Science faith healing are often allowed.

- *Work Loss or Income Continuation Benefits.* When an eligible insured is injured or disabled, he or she is provided with some payments to recover loss of income, if employed at the time of the accident. Payments are limited to a certain amount per week subject to a maximum dollar amount or to a percentage of that person's income during the period of disability, subject to a maximum amount. The benefits do not fully replace the income lost by the injured person.

Some laws require that the work loss amount otherwise payable be reduced by any income earned during the period of disability. All laws require that this benefit be reduced by any amount paid or payable or required to be provided under workers compensation.

- *Essential Services Expenses.* If seriously injured or disabled, an insured may be unable to perform normal services required in or about the home, such as child care, household chores and regular maintenance, and property repairs. When substitute services must be obtained, they are covered under the essential services expenses benefit if the expenses are essential and for a reasonable amount. Usually, if the insured is collecting work loss benefits, he or she *may not* also collect essential services benefits. The insured is entitled to only one form of income benefits.

- *Funeral Expenses.* If an eligible insured dies in a covered auto accident, certain funeral expense coverage often is available, generally for reasonable expenses actually incurred of between $1,000 and $2,000 (depending upon the state) for burial or cremation. Most no-fault laws specify this benefit.

- *Survivors Benefits.* In the event of an insured's death, survivors are entitled to certain benefits representing the economic loss, such as income that would have been earned if death had not occurred. However, the benefits may not fully replace what the decedent might have been earning. Under no-fault laws, the survivor is paid a certain amount per week or quarter, usually until the surviving spouse remarries or dies. This benefit sometimes includes the essential services expenses benefit when that benefit is not separately provided. Or, when essential services expenses are separately provided, the survivors benefits are subject to reduction by the former benefit. In either case, survivors benefits are subject to reduction by the amount of any workers compensation benefits.

Eligible Insureds   All PIP endorsements make no-fault benefits available to the named insured and relatives of the named insured. "Relative" generally is defined to include those who are covered persons under the PAP. Thus, the named insured's spouse is an insured if residing in the same household as the named insured, and so are residents related to the named insured by blood, marriage, or adoption. Also commonly included are minors in the custody of the named insured. All these persons are protected while occupying an owned or nonowned vehicle or when struck as a pedestrian by any vehicle.

In addition to protection for the named insured and relatives, benefits are also usually available to other persons occupying an insured motor vehicle or to pedestrians struck by an insured motor vehicle. Some laws (and hence some endorsements) even provide coverage to other persons occupying a nonowned auto being used by the named insured.

Some variation exists among the endorsements regarding the type of vehicle in or by which the insureds must be injured in order to be covered. Some laws require coverage for any motor vehicle accident, including those involving a motorcycle, auto, truck, or bus. Other laws require coverage only for accidents involving private passenger autos. When coverage is restricted to preclude accidents involving livery conveyances, trucks, and motorcycles, protection is seriously restricted, and recovery for many accidents is available only through the tort system.

Despite these variations, nearly all PIP endorsements require an insured motor vehicle both (1) to be specifically insured by the policy and (2) to have no-fault coverage under the applicable state law. Thus, for example, a dune buggy may be insured under the policy, but unless the law requires it to be insured under the no-fault statute, it would not qualify as an insured motor vehicle.

Exclusions   The rationale for the exclusions in the PIP endorsements is similar to the rationale for the exclusions in the PAP. Generally, PIP endorsements do not apply to any of the following losses:

- Those involving a motor vehicle owned by the named insured or relative that is not specifically insured.

- Those sustained by persons other than the named insured or relative while using an otherwise insured auto without a reasonable belief that they are entitled to do so.

- Those sustained by persons other than the named insured or relative when struck by the insured auto if the accident occurs outside the state where the PIP is written. In other words, out-of-state coverage applies only to named insureds and their relatives, *not* to other occupants of insured autos or to pedestrians.

- Those resulting from the maintenance or use of a motor vehicle as a residence or premises.

- Those intentionally caused or caused while a person is committing a felony or attempting to avoid apprehension by law enforcement agencies.

- Those arising from war, whether declared or not, nuclear radiation, contamination, and similar catastrophic exposures.

- Those sustained by any person (some endorsements make exceptions of the named insured and relatives), which arise during the course of business of selling, repairing, servicing, storing, parking, or otherwise maintaining motor vehicles, unless the conduct giving rise to loss occurs off the business premises.

Whatever else is excluded in PIP endorsements depends on the peculiarities of each state's no-fault law.

Constitutionality Clause   Although not always labeled as such, a constitutionality clause is found in all PIP endorsements. It gives the insurer the right to recompute the premium and void or amend the coverage if a final court's decision should find the no-fault statute invalid or unenforceable in whole or in part. No-fault laws are frequently a subject of debate in many states, and the possibility exists that some laws may be found unenforceable, resulting in insured loss exposures greater than those contemplated when coverage was originally written. The constitutionality clause protects the insurer against such a contingency.

Coverage Under Add-On Plans

States that have add-on plans do not restrict the right to sue. No threshold exists, and the tort liability system remains unaffected. The endorsements of these plans commonly list three optional coverages: (1) medical payments, (2) work loss coverage, and (3) accidental death benefit.

Medical Payments   The medical payments coverage of the PIP endorsements for add-on plans is similar to the medical expense coverage in PIP endorsements of modified no-fault states. However, the add-on plans limit the time within which the exposure must be incurred. This is similar to the time limit of medical payments coverage under the PAP. Also, the medical payments coverage of add-on plans is subject to a limit, selected by the insured, which applies to each person.

Work Loss Coverage   The optional work loss coverage of add-on plans combines the equivalent of work loss coverage and essential services expenses found in PIP endorsements in modified no-fault states. Thus, if the eligible injured person is an income earner, work loss coverage of add-on plans will pay for the income that would have been earned if the person had not sustained bodily injury. If the injured person is not an income earner, the benefits payable are those reasonable expenses incurred for necessary services the injured person would have performed had the person not sustained bodily injury. Either benefit is statutory—that is, the amount payable is specified by law.

Accidental Death Benefit   When accidental death coverage is purchased, the insurer will pay the amount stated in the schedule if the death of an insured is caused by an accident and arises out of the maintenance or use of the motor vehicle. Such coverage applies if death occurs within a specified time (usually one or two years) from the date of accident.

Other Differences   Personal injury protection offered under add-on plans differs from that provided in modified no-fault states in several additional areas. First, most add-on plans do not have separate funeral expenses and survivors benefits coverages. Funeral expenses are included with medical payments coverage. Also, since personal injury protection of add-on plans usually is not compulsory, the endorsements do not have a constitutionality clause. Finally, coverage provided by the add-on plans applies only to the insured motor vehicles described in the endorsement declarations, and each of the three optional coverages is subject to a separate description of insured motor vehicles designated by the insured. For example, when auto medical payments coverage is purchased as part of an add-on PIP endorsement, the insured might be able to elect any one of the following three vehicles as being the insured motor vehicle: (1) an owned auto insured under Part A of the PAP, (2) any motor vehicle owned by the named insured, or (3) a private passenger auto owned by the named insured.

Weaknesses of Current No-Fault Plans

Many different opinions have been expressed regarding no-fault insurance plans. Some people contend that the laws do not go far enough in limiting the right to sue. As indicated, no state has enacted a **pure no-fault law**, which would completely eliminate tort liability claims. The critics allege that modified plans, although they partially restrict the right to sue, are little more than weak compromises between plaintiffs' attorneys and legislators. These compromises, in many instances, have supposedly produced laws that neither reduce tort claims nor pay sufficient personal injury protection benefits to seriously injured auto accident victims. The real culprit, according to these critics, is the inadequate tort threshold—low dollar thresholds that make a mockery of some states' attempts to restrict tort liability claims. An opposing viewpoint is that thresholds restricting tort claims must not be too high because pain and suffering exist even with injuries involving minimal medical costs.

Medical costs and inflation have seriously eroded the effectiveness of existing dollar thresholds. Verbal thresholds seem more effective in reducing tort liability claims. Little or no incentive exists to overuse or abuse medical services, because the amount of medical expenses does not influence the right to sue. Yet, verbal thresholds are less precise than dollar thresholds, which may create a different set of problems—such as determining what types of injury are considered severe enough to allow suit. In addition, some people have gotten around the limitations by being declared seriously injured when they are not.

No-fault insurance was promoted as a plan to reduce insurance premiums. This has not occurred. The so-called no-fault plans that have been introduced are a far cry from pure no-fault insurance. Yet, the public has seen the "no-fault" label attached to coverages that continue to become more costly. Many have become dissatisfied with existing options and have proposed a variety of changes, which are debated at length in state legislatures. Some states have repealed their no-fault laws and returned to the tort system, sometimes requiring that a variety of choices be offered to insureds. Further change and innovation seem inevitable.

Factors Affecting the Cost of Insurance

Some people pay more than others for auto insurance because their expected loss costs are higher or their probability of loss is greater. Insurers have developed rating systems reflecting these various loss probabilities. Rating systems consider a variety of factors to place each insured and auto into a rating class or classification. The premium for an auto insurance policy is based largely on the classification to which each individual insured is assigned.

The following is a brief overview of the traditional rating systems that apply to liability, physical damage, and bodily injury coverages. The discussion is general rather than specific because rating factors vary among insurance companies and states. Some insurers continue to experiment with different rating factors, and some states have banned the use of one or more of the traditional rating factors.

Classification Plans

When an individual driver applies for and receives personal auto insurance, the insurance company, using certain factors, classifies the driver according to the type and amount of risk the driver is determined to represent. The premium charged for the insurance policy is based on this classification. Regardless of the classification or rating system used, it is important for the individual driver to recognize the factors affecting his or her insurance premium and what may be done to move to a classification with a lower premium.

Reasons for Classification

Insurance is a device for distributing the financial impact of losses of the few over a large group, with each group member contributing a relatively small amount as his or her "fair share" of group losses. A basic operating principle of insurance is that this "fair share" should be based on loss potential and that persons paying the same premium for a certain type of coverage should be similar in loss potential—that is, they should be relatively **homogeneous**. Classification is one method to achieve homogeneity. Without it, a driver who uses a ten-year-old station wagon to go four miles down a rural country road to get to church on Sundays would pay the same premium as a driver who uses a brand new luxury car to cross a crowded urban area each day going to and from work. All other factors being equal, the exposures faced by an older vehicle on the rural country road one day a week have much less potential to result in loss than driving a new luxury car in a congested area five days a week. These drivers should not be placed in the same group for the purpose of determining the fair share, because their loss exposures are not homogeneous.

Casual observation by an objective person unfamiliar with insurance and loss sharing would support the contention that all persons should not be charged the same price for the protection received in a particular type of insurance, without regard to the exposure presented. However, a separate classification for each driver is not an appropriate nor feasible alternative. The goal, then, is to achieve **workable homogeneity**—dividing drivers into *relatively homogeneous groups* without creating a system that becomes too burdensome to operate or that results in classifications containing too few drivers. If successfully achieved, workable homogeneity in classification results in insureds being charged fair premiums for the coverage they receive. A number of considerations and forces influence the successful establishment of workable homogeneity within rating classifications at any given time.

Equity

One of the primary reasons for classification is to charge insureds fairly for the insurance protection they buy. Drivers should pay their fair share for the risks to which they are exposed. Because data are collected by insurers when losses occur, insurance companies can determine which factors allow for the most equitable distribution of losses. This point is demonstrated in the development of territorial rates. When automobiles first appeared, no distinction by territory existed, because no data were available upon which to base a rate differential. As experience developed, it became evident that insureds in some geographic locations should pay higher premiums because their loss experience was worse than that at other locations, while other locations experienced fewer losses and should be charged lower premiums. Therefore, rating territories were adopted.

The factors that achieve equity change over time, and thus some rating factors may be eliminated while others are added as new information comes to light through actual loss experience. For example, at one time, auto theft was not the major problem it currently is, and there was no need to install security systems in cars. However, as the risk of theft increased, experience showed that certain antitheft devices reduced the exposure to theft so that an auto owner can now get a premium discount if an acceptable security system is installed in the insured auto.

Competition

One of the strongest pressures encouraging classification development and change has been competition among insurers. An insurer might identify a particular group of insureds who are less prone to loss than others within the classification to which they are all assigned. By separating these insureds into a new classification, the insurance company can charge them less and achieve a competitive advantage in the marketplace. In contrast, the newly identified group might be more susceptible to loss than others currently falling into the same category, and separating them into a higher-rated class would enable the insurer to reduce rates for those remaining in the original class. This approach also makes the insurance company more attractive to some insurance buyers.

Economy and Ease of Administration

Cost is an important consideration in establishing classifications. It is a major reason for differences in classification practices among insurance companies. Some possible classifications can cost more to administer than they develop in benefits.

For instance, assume that an insurance company wants to give a discount to good students but feels that regular reporting of grades would be necessary to verify each student's scholastic performance. The cost to request and handle report cards and administer the program internally might be more than the company would realize from retaining and attracting profitable business from students. As another example, consider the use of driver attitude in auto insurance classification. The mental attitude of a driver is generally accepted as an important factor in determining accident probability. An antagonistic, impatient driver or a lax driver who is inclined to daydream is more likely to have an accident than one who is patient, composed, and attentive. A higher degree of rating equity could be achieved if this factor were part of the classification system and companies using it could gain substantial competitive advantages. However, assuming that a valid, objective, and reliable test even existed, the cost of administering such a program would be high.

Another cost factor influencing the number of classifications is the increased chance of error and misclassification as the number of classes increases. This problem can be demonstrated by considering territory classifications. It is simple to assign one class to a large city, but it becomes more difficult to apply proper classifications when a large number of territories within the city—such as one class per city borough—is used. With one large class, any insured within the city is easily placed in the correct territorial classification. However, the possibility of error increases with the multiplicity of territories in the city. Instead of one simple class, a city may have four or five classes, and the insurer must take more time and make more of an effort to ensure that the driver is placed in the correct classification.

Credibility

The greater the number of classifications, the more difficult it is to achieve credible loss results in any particular classification and to justify rate differentials among classifications. Even if cost and administrative ease were not problems, limits exist on the number of classifications because of the need to support the plan's rates and overall structure with credible data. This support is needed to justify rates with insurance departments in most states.

Consider an example. Suppose County Insurance Company has set up a classification system that results in 100 rating classes, each with one insured. If an insured in any one of these classes experiences a loss during the coverage period, County Insurance Company has no way to judge whether the loss results from a normal exposure or if it is unusual. In other words, County is unable to establish the credibility of the loss results. However, if County had one rating class with 100,000 insureds in it and 40,000 of the insureds experienced a similar type of loss, County could determine that these losses are fairly common occurrences and could place some credibility in the loss results.

Social Acceptability

Increasingly, public perception and acceptance of potential rating factors determine whether or not the factors are actually used. Consider the use of age, sex, and marital status as classification factors. Traditionally, insurers found that drivers between the ages of thirty and sixty-five, female drivers, and married drivers, especially at younger ages, experienced fewer losses and thus were charged lower premiums. However, those favoring change state that, among other things, it is unfairly discriminatory to classify drivers on factors such as age, sex, and marital status. They hold that it is possible to develop equitable insurance rates based on other factors more within the insured's control—such as the number of miles driven, driving record, and accident experience. Movement has been made to eliminate the use of age, sex, and marital status in developing auto insurance rating classifications, and some insurers have experimented with more novel approaches to rating classification. Because of social pressure, the use of age, sex, and marital status as a classification factor is being reconsidered.

The Structure of Classification Plans

Classification plans for most insurance companies traditionally have been based on territory; age, sex, and marital status of operators; and the use of the vehicle. Many plans also include surcharges or credits based on such factors as driving record, scholastic achievement, driver training of youthful operators, number of cars insured, nature of the vehicle, and safety features of the vehicle.

Territory

The degree of density of the driving population, traffic patterns and conditions, and crime, among other factors, influence accident frequency and, to a lesser degree, severity. Insureds in larger cities produce higher average losses than in rural areas, primarily due to higher claim frequency as opposed to claim severity. As a result, one of the first points introduced into auto rating was the practice of isolating geographic areas producing higher loss ratios and altering the rating structure accordingly.

Within each state, territorial subdivisions may be structured by county; city; areas within a city, township, town, village; or ZIP code. The number of rating territories varies from state to state and may also vary in a given state among insurance companies using different classification plans. In general, the number of territories varies directly with population.

In the process of making or revising rates, the various territories within a state are given a rate or rate modification. This territorial rate serves as the base point for all other rates—such as the rate for males, age twenty and twenty-one—developed by the classification plan for that territory. A basic goal of territorial classification is to include within a rating territory areas having roughly similar characteristics and loss experience. A variety of factors may cause differences in loss experience, and hence rates, from one territory to another. Loss frequency and severity can differ because of variations in at least the following factors: population and traffic density, traffic controls, law enforcement, topography, climate, availability of mass transportation, street and highway design and maintenance, wage rates, medical and hospital costs, judicial attitude and conduct, crime rates, claims consciousness, and availability of legal representation.

The basic rating territories used by many insurance companies are those prepared by ISO. These are referred to as "bureau" rating territories. Among other activities, ISO receives loss, premium, and exposure unit data from member companies throughout the United States, compiles and analyzes this information to monitor experience in the territories, recommends changes, and modifies the territorial structure from time to time. Most insurers maintain their own premium and loss data by territory, and some have a sufficient volume of business in their operating areas to develop credible data. The territorial delineations established by ISO and these "independent" insurance companies tend to be similar, but some differences do exist.

Age, Sex, and Marital Status of Operators

Age, sex, and marital status of the identifiable operator(s) of the vehicle traditionally have been important elements in classification. The three items are grouped under one heading because the rating significance of one item may be dependent upon another. As mentioned earlier, the use of these factors has received some criticism.

Youthful operators produce the highest accident frequency. Exhibit 5-4 shows that while the number of teenage drivers is approximately half the number of fifty-five-to-sixty-four-year-old drivers, teenage drivers are nearly twice as likely to have an accident as fifty-five-to-sixty-four-year-old drivers.[5] Within a given territory, teenage drivers are the highest rated (that is, charged the highest premium) auto insurance group. Within the youthful operator group (which in some states can range from age fourteen to age twenty-nine), an inverse correlation exists between age and accident frequency—the lower the age, the higher the frequency. The same relationship appears to exist between age and traffic convictions.

Historically, classification systems have distinguished, particularly at younger ages, between male and female operators. Other things being equal, females traditionally generated lower loss levels than males, and most classification plans resulted in lower rates for females than for males of the same ages. Exhibit 5-5 indicates that, with respect to drivers involved in fatal accidents, males have worse loss experience than females. However, Exhibit 5-6 shows that, per ten million miles driven, female drivers were involved in more auto accidents than male drivers in 1989, 1990, 1991 and 1992.[6] Insurance company rates may reflect this changing trend, depending on their own loss experience by sex and age. Furthermore, differences exist among insurance companies with respect to the use of male-female rating differentials. Most insurers use the differentials only for younger drivers and phase out the rate differences by a certain age category.

Exhibit 5-4
Age-Group Drivers (1992)

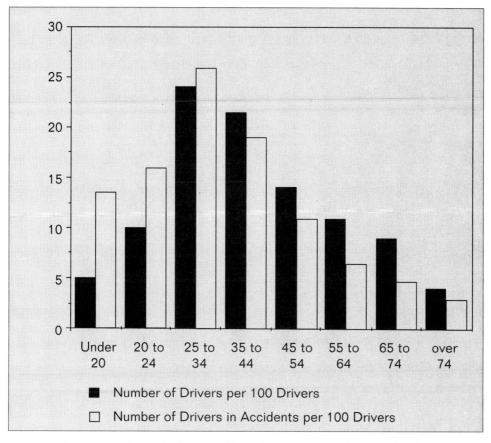

Source: *The Fact Book 1994: Property/Casualty Insurance Facts* (New York, NY: Insurance Information Institute), p. 89.

Youthful operators are generally subdivided into several classifications based on age. Virtually every insurer uses at least two-year groups, and many go so far as to refine youthful driver classifications into one-year age groups. Some insurance companies use a fourfold breakdown for male drivers under age thirty: (1) under age twenty; (2) ages twenty and twenty-one; (3) ages twenty-two, twenty-three, and twenty-four; and (4) ages twenty-five through twenty-nine. Insurers use different combinations depending on their own capabilities, data, and objectives. Obviously, division into more groups decreases the number of insureds within each group. While this may refine the classification plan and present a more accurate reflection of the exposure by age, it can also be that a smaller classification develops too little data to be credible.

Exhibit 5-5

Differences in Fatal Accident Frequency Between the Sexes
1983 through 1992

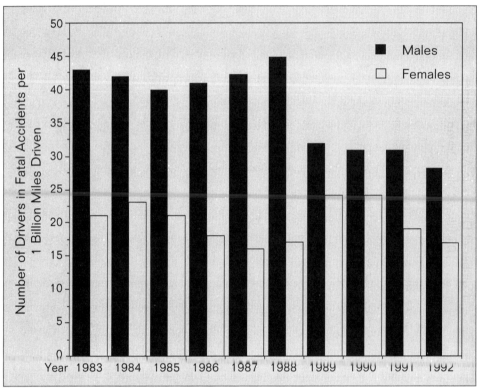

Source: *The Fact Book 1994: Property/Casualty Insurance Facts* (New York, NY:
Insurance Information Institute), p. 90.

Marital status plays an important role in further refining classification plans
for both male and female youthful drivers. Traditionally, rating plans assign
different classes to young married operators whose rates are then lower than
the rates for their unmarried counterparts.

Drivers in the age groups between thirty and sixty-five make up a major
portion of both the driving population and the book of personal auto business
of most insurers. This group is used to set the **base rate** by territory (that is, all
other rate classifications within a territory are keyed to the rate for this group).

For drivers over the age of sixty-five, the loss experience of individual insurance companies has been mixed. Some time ago, most insurers charged more
for elderly drivers than for those in the thirty-to-sixty-five age group. This
practice was discredited as a blanket approach by the analysis of increasing
amounts of data made possible by a larger over-sixty-five population. For

Exhibit 5-6
Differences in Accident Frequency Between the Sexes
1983 through 1992

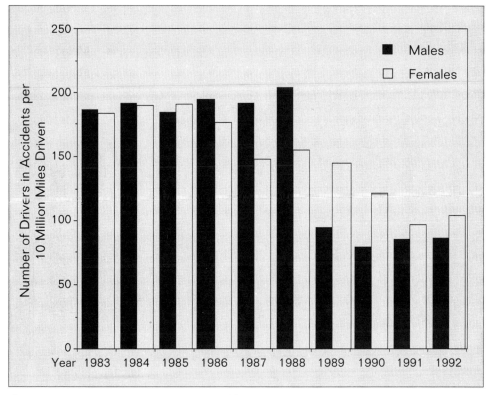

Source: *The Fact Book 1994: Property/Casualty Insurance Facts* (New York, NY: Insurance Information Institute), p. 90.

example, Exhibit 5-4 shows that drivers in the sixty-five to seventy-four age group had the lowest accident frequency in 1991. The over seventy-four age group had an accident frequency slightly higher than the sixty-five to seventy-four age group. Many insurers have substituted credits for surcharges. Some have found that elderly drivers have better liability experience, but poorer collision experience while others have found higher liability *and* collision experience among elderly drivers. At present, no uniformity exists in rating approaches for drivers over age sixty-five.

Use of Vehicles

The term **use** includes a number of factors. As with other classification criteria, insurer practices on use as a classification variable are not standardized, but are generally comparable.

Use of the vehicle enters the picture even before serving as a rating factor, because personal use must be established if the insured is to be eligible for personal auto classification, rating, and forms. Taxis, buses, auto rental agencies, racing cars, and some trucks used in business are ineligible for coverage under most personal auto insurance plans.

For an otherwise eligible vehicle, some business use is permitted, and a separate rate class assigned. Such combination-use vehicles would include, for example, cars owned and used in business by salespersons, insurance producers, real estate agents, or employees of a government or governmental agency and would extend to include a pickup or van owned by an individual and used for personal purposes by a carpenter or other artisan if the business use is limited to driving to and from work and carrying tools and other material to job sites.

Farm use takes a separate classification with the vast majority of insurers. A discount is given to vehicles that are principally garaged on a farm, are not used in any occupation other than farming, and are not customarily driven to and from work or school.

Apart from vehicles subject to farm rates and rates applicable because of business use, what remains are nonfarm vehicles used strictly for pleasure, or for pleasure plus driving to and from work or school. Almost all insurers secure information on whether the car is driven to and from work or school and classify on the basis of this information, but some insurers consider this information too unreliable for rating purposes.

Some insurers classify on the basis of annual mileage driven. Common dividing points are 5,000, 7,500, 10,000, and 15,000 miles per year. An insurer using this criterion for classification may apply it to only some of its rate classes.

Credits and Surcharges

A number of other rating criteria are used by insurers. These are applied as credits and surcharges to the rates otherwise developed through the use of the classification plan. Only the more common are described here.

A **multiple-car discount** is given by most insurers. One common approach is to allow a discount of 10 percent for each car when two or more owned by an insured are covered by the same company. Another approach is to allow a standard discount, for example 20 percent, for the second car and none for the first car. Some insurers give a discount, sometimes called a **fleet discount**, when five or more cars with common ownership are insured by the same insurance company.

Safe driver insurance plans, which allow for lower basic premiums for accident-free driving records and surcharge for accidents, are quite common. Many variations exist, but all are designed to favor the drivers who have not had accidents and to charge more for those who have. The definitions of the accidents considered and the period during which they are counted vary considerably by insurance company and state.

Moving traffic convictions, expressed in the form of surcharges applied to basic premiums, also serve as a rating factor for some insurance companies. Most insurers writing preferred or standard business do not surcharge for citations. Instead, they use citations to define their market by making eligibility for low or preferred rates contingent upon the absence of citations during a stipulated period, or by using citations as a selection tool. However, some insurers have programs for increasing the rate because of convictions for moving violations. As with accidents, differences exist regarding which citations are counted and what time period is used. Differences also exist on the subject of higher surcharges for major convictions such as driving under the influence of alcohol or drugs.

Driver training credits are allowed by many insurers. The theory underlying the credit is a belief that a driver (usually a youthful driver) who has completed an approved driver training course usually will be a better driver than one who has not, although empirical evidence does not support this theory. Minimum hours usually apply, such as thirty hours of classroom education and six hours behind the wheel of a training car. Credits usually average around 10 percent to 15 percent, with the highest discount applying to the youngest classes.

Good student discounts are allowed by some insurers. The theoretical basis for the credit is the relationship among good grades, study time, and personal responsibility. Students who study hard usually do not drive as much as students in general, and good grades tend to indicate that, as a group, good students are responsible. (However, most insurers have not found statistical support for such discounts.) Credits vary by company.

Inexperienced drivers are surcharged by some insurance companies. These surcharges are generally applied to drivers of all ages who have been licensed for less than three years. Surcharges also may be imposed for drivers who claim to have experience but whose driving record cannot be verified, such as when driving has been done in a foreign country. The surcharge is intended to compensate for the lack of an actual driving record as an aid in estimating what may be expected in the future.

Some insurers allow a credit for **safety features** installed in the insured auto. Safety features such as automatic seat belts, airbags, and antilock brakes are designed to prevent an accident and reduce injury involved in an accident. In fact, most states have enacted laws that mandate using seat belts. Safety features reduce the frequency and severity of claims and, therefore, are taken into account in the premium through a credit.

Some insurers allow a discount to policyholders who have been continuously covered for more than a given number of years. Some insurers also allow a so-called "homeowners-auto" discount to insureds who have both their homeowners and auto policies with the same insurance company.

Other Factors Affecting Cost

The classification factors discussed above affect the overall loss experience of each driver and thus the class to which he or she is assigned for rating purposes. A driver may not have control over some of these factors. However, the cost of bodily injury and physical damage coverages is also influenced by factors other than those discussed above, and these factors are within the control of the driver. The following section describes the impact of various factors, specific to bodily injury or physical damage loss exposures, on the cost of coverage against these exposures.

Physical Damage Cost Factors

Although characteristics about the driver, the territory, and the use of the auto do affect the physical damage loss exposure, other factors, especially with respect to the auto itself, also are important. Factors that significantly affect the cost of auto physical damage insurance—collision coverage and other-than-collision coverage—are damageability and repairability, age and original cost, security devices, and deductibles.

Damageability and Repairability

The concept of determining physical damage insurance costs based on damageability and repairability of the auto is not new. However, until the late 1970s, these factors were seldom considered for rating purposes. What has made these two factors important are studies and tests that show unequivocally a direct correlation between the size and model of an auto and its susceptibility to damage. Loss severity can be predicted, to a degree, based on the actual loss experience of similar size and model autos. Each new model is assigned a cost factor depending on the loss potential of similar models.

Studies have also found that auto industry practices and standards affect the damageability and repairability of autos, and therefore affect the cost of auto insurance. For example, federally mandated fuel efficiency standards have had a significant effect on vehicle design, materials, and construction with a resulting increase in repair costs. Bumper standards were lowered from withstanding a five-mile-per-hour crash with no damage to withstanding a two-and-a-half-mile-per-hour crash, resulting in increased repair costs. However, use of non-OEM (original equipment manufacturer) parts, which are parts from discount dealers, has increased and helped to reduce the cost of vehicle repairs.

When considering the purchase of an auto, a driver may first contact his or her insurance company. The insurer will provide the premium information for different makes and models based on the loss experiences of each.

Age and Original Cost

Under the traditional rating system (which most insurers are replacing), the age of the auto and its original cost were primary factors of consideration. Regardless of the model and its susceptibility to damage, all autos within the same price range were classified in the same rating class. As the age of the auto increased, this system led to a reduction in insurance costs. Actually, repairing an older auto generally does not cost less than repairing a new auto, but, since loss severity on an older car is limited to the value of the vehicle, it takes less damage to an older auto to cause a constructive total loss. The insured can take this into account when considering the purchase of a new, versus a used, auto.

Security and Passenger Protection Devices

Theft of vehicles is higher than it was a decade ago, and as a result, a proliferation of security devices to protect autos from being burglarized or completely stolen has occurred. The use of appropriate and successful security devices helps to reduce the chance of theft. These devices also reduce the cost of other than collision physical damage coverage through rate credits for such devices and the reduction in theft loss.

In an effort to reduce the severity of injury to passengers, air bags, automatic seat belts, and similar items have become popular. Although these devices may help to reduce bodily injury costs, they increase the cost of auto repair, and, thus, premiums for physical damage and property damage liability coverages may rise.

Deductibles

Obviously, the lower the deductible, the greater the cost of insurance. At least two reasons explain why deductibles may be desirable:

1. Deductibles can reduce the overall cost of insurance to the insured.
2. Deductibles, if they are high enough, may motivate the insured to exercise a greater degree of loss control.

During recent years, there has been a modest trend toward higher deductibles on auto physical damage coverages.

Bodily Injury Cost Factors

Several factors deal specifically with bodily injury and affect the cost of auto insurance. These factors include the design of autos and passenger restraints and primarily influence the severity of bodily injury losses.

Design of Autos

Just as the design of the automobile influences the amount of damage resulting from an accident and the cost to repair it, the design of a vehicle affects the amount and cost of any bodily injury resulting to the driver and passengers in the event of an accident. Because of the federally mandated fuel efficiency standards, the materials being used to construct autos have become lighter and less resistant to damage on impact. As a result, the occupants of the vehicle are more at risk to suffer bodily injury than they were before these standards were enforced. The reduction of bumper standards has also contributed to an increase in bodily injury to the driver and passengers. This caused bodily injury costs, and the premiums for bodily injury coverage such as medical expenses or personal injury protection, to rise over the past couple of decades, partly in response to the increased risk of damage to autos.

Some new cars continue to maintain more rugged designs and have lower bodily injury loss experience for occupants. A driver might consider such a new car or an older car with a good safety rating when purchasing an auto. However, big, heavy cars tend to cause greater amounts of bodily injury to occupants of other autos and pedestrians with whom the rugged cars collide. The cost of bodily injury liability insurance may be greater for larger vehicles.

Passenger Restraints

Technological advances in passenger restraints have helped to prevent and reduce injury to the driver and passengers. For example, automatic seat belts ensure that the front-seat occupants are not thrown from the car in a collision. Air bags are now available for the driver, and, in some cars, for the front-seat passengers and even rear-seat passengers. They have saved the lives of many individuals involved in head-on collisions. In fact, many individuals involved in such accidents walk away with only minor injuries. Passenger restraints help to reduce the severity of bodily injury, and thus autos equipped with such restraints may qualify for premium credits.

Cost of Health Care

Many individuals may not recognize the impact of increasing health-care costs on the cost of auto insurance. The PAP covers bodily injury in three of its four coverages—Liability, Medical Expenses, and Uninsured Motorists Coverage. Personal injury protection and underinsured motorist coverage are also affected by the cost of medical treatment. As the medical costs of treating an injured motorist or pedestrian increase, the insurer's loss costs also increase, and this directly influences the cost of insurance to the insured.

Ideas for Making Auto Insurance Fairer and More Affordable

Insurance rates have been increasing at a steady rate. The insurance industry is concerned about this trend and is pursuing many ideas in order to reverse the situation. Unhappy customers and increasing rates are not in the industry's best interest, and, therefore, the insurance industry is working hard to make insurance more fair and more affordable for everyone. The following ideas are proposed by the Insurance Information Institute and represent a small sample of the ways by which the goal of fairer and more affordable auto insurance can be attained.

1. *Increase service to consumers.* With more information at their disposal, consumers can make more cost-effective decisions when purchasing auto insurance. For example, many people do not realize how much of an impact the make and model of a car have on the cost of the coverage needed.

2. *Provide low-income consumers with financial assistance.* People who cannot afford traditional auto insurance often drive uninsured, and their accidents are reflected in everyone's insurance rates. Some insurers and consumer representatives are considering the development of limited-coverage, low-cost policies for drivers who need automobile insurance but cannot afford it.

3. *Allow consumers more ways to save money.* Many suggestions have been made in this area, including (1) promoting more competition among repair shops; (2) keeping the auto parts market open to anyone with safe, quality products to offer; (3) offering incentives to consumers to use hospitals and doctors who adhere to fair fee schedules; and, (4) encouraging all insurers to provide special rate discounts and credits. In fact, several of these ideas have been further developed into workable solutions. For example, the development of preferred provider repair networks enables insurers to negotiate directly with repair facilities for lower labor rates for insurance-related repairs that lower insurer's claims costs and thus premiums.[6]

4. *Conduct consumer campaigns for safer cars and highways.* To help reduce the severity of injury and damage, public-private partnerships are recommended to push for air bags, stronger bumpers, antilacerating glass, further development of antilock brakes, and increased side protection on cars, vans, and light trucks. Support should also be given to organizations dedicated to improving auto safety and engineering, such as the Society of Automobile Engineers and the Insurance Institute for Highway Safety.

5. *Encourage highway safety.* Highway safety is key to reducing the cost of auto insurance. Tougher drunk driving laws should be enacted and enforced. All new drivers should be encouraged to take driver's education courses. Seat-belt use should continue to be promoted. Speed limits should be rigorously enforced. The monitoring of truck violations should be increased, since about 10 percent of all driving fatalities occur in truck-related accidents. Tougher penalties should be enacted and enforced for repeat offenders.

6. *Work to decrease auto theft and fraud.* The problems of auto theft and auto insurance fraud are of major concern to the insurance industry. Auto theft and auto insurance fraud are a burden not only to the insurers but also to the insureds, as at least 10 to 25 percent of auto insurance premiums pay for these losses. Law enforcement officials need more support to stem the increase in car thefts. Meanwhile, the insurance industry is continuously working to establish a comprehensive system of fraud detection. Steps have been taken to form interactive data bases on a national level that provide information by vehicle identification numbers for fraud detection, and the data bases are beginning to have an effect on fraud detection. However, other means of preventing and detecting fraud can also be supported. These include (1) mandatory preinspection of vehicles before insurance coverage is purchased to prevent fraudulent claims; (2) peer reviews to penalize those in the medical and legal professions who participate in fraud; and (3) more theft and fraud investigations by agents, claims personnel, and authorities to make the criminals, rather than other insureds, pay for their crime.

Summary

All motorists are expected to be financially responsible for their actions as motorists. Several types of laws have been passed to address problems that result when motorists are not able to pay for the injury and damage they cause while using, maintaining, or owning an automobile, including the following:

• Financial responsibility laws

- Compulsory auto insurance laws
- Unsatisfied judgment funds
- Uninsured and underinsured motorists laws
- No-fault laws

Each of these laws has its merits and its supporters, but none of the solutions is perfect.

Uninsured motorist and underinsured motorist laws require insurers to provide coverages against bodily injury and property damage caused by motorists with inadequate or no auto liability insurance. These coverages provide an additional and timely source of recovery for injured motorists but they do not address the problem of uninsured and underinsured motorists. People continue to drive without auto liability coverage or with inadequate limits.

No fault laws were supported as a way to get financial help to people injured in auto accidents when the financial help was needed, that is, in an efficient manner. However, evidence suggests that no-fault laws are not eliminating tort actions, and, in fact, might be adding to the problem. To get around thresholds, injured motorists exaggerate their injuries so they can sue.

When motorists do obtain insurance to satisfy their financial responsibility requirements, they are classified and charged a premium based on certain characteristics that insurers have determined affect a motorist's risk to the insurer, such as the following:

- Territory
- Age, sex, and marital status of motorists
- Use of vehicle

The classification of motorists allows insurers to better assess the potential losses and charge the insureds a fair premium. Some of these factors are within the insured's control; others are not. However, if the insured is aware of the factors, he or she can take steps to reduce his or her risk and thus the auto insurance premium.

Chapter Notes

1. "Compulsory Auto Insurance," *Data Base Reports* (New York, NY: Insurance Information Institute, October 1987).
2. Many issues regarding uninsured and underinsured motorists coverage and multiple sources of recovery remain unresolved. For more on this, see Insurance Services Office, Inc.; *Uninsured and Underinsured Motorists Insurance: A Perspec-*

tive, ISO Insurance Issues Series, December 1992; and Robert J. Prahl, "Underinsured Motorists Insurance," *CPCU Journal*, December 1993, pp. 219-222.

3. National Underwriter Co., "Development of No-Fault Automobile Insurance," *FC&S Bulletins: Personal Lines Volumes*, August 1991, pp. Noa-1; Insurance Information Institute, "No-Fault Auto Insurance," *Data Base Reports* (New York, NY: Insurance Information Institute, July 1988).

4. "Will Insurers Make the Right Choice?", *Emphasis* (1990/4), a publication of Tillinghast, a Towers Perrin Company.

5. *The Fact Book 1994: Property/Casualty Insurance Facts* (New York, NY: Insurance Information Institute), p. 89.

6. *The Fact Book 1994: Property/Casualty Insurance Facts*, p. 89.

7. "Will Insurers Make the Right Choice?"

Chapter 6

Additional Property and Liability Coverage

Homeowners policies and personal auto policies do not cover some common personal loss exposures. For example, many individuals own homes that they do not live in but that they rent to other individuals and families. These homeowners generally do not qualify for homeowners insurance. However, dwelling insurance programs sponsored by ISO and individual insurers provide landlords with property insurance to cover the loss exposures associated with renting a home to other individuals and families. Dwelling insurance may also be used to cover the loss exposures of owner-occupants of multi-family homes that do not qualify for homeowners insurance. In addition, mobilehomes are a popular form of housing, especially in warmer climates. Mobilehomes may not qualify for homeowners policies because of their value and their construction. Mobilehome policies are available to cover the loss exposures of owner-occupants of mobilehomes.

A couple of common sources of loss exposures for individuals and families involve motor vehicles—specifically, recreational land motor vehicles and watercraft. Homeowners policies and personal auto policies provide limited coverage for these types of vehicles. However, the vehicles can be covered by insurance designed for such exposures.

Another area of concern is that of liability coverage. Although both homeowners policies and personal auto policies provide coverage for certain liability exposures, the coverage may be limited—narrower scope and lower available limits than desired or needed by individuals and families. Personal umbrella insurance and excess insurance provide cost-effective means by which large and unusual liability exposures may be covered.

Even with all of the different policies available and the different classification standards among insurers, many individuals and families find it difficult to purchase insurance for certain exposures. For example, windstorm insurance is either unavailable or unaffordable in many coastal areas, and drivers with poor driving records are often unable to purchase insurance from private insurers. Residual markets for insurance have been instituted, primarily by state or federal statute, which provide insurance to those individuals and families who cannot obtain coverage in the private insurance market.

As pointed out above, property and liability insurance is not limited to homeowners policies, personal auto policies, and their endorsements. Many other loss exposures exist that are either not addressed or not adequately addressed by the policies. This chapter discusses several additional policies and programs for insuring property and liability loss exposures.

Additional Policies for Residential Loss Exposures

As mentioned, landlords and owner-occupants of multi-family dwellings or mobilehomes do not generally qualify for homeowners insurance. The loss exposures faced by these two groups differ from the loss exposures covered by ISO homeowners policies. Dwelling policies and mobilehome policies are available to cover these loss exposures.

Although this text has concentrated on ISO property and liability coverages, the ISO dwelling policies and mobilehome policies are not used by many insurers that offer dwelling insurance and mobilehome insurance. Insurers that offer these coverages may file their policies independently. Therefore, the following discussions of dwelling policies and mobilehome policies focus on general characteristics of the coverages, including descriptions of the most common provisions and how they differ from homeowners policies.

Dwelling Insurance

Although most owner-occupied homes are covered by a homeowners policy, many dwellings do not meet homeowners policy eligibility requirements. For example, a dwelling may not be owner-occupied, or it may be a four-family building in a state where only one- and two-family dwellings are eligible for homeowners coverage. In such cases, the structure and its contents can generally be insured under a dwelling policy.

Applicable Situations

Dwelling policies are designed principally for insuring one- to four-family dwellings, whether owner-occupied or tenant-occupied. However, dwelling policies may also be used for the following:

- Mobilehomes or trailer homes at a permanent location

- In some states, houseboats

- Certain incidental business occupancies if they are operated by the owner-insured or a tenant of the insured location

- Dwellings that do not meet the underwriting requirements for homeowners policies because of age, low value, or poor physical condition

Dwelling Policies

Most dwelling policy programs provide a choice of at least two dwelling policies that differ in the amount and type of coverage available. For example, the 1989 ISO program includes four dwelling forms: the basic form, DP-1; the broad form, DP-2; the special form, DP-3; and the modified coverage form, DP-8. (Although the official form numbers are DP 00 01, DP 00 02, DP 00 03, and DP 00 08, this text continues to refer to the policies as DP-1, DP-2, DP-3, and DP-8.) However, an independent filer may offer only two policies: (1) fire and extended coverage and (2) broad form.

General Provisions

In many instances, dwelling policies are separate package policies that provide coverage for property damage and loss of use. However, some insurers provide dwelling coverages by modifying their homeowners policies. For example, a homeowners policy may be endorsed to allow property coverage for the owner of a dwelling that is usually rented to a family.

Dwelling forms provide narrower coverage than homeowners forms in several respects. For example, under ISO policies, when a homeowners policy is purchased, the insured must accept all the coverages. The insured may not pick the coverages desired and eliminate the remaining coverages—the policy is a complete package offered on an all-or-nothing basis. This does not hold true for ISO dwelling policies. Although the coverages provided by dwelling policies are included in a package, the insured may choose the coverages desired and delete those not needed from the package.

The following examples illustrate how coverage might be arranged for particular insureds:

- An insured who rents an unfurnished house and detached garage to others can purchase coverage (1) on the dwelling and other structures and (2) for fair rental value. (Any equipment of the insured kept at the location and used to service the premises—such as a refrigerator—is considered part of the dwelling.)

- A tenant interested in covering only personal property and additional living expenses can purchase a dwelling policy that includes only coverage for personal property and additional living expense. He or she may also purchase other structures coverage for such property as an outbuilding or a satellite dish.

- A condominium unit owner may purchase personal property coverage. (Endorsements may be added to provide condominium unit-owners coverages as needed for property loss assessments, loss of use of a unit resulting from damage to the condominium building, and damage to certain building items.)

Although coverage on the dwelling and other structures is often similar to coverage provided by homeowners policies, two important differences may exist between the dwelling and homeowners coverage of personal property:

1. The personal property coverage agreement in dwelling forms, unlike that in homeowners forms, may only fully apply to property *"usual to the occupancy as a dwelling"* while it is at the described location. This requirement can be more restrictive coverage than coverage for personal property "usually located at the dwelling." For example, property associated with unusual hobbies, such as mountain-climbing equipment or scuba-diving equipment, may not be covered by a dwelling policy, because most people do not participate in mountain climbing or scuba diving and, thus, the property is not "usual to the occupancy as a dwelling." However, bicycles or cameras are often found at residences and, therefore, may be covered because they are "usual to occupancy as a dwelling." A policy that covers personal property that is usually located at the dwelling generally applies to mountain-climbing equipment, scuba-diving equipment, bicycles, and cameras.

    Most dwelling policies provide limited coverage while the personal property is off the described location. For example, the ISO dwelling forms limit coverage for personal property away from the described premises to 10 percent of the personal property coverage limit.

2. Dwelling policies generally do not automatically presume a relationship between dwelling values and personal property values. Instead, a separate limit must be selected for coverage on the dwelling and coverage on personal property, if each is chosen.

The fundamental differences between homeowners forms and dwelling forms are that dwelling forms generally do not include theft insurance, liability coverage, or medical payments coverage unless they are added by supplemental forms. As noted earlier, the dwellings that are covered by dwelling policies tend to be older, in less safe neighborhoods, or in poorer condition than those dwellings that meet the qualifications for homeowners policy coverage. Dwellings covered by dwelling policies, unlike those covered by homeowners policies, also may be occupied by persons other than the owners. These types of dwellings generally represent a greater risk of loss by theft as well as an increased possibility of bodily injury that may result in liability or medical expenses. For example, tenants can remove appliances and furniture from a rental unit. A house that is in poor condition may have a loose step that gives way and injures a guest. Thus, insurers limit the coverage available on the general dwelling forms and allow insureds who qualify to endorse the coverages they require.

Theft Coverage

Theft coverage on personal property can often be added to a dwelling policy by endorsement. Although these endorsements vary, they typically cover loss to personal property caused by theft, including attempted theft (vandalism or malicious mischief resulting from theft or attempted theft is often covered by an unendorsed dwelling policy). Theft coverage may apply to personal property owned or used by the named insured and resident relatives, or only to property owned or used by the named insured. Theft endorsements usually cover theft of property from the insured premises and may have an option for off-premises coverage.

Theft coverage endorsements generally contain special limits of liability that often apply to personal property coverage under homeowners policies. However, business property is usually completely excluded. Other types of property typically excluded by theft endorsements are aircraft; motorized land conveyances; animals; property of tenants, roomers, or boarders not related to the insured; credit cards; property separately described and specifically insured by other insurance; and property while under the following circumstances:

1. At another location owned by, rented to, or occupied by any insured except while an insured is temporarily residing there
2. In the custody of a laundry or tailor except for loss by burglary or robbery
3. In the mail
4. Unlikely to be located on premises that are not owner-occupied

Some of these excluded items are money, coins, and medals; securities, personal records, and stamps; and jewelry and furs.

Liability Coverage

Personal liability insurance can be issued as a supplement to a dwelling policy. The provisions of personal liability coverage are in most respects identical to those contained in homeowners policies. They provide personal liability coverage; medical payments to others coverage; and additional coverages for claim expenses, first aid expenses, and damage to the property of others.

Loss Settlement

Dwelling forms usually provide for loss settlement on the basis of actual cash value (ACV) for personal property, carpeting, domestic appliances, awnings, outdoor antennas and outdoor equipment, and structures that are not buildings. Loss settlement is typically provided on a replacement cost (RC) basis for dwellings and other buildings. However, some dwelling policies cover all property, including buildings, on an ACV basis.

Mobilehome Insurance

Designed commonly for year-round living, mobilehomes are more characteristic of dwellings than of recreational vehicles used as temporary living quarters. The chief similarity between mobilehomes and travel trailers is their mobile nature. However, mobility serves a different purpose for each. Travel trailers are designed to be conveniently moved from place to place and to provide some basic living needs with limited accommodations. In contrast, mobilehomes usually are too large to be moved conveniently. Once they have been towed by specially-built conveyances to the selected site, mobilehomes are commonly placed on foundations—often permanently. Although capable of being moved, mobilehomes, once placed on a site, usually are sold in place rather than moved again.

Mobilehome Exposures

Once placed on permanent foundations, mobilehomes are much like houses from the standpoint of exposures to loss. However, the following exposures are of special importance to mobilehomes:

- *Susceptibility to damage or destruction by windstorm.*   Despite the fact that a mobilehome may be placed on a permanent foundation, the unit generally is lighter than a house. A mobilehome is more likely than a house is to be blown off its foundation or carried away by a severe storm. To reduce the possibility of windstorm damage, mobilehomes usually require **tie downs**, loss control devices that anchor the frame of the unit to its foundation or the ground. Sometimes as added protection, cables are placed over the unit and secured to the anchors. Tie downs are often required as a condition of insurance.

- *Concentration in mobilehome parks.* Mobilehomes in some mobilehome parks are quite close to each other, and this concentration increases the likelihood of fire spread, or windstorm damage when mobilehomes are blown into one another.

- *Portability.* Despite their size, mobilehomes can be moved. Although a commercial mover must usually be engaged, the mobilehome owner is exposed to possible loss by collision or upset of a unit being transported.

Mobilehome Policies

For a number of years, mobilehome insurance was available only from a few insurers that specialized in that market. Markets were limited, because mobilehomes at one time were cheaply constructed and lacked safety standards now required by law. Also, many of the mobilehomes were small and capable of being easily moved, causing excessive exposure to loss during transportation. However, recent growth in mobilehome popularity, sturdier and safer construction, and more favorable loss experience have enticed additional insurers into the market.

Most insurers that provide mobilehome coverage are independent filers. The insurance policies filed by these insurers are generally package policies that include property and liability coverage similar to those provided by homeowners policies. However, some insurers provide coverage for mobilehomes through modified homeowners policies. For example, ISO adds a *mobilehome endorsement* to an HO-2 or an HO-3.

To be eligible under most mobilehome insurance policy programs, requirements, such as the following, must often be met:

1. The mobilehome must be designed for portability and year-round living, but be at least ten feet wide and forty feet long.

2. The mobilehome must be owner-occupied and used exclusively as a private residence on owned or leased land. (If the mobilehome is not owner-occupied, it can be insured under a dwelling policy. Tenants' property may be insured under a renters' policy.)

3. The mobilehome must not be occupied by more than one additional family or more than two roomers or boarders.

Mobilehome policies, whether stand-alone package policies or modified homeowners policies, are designed to meet the unique needs of mobilehome owners. The rest of this section concentrates on the distinctive features of mobilehome insurance policies.

Coverage on the Dwelling

For efficient use of space, mobilehomes often have more built-in furniture than the typical home. Under mobilehome insurance, the definition of "the dwelling" usually includes permanently installed floor coverings, appliances, dressers, and cabinets. Also included as part of the dwelling are structures and utility tanks attached to the mobilehome. Examples of covered structures are a small storage shed, a carport, and a building addition of one or more rooms. Many mobilehome policies also cover, as part of the dwelling coverage, other structures that are not attached to the mobilehome, such as a garage, storage shed, or pool.

Coverage for Personal Property

As mentioned, mobilehomes are manufactured with many built-in accessories and furniture that are covered as part of the dwelling. This reduces the amount of insurance needed to cover personal property, and thus, the limits of coverage available for personal property are typically lower than those available for personal property under homeowners policies. However, special limits similar to those that appear in homeowners policies usually apply to certain types of property, such as money, securities, watercraft, firearms, and jewelry.

Coverage for Loss of Use

Mobilehome policies generally include coverage for additional living expenses and fair rental value. Also covered is "**prohibited use**," under which additional living expenses or fair rental value is covered if a civil authority (such as the fire department) prevents the owner-occupant from using his or her mobilehome because of physical damage to a neighboring mobilehome or premises. This coverage can be especially valuable for mobilehome residents, since mobilehomes in mobilehome parks are often close together and vulnerable to "prohibited use" loss.

Property Removed

Mobilehome policies often include coverage for "**property removed**." Under this provision, the named insured will be reimbursed (possibly to a specific limit, such as $500) for reasonable expenses he or she incurs for removal and return of the mobilehome to prevent its damage when it is endangered by a covered peril. During the move and while the mobilehome is at its temporary location, the mobilehome policy continues fully in force for a limited period of time, generally thirty days. Moving a mobilehome that is on a permanent foundation is not always possible, but if removal is feasible, the insured will be reimbursed for his or her reasonable expenses. Thus if a fire threatens the mobilehome and the insured moves it to another location until the threat of fire is eliminated, the insurer will cover the expenses of the move and will protect the mobilehome against covered perils at its temporary location, subject to the policy's dollar and time limits.

Perils Covered

Mobilehomes may be written on a named perils basis or a special basis. Most mobilehome insurers offer broad named perils coverage with the option of purchasing "all-risks" coverage for the dwelling and possibly for personal property. ISO, for example, allows the mobilehome endorsement to be added to either an HO-2—Broad Form or an HO-3—Special Form.

Actual Cash Value Coverage

Many mobilehomes quickly depreciate to the extent that replacement cost (RC) coverage would be inappropriate. Therefore, many mobilehome policies provide actual cash value (ACV) coverage. Under ACV coverage, the insurer's obligation is limited to the *lowest* of the following amounts:

1. The cost of repairing the damage
2. The cost of replacing the damaged property with similar property, not necessarily from the same manufacturer
3. The ACV of the damage
4. The applicable limit of coverage

Transportation Coverage

When necessary, collision coverage is available to cover the mobilehome and its contents against damage by collision or upset while being transported from one location to another. An endorsement may be purchased that provides such coverage for a specific time period, such as thirty days. The endorsement usually extends coverage, during the move, on the dwelling and other structures to apply anywhere in the continental United States or Canada.

Lienholder's Single Interest Coverage

Coverage may be, and often is required by the lienholder to be, included under the mobilehome policy to protect a lienholder's interest in a mobilehome and its equipment against an exposure unique to this kind of movable property— physical movement of the property beyond the lienholder's reach.

The need for this coverage can be illustrated by an example. Moe and Lilly purchase a mobilehome with a small down payment. The seller loans Moe and Lilly the remainder of the purchase price and is therefore added to the mobilehome policy as a loss payee (in other words, in the event of a covered loss the seller will be paid the amount of his or her interest in the mobilehome), but the lienholder's interest is not covered by the policy. Moe is subsequently laid off from his job. Being heavily in debt and unable to meet their financial obligations, Moe and Lilly decide to move their mobilehome out of state and not to make any further payments on it. If they do this, the seller would have no protection for loss of the unpaid balance due on that property, because the only protection provided to the loss payee is for property that is damaged or destroyed by an otherwise covered peril.

When the **lienholder's single interest coverage** is provided by the policy, the vendor, loss payee, or lienholder also receives coverage for its interest in the property against loss by such perils as collision, conversion, embezzlement, and secretion. Thus, if the lienholder's single interest coverage had been covered under Moe and Lilly's mobilehome policy, the seller would have been reimbursed by the insurer for the amount owed by Moe and Lilly.

Additional Policies for Vehicular Loss Exposures

Although the personal auto policies provide fairly comprehensive coverage for personal auto loss exposures—and homeowners policies allow some coverage for land motor vehicles and watercraft—a large segment of vehicular exposures is still not covered by either of these policy programs.

Recreational Vehicles

Although the loss exposures resulting from the ownership, maintenance, or use of recreational vehicles are similar to those arising from the operation or ownership of automobiles, enough difference exists between these exposures that another form of insurance is often necessary to adequately cover the exposures. This section first discusses the different types of motorized land vehicles and then describes the differences in their loss exposures from those of a personal auto and the types of insurance that can be purchased to cover the unique exposures.

Vehicle Types

A wide variety of recreational vehicles exist. The following paragraphs briefly describe some of the more popular types of motorized land vehicles that generally do not qualify for personal auto insurance.

Motorcycles and Other Two-Wheeled Vehicles

Motorcycles, commonly designed for use on public roads and subject to motor vehicle registration, typically are two-wheeled vehicles, although a sidecar with an additional wheel for support can be attached. These vehicles, used for business and pleasure, are gasoline powered, capable of fast acceleration and high speeds, and undoubtedly the highest priced among all two-wheeled motor vehicles available.

Minibikes are miniature motorcycles with low speed potential. Built to carry only one person, these recreational vehicles are commonly operated by children and teenagers.

Trail bikes are also motorized, although they are somewhat larger and more powerful than minibikes. Although intended for special trails, they are versatile enough to be used in rugged terrain.

Mopeds are motorized bicycles that require pedaling to get them started. In some states, mopeds are considered to be motorcycles and are therefore subject to motor vehicle registration.

Motor Homes and Recreational Trailers

Motor homes are driveable units in which living quarters, with all the conveniences of home, form an integral part of the vehicle. They probably are the most expensive class of any motorized land recreational vehicle to buy and the most expensive to operate. Within this class, though not as large and as homelike as the usual motor home, are truck-mounted campers. One advantage of a truck-mounted camper is that the camper unit can be attached to and removed from the truck without much difficulty. The motor home and truck-mounted unit are designed for use on public roads.

The principal characteristic of **recreational trailers** is that, to be mobile, they must be towed by private passenger autos or trucks. Within this class are travel trailers, which can be as long as thirty feet and as expensive as smaller motor homes. Camping trailers are also in this class. These range from fully enclosed units with some living facilities to compact fold-out tent trailers with limited facilities.

Other Recreational Vehicles With More Than Two Wheels

All-terrain vehicles (ATVs), equipped with four or six oversized or balloon tires, are versatile vehicles designed for use on rugged terrain and in shallow water, although they can be operated on sand and snow as well. Depending on the user's needs, ATVs can be equipped with crawler treads rather than wheels.

Dune buggies are similar in versatility to ATVs, but they are usually private passenger autos that have been modified for use on sand or rough terrain.

Go-carts or midget autos are usually equipped with small gasoline-powered engines similar to those in power mowers, and are usually large enough to carry only the operator. Though generally designed for low-speed racing, they can be "souped up" to run at high speeds.

Golf carts may have three or four wheels, although commonly they have three wheels. These are low-speed vehicles, usually electrically powered and de-signed to carry two passengers and their equipment. Though golf carts are designed for use principally off public roads, their incidental use on public roads is sometimes necessary. Golf carts are principally designed for use on a golf course, but they are increasingly being used for transportation in retire-ment communities, airports, hotels, and other public facilities.

Snowmobiles

Snowmobiles are popular in all areas of the United States offering a reasonable annual snowfall. These vehicles usually have a single wide track or tread in the back connected to a gasoline engine. The steering mechanism is attached to two flexible skis supporting the front of the vehicle. Most snowmobiles are designed to carry one or two people and may be able to tow a sled.

Difference From Auto Loss Exposures

Many of the loss exposures of recreational vehicles are similar to those of autos. Thus, a person is exposed to loss by reason of ownership, maintenance, operation, or use of such vehicles. Loss exposures include the possibility of bodily injury to the owner or operator, property damage to the vehicle, and liability for injury to another person or damage to another's property. The differences in the loss exposures of recreational vehicles and private passenger autos exist primarily in the potential severity of bodily injury and the fre-quency of property damage and bodily injury.

Recreational vehicle bodily injury exposures are often more severe than auto bodily injury exposures for at least three reasons:

1. *Use of a recreational vehicle as a residence or premises as well as a means of transportation*—such as with a motor home. Although recreational vehicle manufacturers generally adhere to various safety codes, the light construc-tion of some camping vehicles increases the risk that a traffic accident will result in injury. In addition, the use of propane and campfires for cooking leads to the possibility of serious injury in a vehicle fire.

2. *Less protection for occupants.* Many of the safety regulations that apply to private passenger autos do not affect motor homes and other types of recreational vehicles. In addition to the lighter construction of campers,

some recreational vehicles—such as motorcycles and dune buggies—simply do not shield the occupants from danger as does an enclosed auto.

3. *Use of vehicle for off-road, recreational purposes.* Vehicles designed for off-road use are often carelessly used. They are pressed to the limit and operated at dangerous speed across unfamiliar ground. Careless use tends to increase the possibility of bodily injury to the occupants.

Recreational vehicles are also exposed to a wider variety of physical damage loss exposures than are most private passenger autos. Collision is a common form of loss for both autos and recreational vehicles, but collision damage to recreational vehicles tends to be more frequent, per miles driven, than for personal autos. Trailers, for example, can jackknife and collide with the vehicles that tow them. Faulty hitches or hitches that become unsecured may cause runaway trailers that can collide with other vehicles and objects. Camping vehicles may have a greater exposure to flood or windstorm damage because campsites are often located in flood plains or in wooded areas. In addition, the careless use of recreational vehicles can increase the possibility of property damage, to both the vehicle and the property of others.

Insurance for Recreational Vehicles

Although recreational vehicles may provide hours of enjoyment, they create loss exposures that are generally not covered by homeowners policies or personal auto policies, because those exposures are different from the ones associated with home ownership and personal autos. The homeowners liability coverage can be broadened to include limited liability coverage for certain recreational vehicles. Several ISO PAP endorsements are also available to cover these exposures. However, a substantial portion of the recreational vehicle insurance market is handled by insurers that specialize in that line. These insurers use independently filed forms that differ considerably from the PAP endorsements. The following discussion considers both the ISO endorsements and independently filed forms.

ISO Endorsements to Homeowners Policies

In some instances, an insured may wish to add coverage for miscellaneous type vehicles under a homeowners policy. Only liability coverage for snowmobiles and certain incidental vehicles can be broadened under homeowners policies. Other recreational vehicles, such as mopeds, trail bikes, and dune buggies, which may be used away from any insured location, must be covered under an endorsement to the PAP or with an independently filed form.

Liability coverage for the use of any snowmobile *on an insured location* is automatically covered under homeowners policies. However, to obtain personal liability and medical payments to others coverage for snowmobiles *owned by an insured and used away from an insured location*, it is necessary to attach a **snowmobile endorsement** (HO). This endorsement extends the definition of "insured" to include any person or organization legally responsible for the use of a snowmobile owned by an insured, as well as any person or organization using or having custody or possession of the vehicle with the insured's permission. Vicarious parental responsibility (the responsibility of parents for their children's actions) is specifically covered. Specifically excluded are certain exposures requiring special coverage, such as (1) snowmobiles subject to motor vehicle registration and (2) use of snowmobiles for prearranged racing contests or for business purposes.

An **incidental motorized land conveyances endorsement** can be used to extend the policy's liability and medical payments coverages to certain vehicles not covered by Section II of ISO homeowners policies. The endorsement does not apply to motorized bicycles, mopeds, or motorized golf carts or to any conveyance (1) capable of traveling more than fifteen miles per hour, (2) subject to motor vehicle registration, (3) while being used to carry persons for a charge, (4) while being used for business purposes, (5) while rented to others, or (6) while being operated in racing. Many vehicles eligible for this endorsement qualify for coverage under the basic Section II coverage when they are (1) not owned by an insured or (2) not on an insured location. Consequently, the principal application of the endorsement is to cover eligible vehicles while they are away from an insured location.

ISO Endorsements to the PAP

When an individual or family otherwise qualifies, insurance on recreational vehicles can be purchased using endorsements to the PAP—the miscellaneous type vehicle endorsement, the miscellaneous type vehicle (motor homes) endorsement, and the snowmobile endorsement.

Miscellaneous Type Vehicle Endorsement   This endorsement amends the PAP with provisions appropriate for covering a vehicle that meets the definition of **miscellaneous type vehicle**—including motor homes, motorcycles or similar vehicles, ATVs, dune buggies, and golf carts—as defined by the endorsement. The definition also includes private passenger autos owned jointly by two or more relatives other than husband and wife or by two or more individuals residing together. The "miscellaneous type vehicle" and the coverages for which it is insured must be named in the endorsement schedule depicted in Exhibit 6-1. The coverages available under the endorsement are liability, medical payments, uninsured motorists, and physical damage. The insured represented in Exhibit 6-1 has chosen $100,000 worth of liability

Exhibit 6-1

Miscellaneous Type Vehicle Endorsement

SCHEDULE			
Description and Type of Vehicle	Passenger Hazard Excluded		
1. 1982 Harley Davidson Motorcycle	Yes ☒		No ☐
2.	Yes ☐		No ☐
3.	Yes ☐		No ☐

Coverage is provided where a premium and a limit of liability is shown for the coverage.				
			Premium	
Coverages	Limit of Liability	Veh. 1	Veh. 2	Veh. 3
Liability	$100,000 Each Accident	$285		
	$ Each Accident		$	
	$ Each Accident			$
Medical Payments	$ 5,000 Each Person	$ 34		
	$ Each Person		$	
	$ Each Person			$
Uninsured Motorists	$100,000 Each Accident	$150		
	$ Each Accident		$	
	$ Each Accident			$
Collision	$ Less $ Ded.	$		
	$ Less $ Ded.		$	
	$ Less $ Ded.			$
Other Than Collision	$ Less $250 Ded.	$ 50		
	$ Less $ Ded.		$	
	$ Less $ Ded.			$
	Total Premium	$519		

coverage, $5,000 worth of medical payments coverage, $100,000 worth of uninsured motorists coverage, and OTC coverage with a $250 deductible.

The endorsement amends the regular PAP definition of "your covered auto" to include only the following:

- Any "miscellaneous type vehicle" scheduled in the endorsement schedule or policy declarations.

- Any newly acquired private passenger auto, pickup, van, or "miscellaneous type vehicle" subject to reporting requirements like those in the unendorsed PAP. To illustrate, suppose Emily owns an ATV and insures it with a miscellaneous type vehicle endorsement to her PAP. She then buys—within the policy period—a new motor home as an additional vehicle. She must report this acquisition to the insurer within thirty days of the purchase for it to be covered by the existing endorsement. If she had acquired a new ATV as a replacement for her old ATV, she would only have had to notify the insurer within thirty days if she wanted to cover it for physical damage.

- Any owned or nonowned trailer as defined in the PAP.

- Any "miscellaneous type vehicle" or auto not owned by the named insured while used as a temporary substitute for any other covered auto or vehicle that is out of normal use because of its breakdown, repair, servicing, loss, or destruction.

The miscellaneous type vehicle endorsement amends Part A—Liability Coverage provisions of the PAP in three ways:

1. It replaces the definition of "insured" with a narrower definition. Insureds under the endorsement for purposes of liability coverage are (a) the named insured and family members for the ownership, maintenance, or use of a covered vehicle, (b) any other person using a covered vehicle, and (c) any person or organization legally responsible for the acts or omissions of the persons named in (a) or (b) for the use of a covered vehicle. Thus, the endorsement does not cover anyone for the use of a nonowned vehicle unless it qualifies as a covered vehicle—that is, a nonowned trailer or a temporary substitute.

2. It modifies the liability exclusion relating to vehicles with fewer than four wheels. The effect is that a vehicle with fewer than four wheels is insured for liability coverage under the endorsement.

3. It adds a **passenger hazard exclusion** that can be activated if the appropriate entry is made in the endorsement schedule or policy declarations. When the exclusion is activated, no liability coverage exists to cover the bodily injury sustained by anyone occupying the described vehicle.

The endorsement also amends the medical payments coverage by allowing coverage for bodily injury resulting from the use of a vehicle with fewer than four wheels if it is covered for medical payments in the endorsement.

With respect to physical damage coverage, the endorsement modifies the usual PAP limit of liability provision. The insurer will pay the actual cash value, the repair or replacement cost, or the stated amount shown in the schedule or declarations—whichever is *least.*

Miscellaneous Type Vehicle (Motor Homes) Amendment When a motor home is insured, both the miscellaneous type vehicle (motor home) amendment and the miscellaneous type vehicle endorsement are used. The **motor home amendment** adds certain exclusions that apply while an insured motor home is rented to a person or organization other than the named insured. Many motor home owners lend or rent their vehicles to others, and, generally speaking, this added exposure increases the probability of loss.

The amendment contains two general exclusions:

1. When the motor home is leased or rented to or used by a person other than the named insured, the policy will not provide any coverage except for liability coverage to the financial responsibility or compulsory limits that apply in the state where the motor home is principally garaged. However, additional liability coverage, medical payments coverage, and physical damage coverage may be provided if (a) the motor home is named in the amendment's schedule (the schedule is similar to that appearing in Exhibit 6-1 for the miscellaneous type vehicle endorsement), (b) the desired coverages are selected, and (c) an additional premium is paid.
2. Regardless of whether the motor home is shown in the amendment's schedule, coverage is eliminated for "fraudulent acquisition" (theft) of a motor home by the party that is renting or using the motor home or has it in his or her care.

Snowmobile Endorsement The **snowmobile endorsement** (PAP) is designed for those land motor vehicles used mainly off public roads on ice or snow for pleasure purposes—other than practicing for or participating in any race or other speed contest—including any trailer designed for being towed by the snowmobile. Any trailer used to transport the snowmobile is not covered by the endorsement, because the PAP covers such units. As with the previous two PAP endorsements, the snowmobile must be listed in an endorsement schedule with the desired coverages. The PAP endorsement allows for broader coverage than the HO endorsement.

The named insured and resident family members are covered while using *any* snowmobile. Other persons are covered only while using the snowmobile owned by the named insured or resident family members, or its temporary substitute. Coverage for others does not apply if the snowmobile is rented or leased to the named insured.

Liability, medical payments, uninsured motorists, and physical damage coverages can be purchased. A passenger hazards exclusion—which excludes liability coverage with respect to a person injured while occupying or being towed by the snowmobile—is generally optional but may be required by some insurance companies. As might be expected, premiums are reduced when the passenger hazard is excluded.

The snowmobile endorsement contains several standard exclusions:

- Liability coverage is not provided for *any* person maintaining or using a snowmobile in *any* business.

- Medical payments coverage is not provided for any person occupying a snowmobile while it is being used in the business *of any insured.*

- Medical payments coverage also does not apply to a person occupying any snowmobile while it is rented or leased to *any party other than the named insured.*

The snowmobile endorsement also modifies the physical damage coverage limit of liability provision. As in the miscellaneous type vehicle endorsement, the insurer will not pay more than the actual cash value, the repair or replacement cost, or the stated amount shown in the schedule or declarations—whichever is *least*.

Independently Filed Recreational Vehicle Policies

While ISO provides homeowners and PAP endorsements for covering recreational vehicles, many insurers that specialize in recreational vehicle insurance use independently filed forms that differ considerably from the homeowners or PAP (plus endorsements) approach described above. Independently filed forms may be specifically designed for one particular class of recreational vehicles—such as snowmobiles—or they may be designed to insure a wider range of vehicles—such as motor homes, camping and travel trailers, and camper bodies. In many cases, the coverage may be broader than that provided by the ISO endorsements.

Non-ISO coverage features that may be found in some independently filed recreational vehicle policies include the following:

- A limited amount of coverage for personal property and household furnishings used with a motor home or camper trailer

- So-called **vacation expense coverage**, which helps to defray part of the additional costs incurred by an insured whose vehicle or trailer becomes uninhabitable because of damage or destruction while on vacation away from home—such as the cost of a motel room or meals

- Coverage for snowmobiles while used in informal races, subject to an increased physical damage deductible

Another non-ISO coverage feature is a **lay-up provision**. Because a number of recreational vehicles—especially snowmobiles—are used only in certain seasons, insurance on them, with the exception of OTC coverage, is not required when the vehicles are actually in storage, so that recreational vehicle owners who have a lay-up provision pay a premium for only a portion of the year. For example, if a snowmobile policy containing a lay-up provision is written for a one-year period, the insured is asked to specify a period, typically six months, during which the snowmobile is likely not to be used. All coverages, except comprehensive physical damage, are then automatically suspended for that period. If weather conditions warrant use of the snowmobile, coverage is provided for such use even during the suspension period, presumably for an additional cost. In practice, an insurer's rates for snowmobiles or other recreational vehicles may consider seasonal limitation even in the absence of a lay-up provision.

Insurance for Watercraft

Watercraft come in many shapes, sizes, and values—including dinghies, rafts, rowboats, kayaks, canoes, jet skis, outboard and inboard motorboats, speedboats, houseboats, sailboats, and yachts. Watercraft loss exposures are similar to loss exposures for recreational vehicles for two reasons:

1. *They are used for recreational purposes.* Like recreational vehicles, personal watercraft are generally used for pleasure. They are a means for relaxation. Therefore, operators may be less concerned with being careful than with enjoying themselves. Thus, they might speed through open water and waterways, ignore nearby boats and swimmers, and drink alcohol while operating watercraft. In 1992, 60.7 percent of all boating accidents occurred on Saturdays or Sundays, and 71.5 percent occurred in the months of May, June, July, or August.[1]

2. *Few restrictions apply to their operation.* Operators of watercraft are generally not licensed and may have little experience. They do not have to prove that they know either the "rules of the water" or how to operate a watercraft safely. In 1992, 15.5 percent of watercraft accidents involved operators with less than twenty hours of experience, and 30.7 percent of the accidents involved operators with one hundred hours or less of experience.[2] Drunken operation of watercraft is not as well-policed as drunken driving of autos. Also in 1992, 20.3 percent of all boating deaths involved alcohol.[3] However, the Coast Guard is increasing its efforts to educate watercraft operators and increase waterway safety, and in 1992, 347,278 persons enrolled in public safe boating courses offered by the Coast Guard Auxiliary, a civilian volunteer organization that promotes

safety in recreational boating in the United States. The Auxiliary also conducted 284,142 Courtesy Marine Examinations. In these examinations, at the request of recreational boat owners or operators, the boat's safety-related equipment is checked for compliance with safety regulations.[4]

Watercraft losses can be caused by perils occurring on land as well as by "perils of the seas." Land perils—which can affect watercraft while either on land or in the water—include fire, lightning, windstorm or hail, explosion, earthquake, vandalism or malicious mischief, and theft. In contrast, **perils of the seas** are generally defined as fortuitous causes of loss peculiar to the sea or other bodies of water. These causes of loss include abnormally high winds and rough seas, collision with other vessels or objects, stranding, capsizing, and errors in navigation. Exhibit 6-2 identifies several causes of loss as well as the number of accidents, the number of fatalities and injuries, and the dollar amount of property damage resulting from each cause in 1992.

Exhibit 6-2
1992 Boating Accident Statistics

TYPE OF ACCIDENT	TOTAL	FATALITIES	INJURIES	PROPERTY DAMAGE
Grounding	341	16	203	$ 3,140,600
Capsizing	458	248	222	2,912,300
Swamping/Flooding	323	82	93	1,120,200
Sinking	202	30	25	1,353,900
Fire or Explosion of Fuel	194	1	213	3,126,100
Other Fire or Explosion	101	3	22	11,043,600
Collision with Another Vessel	2,203	79	1,369	5,778,600
Collision with Fixed Object	839	74	503	5,389,300
Collision with Floating Object	211	5	83	633,200
Falls Overboard	431	212	257	84,200
Falls Within Boat	167	3	172	43,200
Struck by Boat or Propeller*	116	8	111	2,200
Fallen Skier	299	9	293	3,800
Other Casualty; Unknown	163	46	17	135,500

* Of the 116 accidents involving "Struck by Boat or Propeller," 39 involved a boat strike and 62 involved a propeller strike. The remaining 15 accidents did not provide sufficient information to determine whether the victim was struck by the boat or the propeller.

Boating Statistics 1992 (Washington, DC: U.S. Department of Transportation, June 1993, p. 8).

The owners and operators of watercraft may experience physical damage loss to their watercraft or medical expenses associated with injury to themselves while using their watercraft. Physical damage losses may be minor, such as a broken oar, or may involve thousands of dollars, such as a thirty-seven foot sailboat destroyed in a hurricane. Medical expenses may also be minor, such as for removing a fish hook from the operator's foot, or may involve long periods of rehabilitation and physical therapy.

The ownership and use of watercraft create both bodily injury and property damage liability exposures. Bodily injury liability may involve passengers in the owned watercraft, occupants of other watercraft or objects (such as other boaters standing on piers and people dining in floating restaurants), or people in the water (such as swimmers, scuba divers, or water skiers). Property damage liability may result from collision with other watercraft or objects (such as docks, bridges, and buoys). A boat owner may also be held liable for damage caused to another watercraft that is pushed into a pier or another boat by the wake of his or her boat.

Boat owners may also be exposed to liability for wreck removal. If a watercraft is damaged to the point at which it cannot be operated or sinks, the owner is usually required to remove the wreck from the waterway. This exposure is distinct from the physical damage exposure; apart from any loss in value of the watercraft, the owner is legally responsible for removing the wreck.

The ownership and operation of watercraft are subject to **admiralty (or maritime) law** and fall under federal jurisdiction, with few exceptions. Admiralty law does not apply in areas such as contracts for the sale or manufacture of watercraft or contracts for service to watercraft that are laid up. Losses under these contracts are subject to the law in the state or jurisdiction where the loss occurs. In most other contractual and civil liability suits involving watercraft, admiralty law applies in the federal courts. This distinction is important because the remedies available to injured parties under admiralty law may differ from those available under state law.

For example, under admiralty law, a court may grant a **maritime lien** to an unpaid supplier of services or goods, or to an unpaid member of the crew. The lien gives the injured party a property interest in the watercraft to the amount of liability, which is often not yet determined. Thus, the owner of the watercraft may not dispose of it until the suit is settled and the required damages are paid. In addition, admiralty remedy is usually monetary. The court does not have the power to order specific performance or an injunction.

Inadequacies of Watercraft Coverage Under Homeowners Policies

The watercraft coverage provided by homeowners policies is discussed in

Chapters 2 and 3. In many cases, the coverage provided is inadequate for the following reasons:

- Property coverage for watercraft is subject to the following deficiencies:
  - The causes of loss covered under homeowners policies do not include most "perils of the seas."
  - A sublimit of $1,000 applies to watercraft covered under Section I.
  - Damage to watercraft caused by windstorm or hail is not covered if the property is not in a fully enclosed building at the time of loss.
  - Theft of watercraft is not covered when the property is off the residence premises at the time of the theft.
- Bodily injury or property damage liability resulting from the following watercraft is not covered:
  - Inboard motor boats owned by an insured
  - Inboard motor boats with more than fifty horsepower, rented to an insured
  - Outboard motorboats with more than twenty-five horsepower, whose motors are owned by an insured
  - Sailboats twenty-six feet or longer, owned by or rented to an insured

Outboard Motorboat Floater

When owners of outboard motorboats find that personal liability coverage of homeowners policies fits their needs but a broader form of physical damage insurance is required, an **outboard motorboat floater endorsement** can be used to complement coverage.

Most outboard motorboat coverage is on an "all-risks" basis for whatever property the insured may desire to insure—boat and attached motor, separate motors, boat equipment, or boat trailer. The exclusions vary by endorsement. Furthermore, except for equipment—such as covers, oars, life preservers, and fire extinguishers—the boats, motors, and trailers have to be scheduled. Coverage is usually on an ACV basis, although replacement cost coverage is available from a number of insurers.

Watercraft Endorsement

In some cases, the insured may find that appropriate coverage requires adding the **watercraft endorsement** to the homeowners policy. The watercraft endorsement, for an additional premium, expands coverage for personal liability and medical payments to others for bodily injury and property damage that results from three types of situations:

1. The ownership, maintenance, or use—including the loading and unloading—of watercraft

2. The entrustment of watercraft to any persons by an insured

3. Vicarious liability for the actions of a child or ward below the age of majority for the use of watercraft

In each case, the watercraft involved must be described in the endorsement. Watercraft covered by the endorsement may exceed the size and horsepower limitations found in the homeowners policy.

The endorsement coverage is subject to three exclusions:

1. No coverage is available for bodily injury to an employee of any insured whose principal duties involve the maintenance or use of watercraft, such as a captain or a cabin steward

2. Coverage does not apply to bodily injury or property damage occurring while the watercraft is rented to others or being used to carry others for a fee

3. With the exception of sailboats and log cruises, coverage does not apply to the watercraft while used to practice for or compete in an organized race or other speed contest

Policies for Personal Watercraft

As discussed earlier, many individuals and families find the coverage provided by homeowners policies, with or without the watercraft endorsement, inadequate. Free-standing package policies are available that address the various property and liability loss exposures involved with owning and operating watercraft. Although the policies tend to vary from insurer to insurer, the coverages available have common characteristics.

These package policies are frequently referred to as **boatowners policies** and **yacht policies**. Boatowner policies are typically used to cover smaller watercraft, and yacht policies are generally provided to cover larger watercraft. The qualifications for "small" versus "large" boats are determined by the insurer. "Small" boats are often underwritten in the personal lines division, whereas "large" boats (or yachts) are frequently handled by the insurer's ocean marine department. Because the main difference between boatowner policies and yacht policies is in eligibility requirements rather than in coverage, these policies will be discussed simultaneously in the section that follows.

The coverages usually provided by boatowners and yacht policies are physical damage and liability. Medical payments, uninsured boat, and employers liability insurance may also be available. Losses are usually covered for ACV with a deductible, although RC coverage may be endorsed to the policy.

Physical damage insurance generally covers the hull, motors, trailers, and equipment and accessories used to operate or maintain watercraft. Coverage is typically written on an "all-risks" basis, although named perils coverage may be used for underwriting reasons. The usual exclusions for physical damage insurance are war, nuclear hazard, wear and tear, race or speed contest, and mechanical or electrical breakdown. Also excluded are loss resulting from the repair or service of the property (except ensuing fire or explosion), business use, and loss resulting from the dishonesty of persons to whom the property is entrusted (except carriers for hire).

Liability coverage gives the insured protection against liability as the result of bodily injury sustained by others, including persons on other watercraft involved in a collision with the insured's vessel, and property damage liability for incidents when the insured's watercraft damages other watercraft, wharves, docks, and other property. Defense costs are typically also covered. The usual exclusions of liability coverage are contractual liability, employers liability and workers compensation, race or speed contest, war and nuclear hazard, business use, and intentional acts of an insured.

Liability coverage generally includes a provision that deals with the removal or destruction of a wrecked or sunken watercraft. If such actions are required by law or governmental authority, the insurer will pay the reasonable costs of removing or destroying the watercraft.

Medical payments coverage is similar to that provided by both the homeowners policies and the PAP. It is usually limited to $1,000 per person and may be increased for an additional premium. The insured does not have to be at fault for his or her coverage to pay for bodily injury. The coverage may apply to injured persons on board the insured boat as well as to those entering or leaving the insured boat and may also be extended to cover those people on other boats, in the water, or on land who are injured in an accident involving the insured boat. However, injury to employees of the insured is generally not covered.

Uninsured boat coverage is modeled after the uninsured motorists coverage provided by auto insurance policies. It pays for the bodily injury damages to an insured that the insured is legally entitled to receive from another boat owner or operator who does not have watercraft liability insurance or whose insurer is insolvent. The coverage also applies to bodily injury arising from a hit-and-run boating accident.

Although it is unlikely that an owner or operator of a personal pleasure boat will have any employers liability exposures with respect to the pleasure boat, coverage is available to the boatowners or yacht policy if needed. For example, a large yacht owner may have a paid captain and a cabin crew. Coverage for liability assessed under the *Jones Act* (a maritime law that gives crew members of a vessel the right to seek recourse from their employer in the event that they are injured while in service of the vessel) or under general maritime law may be endorsed to the yacht policy.

Boatowners and yacht policies may also contain a provision that covers the insured's liability assessed under the Longshore and Harbor Workers' Compensation Act, which governs the workers compensation for certain maritime employments. Because this act specifically excludes crew members, the chances of a pleasure boat owner's requiring such coverage are minimal.

Boatowners and yacht policies are subject to warranties or promises relating to certain conditions concerning use. Noncompliance with these warranties may result in higher premiums or in no coverage, depending on the nature of the warranties. The following warranties are often found in boatowners and yacht policies:

- *Pleasure Use.* The insured must promise that the watercraft will be used only for pleasure purposes. The insurer requires this warranty to avoid covering the more hazardous exposures of commercial use.

- *Lay-Up.* Under a **lay-up warranty**, the insured declares the period when the watercraft will not be in use, such as during the winter months. If an insured desires to use the watercraft within that period, permission must be obtained from the insurer in order for coverage to be applicable.

- *Navigational.* **Navigational warranties** limit the use of the vessel to a described geographical area. For example, a small boat might be limited to a particular lake or river. In some cases (particularly under yacht policies), the watercraft may be operated outside the boundaries agreed to in the policy if the insurer is notified and an additional premium is paid.

Some policies may also contain warranties to the effect that the watercraft will not be used for water-skiing; or, if used for that sport, the watercraft must have at least two occupants—one to operate the boat and the other to observe the skier.

Personal Umbrella Liability Insurance

"Personal excess liability," "personal umbrella," and "personal catastrophe liability" are among the many terms used to describe a type of insurance that provides individuals and families with broad liability protection over and above a basic liability insurance program. This protection applies to a wide range of liability loss exposures confronting individuals—such as premises hazards, incidental business pursuits, contractual exposures, and personal activities. It also may include coverage for exposures arising out of the ownership and use of autos, recreational vehicles, and watercraft. Personal umbrella policies serve two major purposes:

1. They provide excess liability limits over underlying liability coverage.
2. They cover some of the liability exposures excluded by underlying liability policies.

Standard forms and rates do not exist for personal umbrella insurance. Prospective purchasers, therefore, should compare the premium costs against the coverages these policies provide. Important considerations include not only what may specifically be covered, but also what may specifically be excluded from coverage, as well as what coverages and limits may be required on underlying policies. If the wording of a personal umbrella policy provision varies from that of underlying coverage, gaps can exist in the overall protection.

Traditionally, the term "personal excess liability" referred to policies that only provided excess limits over underlying liability coverages. Although this may still be true for some such policies, the term may also denote a personal umbrella policy that provides excess as well as additional coverage. The insured must be especially careful to consider the coverage provided by a personal excess liability policy.

General Application of Personal Umbrella Liability Insurance

Personal umbrella liability insurance provides catastrophe coverage. It is not a substitute for primary insurance, nor does it cover all liability losses. It is designed, first, to be used to insure losses that exceed primary or underlying insurance limits, such as the liability coverages on the homeowners policies or the PAP. Second, it covers the low probability losses not usually covered by primary insurance. For example, slander is not covered by the Coverage E—Liability section of homeowners policies, because slander is not a common loss exposure for most individuals. However, personal umbrellas often cover liability arising from slander.

Most insurers require underlying primary personal liability insurance (Section II of a homeowners policy or a separate personal liability policy) of at least

$100,000. Auto liability insurance requirements of at least $300,000 single limit (or $250/500/50 split limits) also are common. When a known exposure exists, insurers also require underlying employers liability insurance of $100,000 or more and watercraft liability insurance of at least $100,000. For example, if Gigi has her own chef and a live-in personal attendant, her insurer would probably require Gigi to carry an employers liability policy with a limit of at least $100,000 before the insurer would allow Gigi to purchase an umbrella.

The limits of liability under personal umbrellas commonly range from $1 million to $5 million. In addition, personal umbrellas require insureds to retain part of the losses covered by the umbrella but not by the underlying coverages. These **self-insured retentions** (SIRs) vary by policy from $250 to $10,000.

It is important to understand how the policy limits and SIRs are applied in relation to (1) losses covered by underlying liability policies, (2) losses excluded by underlying policies, and (3) losses excluded by both the umbrella and underlying policies. The following examples involve the liability insurance package detailed in Exhibit 6-3.

When an underlying liability policy covers a loss exposure that is also covered by a personal umbrella policy, the umbrella policy, subject to its limits, ordinarily pays for the amount of the covered loss that exceeds the limits of the underlying liability coverage. For example, Connor has $100,000 in personal liability coverage under his HO-3 policy and a $1 million limit on a personal umbrella. He is legally liable for an accidental fire that caused $110,000 in damages to his neighbor's home. Connor's HO-3 personal liability insurance would pay $100,000 and the umbrella policy would cover the remaining $10,000. The SIR would *not* be deducted from the remaining $10,000.

If a loss is covered by the personal umbrella policy but is not covered by an underlying liability policy, the umbrella insurer would pay only for the amount of the loss, subject to its limit of liability, that exceeds the SIR. The SIR for Connor's umbrella policy is $250. In addition to Connor's liability for property damage to his neighbor's home, he is also found liable for slandering his neighbor in an argument following the fire. His homeowners policy does not cover slander, but his umbrella policy does. His umbrella insurer will pay the $50,000 in damages less the $250 SIR, or $49,750.

When a personal umbrella policy contains an exclusion that is also found in the underlying insurance, the insured obviously has no applicable insurance protection under either policy. So, if the fire officials determine that Connor intended to set fire to his neighbor's house, neither the homeowners policy nor

Exhibit 6-3
Connor's Personal Liability Coverages

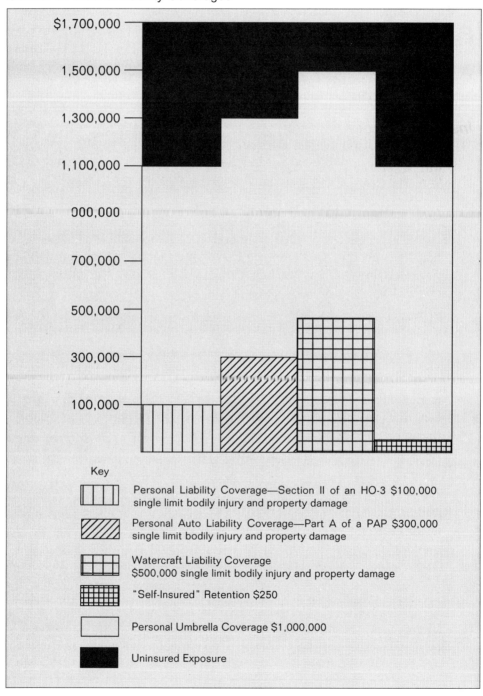

Key

Personal Liability Coverage—Section II of an HO-3 $100,000 single limit bodily injury and property damage

Personal Auto Liability Coverage—Part A of a PAP $300,000 single limit bodily injury and property damage

Watercraft Liability Coverage $500,000 single limit bodily injury and property damage

"Self-Insured" Retention $250

Personal Umbrella Coverage $1,000,000

Uninsured Exposure

the personal umbrella will pay for the damages resulting from Connor's intentional act.

Personal Umbrella Policy Provisions

Much diversity exists among personal umbrella liability policies. The comments that follow describe some of the more common approaches to insuring clauses, key provisions and definitions, and exclusions.

Insuring Clauses

The insuring clauses of many personal umbrella policies state that the insurer will pay on behalf of the insured the *ultimate net loss* in excess of the *retained limit*. The definitions of these two terms are of obvious importance.

Ultimate Net Loss

Ultimate net loss is defined as the amount actually paid or payable for the settlement of a claim for which the insured is liable after deductions are made for all recoveries and salvage. The ultimate net loss may or may not include defense costs.

When the term is defined to include defense costs within the limit of liability, it usually does not include costs (1) covered by underlying insurance, (2) incurred in defending a claim not covered by underlying insurance, or (3) incurred by the umbrella insurer as any of the following: costs taxed against the insured, interest accruing on any judgment, premiums on appeal or release of attachment bonds, and reasonable expenses incurred by the insured at the insurance company's request in the defense of any suit. Thus, only the costs incurred by the umbrella insurer to defend its insured above the defense cost obligations of the underlying insurer remain in the ultimate net loss amount.

Although oversimplified, the following example illustrates this basic point. Assume that an insured has a personal umbrella policy with a limit of $1 million and a personal liability policy with a $500,000 limit. A claim is made against the insured for $1.5 million in damages, which the court ultimately awards. The insurer of the underlying policy pays $500,000 as its share of the damages assessed against the insured and assumes its costs of defense. In defending the insured for the remaining amount, the umbrella insurer incurs $10,000 in defense costs. The ultimate net loss in this case, therefore, is $1,010,000, as calculated in Exhibit 6-4. In this case, the umbrella insurer pays $1 million (its limit of liability), and the insured is responsible for the remaining $10,000.

When ultimate net loss is defined to exclude defense costs from the limit of liability, the insured normally receives protection for its defense costs in addition to the applicable limit of the umbrella liability policy. If the insured in the preceding example had a personal umbrella policy that covered defense costs in addition to the applicable limit of liability, the umbrella insurer would have paid the $1 million judgment from the policy limit, plus the $10,000 in defense costs as an additional amount, for a total of $1,010,000.

Exhibit 6-4
Ultimate Net Loss Calculation

Judgment awarded	$1,500,000
Personal liability policy limit	500,000
Remaining for umbrella coverage	1,000,000
Defense costs incurred by umbrella insurer	10,000
Ultimate Net Loss	1,010,000
Personal umbrella policy limit	1,000,000
Insured's responsibility	$ 10,000

Generally, personal umbrella liability policies, whether including or excluding defense costs as part of the ultimate net loss, provide "first dollar" defense coverage when loss is not covered by underlying insurance. Such defense costs are also considered in addition to the applicable limit of the umbrella policy. For example, an insured has a personal umbrella liability policy with a limit of $1 million subject to a $2,000 SIR and is faced with a suit for $30,000 in damages not covered by underlying insurance. If judgment is made for the full amount of damages and the umbrella insurer incurs defense costs of $5,000, the ultimate net loss is $30,000 less the $2,000 SIR, or $28,000. The defense costs, payable in addition to the applicable limit of liability, would be paid in full by the insurer.

Retained Limit

The **retained limit** can represent either the amount recoverable under any valid and collectible underlying insurance or the amount stated in the personal umbrella policy declarations as the SIR. It is the amount of the liability claim that the umbrella insurer will not cover.

Maintenance of Underlying Insurance Condition

One of the more important provisions of personal umbrella liability policies is the **maintenance of underlying insurance condition**. Under this condition, the insured is required to maintain in full force, without change, all the underlying policies specifically listed on the declarations page of the personal umbrella policy. If the insured fails to maintain those underlying policies, the personal umbrella liability policy operates as though the underlying coverage were still in force. The umbrella insurer will pay no more for any loss than it would have been required to pay if the insured had maintained the underlying policies.

For example, assume that Henry has a personal umbrella liability policy with a $1 million limit and a $250 SIR. He declares to the insurer of the umbrella policy that he has personal liability insurance under his homeowners policy with a limit of $100,000 and an auto liability policy with a $300,000 limit. While on a hunting expedition, Henry accidentally shoots and wounds one of his friends. When Henry returns home, he learns his homeowners policy has been canceled for nonpayment of premium with the cancellation becoming final before the shooting incident. Henry is subsequently sued by his former friend, who obtains a judgment for $150,000. Since Henry's homeowners policy was not in force at the time of the incident, $100,000 of the loss that would have been covered by the homeowners policy will have to be retained by Henry. Henry cannot look to his personal umbrella insurer to pay the full amount of the loss. The umbrella insurer is liable only to the extent that it would have been liable had Henry maintained the homeowners policy as required by the maintenance of underlying insurance condition. The umbrella insurer will pay only $50,000 plus the umbrella insurer's share of defense costs.

Coverage Definitions

Umbrella policies usually cover claims arising out of personal injury and property damage.

Personal Injury

While personal injury is not uniformly defined among personal umbrella policies, virtually all such policies define personal injury to include bodily injury. Whatever else is included with the definition of personal injury varies among umbrella policies. Many policies define personal injury to include mental anguish, false arrest, wrongful eviction, libel, slander, defamation of character, and invasion of privacy; assault and battery not committed by or at the direction of the insured; and care, loss of services, and death resulting from any of the foregoing. Other personal umbrella policies define personal injury also to include shock, mental injury, wrongful entry, and humiliation.

Property Damage

Most personal umbrella policies define property damage as physical injury to or destruction of tangible property, including loss of use of property resulting from such physical injury or destruction. Some personal umbrella policies also define property damage to include loss of use of tangible property that has not been physically injured or destroyed. For example, suppose Willy, while driving to work, collides with a propane truck in front of a department store. Willy's PAP limits are exhausted by the bodily injury claim paid to the truck's driver. The department store is not damaged, but since it cannot open for one day while the accident is cleared and investigated, the store loses $50,000 as a result of lost sales. If Willy's personal umbrella allows coverage for loss of use of property that is not physically damaged, the store may recover the $50,000 of lost income from Willy's insurer, subject to available limits.

Exclusions

Although personal umbrella policies provide broad liability coverage, they contain a number of exclusions, as summarized below.

Intentional Injury

Personal umbrella liability policies typically exclude coverage for acts committed by or at the direction of the insured with intent to cause personal injury or property damage. However, many policies state that the exclusion does not apply to the following:

1. *Assault and battery committed to save life or property.* Under the law, a person is granted the privilege of acting reasonably in self-defense. Thus, an insured who causes physical harm in an effort to defend against an attack or an impending attack is covered in the event of suit by the attacker for assault, battery, trespass, or other intentional tort.

2. *Acts committed to prevent or eliminate danger in the operation of motor vehicles or watercraft.* For example, if Arthur is faced with a choice between hitting a child or running into a fence with the borrowed auto he is driving, he will choose to run into the fence. This is an intentional act that results in property damage to the car and the fence, but it was done to save the life of a child. In this case, Arthur's personal umbrella policy would cover the liability for the property damage, if needed.

As noted earlier, personal umbrella policies specifically cover liability for personal injury offenses such as false arrest, false imprisonment, wrongful eviction, and, in some cases, even malicious prosecution. These offenses are frequently committed with intent to cause injury. Thus, in the case of some personal injury offenses, application of an intentional injury exclusion may be problematic.

A solution used in some personal umbrella coverages, similar to that used in the ISO personal injury coverage endorsement to the homeowners policies, is to restrict the intentional injury exclusion to bodily injury and property damage and add one or more exclusions that more appropriately address personal injury offenses. One such exclusion eliminates coverage for personal injury arising from the violation of a penal statute or ordinance by or at the direction of the insured. Another exclusion eliminates coverage for libel, slander, or defamation arising from statements made by the insured with knowledge that the statements are false.

Fellow Employee Suits

Some personal umbrella policies deny protection to any insured, other than the named insured, who causes injury to a fellow employee during the course of employment as a result of the use of an auto, watercraft, or aircraft. Generally, the rationale for this exclusion is to make workers compensation insurance, rather than auto, watercraft, or aircraft insurance, the exclusive remedy of an employee injured by the negligence of a fellow employee while both are working within the scope of their employment.

The problem with this exclusive remedy rule is that it usually insulates only the employer. An injured employee may still be permitted to sue and recover from a negligent fellow employee. When such suits are allowed, an employee confronted with a suit is likely to be without protection. To give an individual some form of protection against such suits, coverage may be granted under the personal umbrella by an exception to the exclusion only for the named insured or the removal of the exclusion from the policy.

Property Owned or in Care, Custody, or Control

The umbrella is intended to provide liability coverage, not property coverage. Therefore, all personal umbrella policies exclude coverage for damage to property owned by the insured. Most also exclude damage to property to the extent that the insured has agreed contractually to insure the property. Such contractual obligations can be insured by obtaining property insurance.

The liability coverages of homeowners policies and the PAP exclude damage to property rented to, used by, or in the care, custody, or control of the insured. Most personal umbrella liability policies, in contrast, apply the "care, custody, or control" exclusion to nonowned aircraft and, possibly, to nonowned watercraft. The "care, custody, or control" exclusion does not apply to any other property.

Recreational Vehicles

Some personal umbrella policies exclude personal injury or property damage arising from the ownership, maintenance, or use of recreational vehicles.

Generally, a recreational vehicle is defined in the umbrella policy as a golf cart, snowmobile, and any other land motor vehicle designed for use principally off public roads. Policies that exclude this exposure usually provide excess liability protection if underlying insurance exists with at least the minimum required limits. In some cases, the umbrella policies flatly exclude without exception recreational vehicles used for speed contests.

Aircraft and Watercraft Liability

Most umbrella policies exclude liability for property damage to aircraft rented to, used by, or in the care, custody, or control of the insured—an exposure for which aircraft insurance is available. Some policies also exclude liability for property damage to watercraft in the care, custody, or control of the insured. Watercraft insurance can be purchased to cover the exposure.

In addition, most umbrella policies exclude *any* liability arising from the ownership, maintenance, use, loading, or unloading of aircraft, including aircraft chartered without a crew. Generally, when individuals and families have these exposures, an aircraft policy is purchased, because it can offer higher primary coverage limits than are normally available under umbrella contracts. However, some umbrella policies do cover certain aircraft exposures, such as coverage for an insured who occupies a nonowned aircraft other than as a pilot or member of a crew or for an insured employer whose employee (who is neither covered by nor required to be covered by workers compensation) is injured during the course of employment in an aircraft-related venture.

Liability arising from the ownership, maintenance, use, loading, or unloading of watercraft is generally not excluded—and thus, is covered—by personal umbrella policies. However, the insured must usually maintain underlying homeowners coverage or a separate watercraft policy.

Business Pursuits

Virtually all umbrella policies exclude personal injury or property damage arising from business pursuits other than the ownership, maintenance, use, loading, or unloading of autos (in some cases limited to private passenger autos) and, in some policies, aircraft and watercraft.

Some umbrella contracts make no exceptions to this exclusion; other personal umbrellas cover, by exception to the business pursuits exclusion, (1) liability arising out of activities ordinarily incident to nonbusiness pursuits and, in some cases, (2) certain types of business activities. For example, some umbrellas provide coverage to persons who are involved in civic activities other than as regular employment. Another form of protection provided by some policies is directed toward students who are members of the household and who work part time or during the summer months. A few policies even provide coverage against business pursuits if underlying insurance is maintained for that exposure.

Professional Liability

At one time, some personal umbrella insurers offered to provide excess protection against any professional liability exposures of insureds if underlying insurance was in force. However, at present, this is the exception rather than the rule.

An increasingly common exclusion eliminates coverage for liability arising from an insured's activities as a director or officer of a corporation or association other than a nonprofit organization. Directors and officers (D&O) liability coverage is available under separate directors and officers liability policies.

Obligations Under Workers Compensation and Similar Laws

All personal umbrella policies exclude any obligation payable under a workers compensation, unemployment compensation, disability benefits, or similar law. The purpose of this exclusion is to avoid duplicating benefits more appropriately provided elsewhere.

Nuclear Energy Liability

All personal umbrella policies contain a nuclear energy liability exclusion. It excludes coverage for any personal injury or property damage when an insured under a personal umbrella contract is also an insured under any nuclear energy liability policy, or would have been an insured under any such policy had that policy not exhausted its limit of liability.

Residual Insurance Markets

Many individuals and families cannot get the insurance they need or desire from a private insurance company. To address the loss exposures that private insurers are not able to cover because those exposures are too severe or otherwise undesirable, shared or residual market programs have been established to make insurance available to cover these potentially catastrophic losses.

This section describes four residual market programs for residential property: the National Flood Insurance Program (NFIP), the Fair Access to Insurance Requirements (FAIR) plans, federal crime insurance plans, and beach or windstorm plans. In various ways, each of these programs is designed to provide coverage against certain perils in situations in which the loss exposure is too severe to be handled voluntarily by private insurers in the standard market.

The section also discusses the four mechanisms for providing residual market auto insurance: auto insurance plans, reinsurance facilities, joint underwriting associations (JUAs), and state funds. Each of these systems allows drivers with high loss potential, who could not otherwise purchase auto insurance, to purchase at least a minimum amount of auto insurance.

National Flood Insurance Program

In response to a general need for flood insurance, Congress passed the National Flood Insurance Act of 1968. The act delineated the operation of a national program for providing flood insurance. The Housing and Urban Development Act of 1969 amended the National Flood Insurance Act to provide coverage for mudslides as well.

The program was further amended by the Flood Disaster Protection Act of 1973. This act put constraints on the use of federal funds for property in flood-prone areas unless the property is protected by flood insurance. No lender who is federally insured or financed can lend money on property in a flood-prone area unless the property is covered by flood insurance—even when making a conventional loan—if the community is participating in the **National Flood Insurance Program (NFIP)**. If the property is in a flood-prone area and the community is not participating in the NFIP, a lender may make a conventional loan—not a federally backed loan—but must notify the borrower that federal disaster relief may be unavailable.

In January 1991, the NFIP added the **Mortgage Portfolio Protection Program (MPPP)**. This program allows mortgage lenders to force, if necessary, existing mortgagors to purchase flood insurance on their mortgaged property if it is located in a flood zone and is not covered by flood insurance. The lender must give the mortgagor adequate notice that flood insurance is now required and, if the mortgagor does not purchase it, the lender may purchase it for the mortgagor. If the lender must buy the coverage, the mortgagor is charged for the coverage, at a cost much more expensive than if the mortgagor had made the purchase.

Organization of the NFIP

Since 1978, the Federal Insurance Administration (FIA), an arm of the Federal Emergency Management Agency (FEMA), has managed the NFIP through the administrative services of a private contractor. It is the contractor's responsibility to maintain all policyholder records and funds.

Financial and statistical reports on the program's performance are prepared by the contractor and submitted to the FIA. The National Flood Insurance Fund, run by the FIA, is the sole insurer. Local adjusting firms assist in settlement of insured flood losses.

Flood insurance is marketed by licensed insurance agents and brokers in communities enrolled in the NFIP. Under the **Write Your Own (WYO)** program, a number of insurance companies have arranged to sell NFIP policies and adjust flood claims under their own names. The FIA determines rates, coverage limitations, and eligibility. The private insurer collects premiums, retains a commission, and uses the remainder of the premium to pay claims when they arise. If flood losses exceed the amounts the insurer holds to pay flood claims, the federal government makes up the difference. However, if income to the insurer exceeds losses, the insurer pays the excess to the federal government. The majority of NFIP policies in force are issued by insurance companies participating in the WYO program.

FEMA operates regional flood insurance specialist offices. In addition, each state has a state coordinating agency for flood insurance that works with FEMA in establishing flood controls and implementing flood prevention measures.

Determination of Flood Insurance Availability

For the residents of any area to become eligible for flood insurance, one of two procedures must be followed. Under one approach, the community takes the initiative and makes an application to the FIA to be included in the flood insurance program. Under the second approach, FEMA determines that an area is flood prone and notifies the community that it must comply with federal flood program standards. The community has the option of making the appropriate application, contesting its designation as a flood-prone area, or not participating in the program.

Once an application for flood insurance has been submitted to the FIA and all the necessary information has been provided by the community, a flood hazard boundary map is prepared (if one has not already been prepared). The **flood hazard boundary map** is a temporary map designed to identify flood-prone areas in the community. The map is sent to the community and all the participating agencies, the servicing company, the state coordinating agency, the state insurance commissioner, the regional FEMA flood specialist, and other federal agencies.

Flood Insurance Programs

Two federal flood insurance programs are in place: emergency and regular.

Emergency Program

After a community has submitted its application and is designated by the FIA as a flood-prone area, considerable work is involved in preparing flood insurance rate maps and in developing actuarial rates that are exposure-related and presumably self-supporting without federal subsidy. In the interim, owners of residential and business property within areas of qualified communities can secure insurance through the **emergency program**. This first layer of flood insurance is available for buildings and contents at *subsidized rates*. Only four emergency rates are used: one for residential buildings, one for residential contents, one for nonresidential buildings, and one for nonresidential contents. These rates, which apply per $100 of insurance, are uniform in all eligible communities. The maximum amount of first layer insurance under the emergency program for residential property is shown in the first two columns of Exhibit 6-5. The following example illustrates how these limits apply.

Exhibit 6-5
Maximum Limits of Flood Coverage

Building Type	Emergency Building	Emergency Contents (per unit)	Regular Building	Regular Contents (per unit)
Single Family Residential				
States and jurisdictions other than Alaska, Guam, Hawaii and U.S. Virgin Islands	$ 40,000	$10,000	$185,000	$60,000
Alaska, Guam, Hawaii, and U.S. Virgin Islands	$ 50,000	$10,000	$185,000	$60,000
Other Residential				
States and jurisdictions other than Alaska, Guam, Hawaii, and U.S. Virgin Islands	$100,000	$10,000	$250,000	$60,000
Alaska, Guam, Hawaii, and U.S. Virgin Islands	$150,000	$10,000	$250,000	$60,000

Helen owns a home in a flood-prone area along the Mississippi River. The home is valued at $60,000; the contents of the home are worth $19,000. The community in which Helen lives has qualified under the emergency flood insurance program. Therefore, Helen can insure her house for $40,000 and the contents for $10,000—the maximum limits available.

Once the first layer of insurance coverage has been made available to individuals in a flood-prone area through the emergency program, they cannot obtain federal or federally insured money for new construction unless flood insurance is purchased. New construction includes not only new buildings but also repair, reconstruction, or improvement to a building amounting to 50 percent or more of the building's market value prior to the project's start or, if the project is necessary to restore a damaged building, the building's market value at the time of the damage.

Regular Program

After FEMA completes its assessment of a community's flood-prone area, establishes an accurate **flood insurance rate map (FIRM)**, and promulgates actuarial rates, the community is converted from the emergency program to the regular program. The FIRM specifically recognizes **special flood hazard areas**—areas that are subject to a flood that has a 1 percent chance of occurring in any given year. The conversion from the emergency to the regular program is dependent on the community's enacting and enforcing flood plain management regulations.

Under the regular program, residents of the community are eligible for a second layer of insurance. The maximum amount available to each resident is the amount shown in the last two columns of Exhibit 6-5. However, a community's failure to convert to the regular program results in its suspension from the program and in a lack of eligibility for *any* flood insurance.

The continuation of the above example illustrates how the regular program's coverage limits function. Recall that Helen's home is valued at $60,000 and her contents are worth $19,000. Under the emergency program, she has $40,000 of insurance on the dwelling and $10,000 coverage for its contents. Once the community is under the regular program, Helen can apply for full coverage because the maximum available limits under the program should be $185,000 for a single-family home and $60,000 for contents.

Flood Insurance Policies

Two flood insurance policies have been available since the inception of the NFIP. The **dwelling and contents form** is used for any dwelling having an occupancy of no more than four families, such as single-family homes, town houses, row houses, and individual condominium units. The **general property form** is used for all other occupancies, that is, multiresidential and nonresidential. Both policies are designed to protect the insured against direct loss to real and personal property from the peril of flood. Indirect loss, such as additional living expenses, rent, rental value, and enforcement of any ordinance or law regulating the construction, repair, or demolition of buildings, is not covered.

For purposes of coverage, **flood** is defined as:

A. A general and temporary condition of partial or complete inundation of normally dry land areas from:

1. The overflow of inland or tidal waters

2. The unusual and rapid accumulation or runoff of surface waters from any source

3. Mudslides or mudflows that are proximately caused by flooding

B. The collapse or subsidence of land along the shore of a lake or other body of water as a result of erosion or undermining caused by waves or currents of water exceeding the cyclical levels that result in flooding as defined in A-1 above.

Not covered by this peril is loss by rain (unless excessive rain causes a mudslide or flood), snow, sleet, or water spray. Any freezing, thawing, or loss by weight of ice or snow is not covered unless such loss occurs simultaneously with a flood. Any damage caused by conditions within the control of the insured is not covered. Also not covered is any damage caused by conditions such as design or structural defects, unless caused by flood. A hillside cottage supported by steel piers that slip because of loose, excessively wet ground caused by rain or melting snow *would not* be covered. However, the property damage *would* be covered if the excessively wet ground is caused by flood waters.

While no coverage applies to damage from normal erosion along a river bank, lake shore, or other body of water, coverage does apply for unusual erosion and for flooding that is not "temporary" but that results from rising water levels that do not recede (such as rising levels of the Great Lakes). Loss by theft, fire, windstorm, explosion, earthquake, or landslide is not covered. And while any loss by earth movement is outside the scope of coverage, such a loss is covered when caused by mudslide or erosion otherwise covered by the policy. The policy also contains the usual exclusions of loss by war, nuclear radiation, and off-premises power failure.

The dwelling building and contents flood policy for dwellings of one to four families contains two major coverage divisions: dwelling and contents. In addition, several clauses further define the coverage.

Dwelling Coverage

The dwelling coverage of the flood policy includes protection not only for the residential building occupied principally for dwelling purposes, but also for any additions attached to it. Building equipment, fixtures, and outdoor equipment used in the service of the premises are covered while contained in an enclosed structure on the same or adjoining premises, and such equipment is also covered if it is used in the construction, alteration, or repair of the dwelling or other structures.

A "dwelling extension" allows the insured to apply up to 10 percent of the coverage on the dwelling for damage to a detached garage or carport located on the insured premises. Such structures cannot be used for commercial, industrial, boat storage, or farming purposes and cannot be leased or rented to others except for private garage purposes. This 10 percent extension is contained within the policy limit, not in addition to it. The extension merely gives the insured flexibility in applying the insurance limit. For example, if Sam has a policy covering a dwelling for $50,000, he would have up to $5,000 coverage on its detached garage. If this other structure is valued at $7,000, Sam can purchase a separate flood policy for $7,000 worth of coverage if he wants to insure the garage for its full insurable value.

Contents Coverage

Coverage is provided for "contents incidental to the occupancy of the building as a dwelling." In order to be covered, the contents must belong to the insured or to members of the insured's family who reside with the insured. Coverage extends to property for which the insured may be held liable. The property of servants or guests is covered at the insured's option while the property is located in the enclosed structure on the insured premises. Contents coverage is excess over specific coverage on personal property that insures against the peril of flood. Generally, an individual or family will not have other flood coverage except under a personal property floater endorsement or policy.

The contents coverage includes a 10 percent benefit extension that is available to tenants and condominium unit owners. Ten percent of the amount of insurance applicable to contents can be applied to improvements, alterations, and additions to the dwelling and other structures if the insured is not the owner of the premises. When the policy covers a condominium unit, 10 percent of the coverage can be applied to interior walls, floors, and ceilings considered to be the unit owner's property. The 10 percent extension is not additional protection. Like the dwelling extension discussed above, the extension for improvements, alterations, and additions is an alternative means of using the policy limit.

Debris Removal

The cost of removing debris following a loss is covered under the flood policy. This coverage does not increase the policy's limit of liability. Instead, loss to property and debris removal expense is subject to the amount of insurance applying to the property covered. For example, Alex has a flood dwelling and contents policy under the regular program with $70,000 worth of coverage on his dwelling and $15,000 worth of coverage for his contents. A flood causes $50,000 in damage to his dwelling and $13,000 in damage to his contents. It will cost him $10,000 to remove the dwelling debris and $3,000 to remove the contents debris. His flood policy will cover the $60,000 in dwelling damage and debris removal under the dwelling coverage and only $15,000 of the contents damage and debris removal under the contents coverage. Alex must retain the remaining $1,000 of contents debris removal.

Property Not Covered

Excluded from flood policy coverage are the following types of property:

- Accounts, bills, currency, deeds, evidences of debt, money, securities, bullion, manuscripts, valuable papers or records, and coin or stamp collections

- Fences, retaining walls, seawalls, outdoor swimming pools, bulkheads, wharves, piers, bridges, and docks

- Property in the open

- Land values, lawns, trees, shrubs, plants, growing crops, and livestock

- Underground structures and equipment

- Walkways, driveways, patios, and other surfaces outside the exterior walls of the building

- Animals, birds, and fish

- Aircraft, watercraft, motor vehicles not used to service the premises, trailers on wheels, and business property

The policy also excludes coverage for contents and finished walls, floors, and ceilings in a basement area. This exclusion eliminates coverage for losses that can be controlled through improved building design and use. For elevated buildings (buildings built on "stilts," where the first floor is located the distance of one story off the ground) sometimes found in flood-prone areas, coverage does not apply to enclosures and building components below the lowest elevated floor if the building was constructed after the community entered the regular program.

Replacement Cost Coverage

Replacement cost coverage is provided only for single-family homes occupied as a primary residence. (Second homes are covered only for ACV.) The RC coverage of the flood insurance policy is the same as that found in homeowners policies, with one additional consideration. The insured is required to purchase insurance equal to at least 80 percent of the replacement cost of the dwelling, or the *maximum amount of insurance* available (as shown in Exhibit 6-5), whichever is *less*. If the amount of insurance is in compliance with this requirement, the insured will be paid the full amount to repair or replace the dwelling up to the policy limit. If the amount of insurance is not in compliance with this requirement, the insured will be paid the larger of the calculated proportion of the replacement cost or the actual cash value of the damaged property. The proportion is determined as follows:

$$\frac{\text{Amount of insurance purchased}}{\text{80 percent of the dwelling's total replacement cost}}$$

However, if 80 percent of the dwelling's replacement value is greater than the maximum amount of insurance available under the NFIP, the available limit replaces the 80 percent figure.

For example, Dick and Ellen own a home on the Ohio River in a community recently declared a flood-prone area. The replacement cost of their house is $100,000. Under the replacement cost rule, Dick and Ellen are required to maintain at least $80,000 worth of insurance on the dwelling. But, because they are subject to the emergency flood program, the maximum insurance they can and do purchase is $40,000. In the event of a covered flood loss, they will receive full replacement cost coverage to the $40,000 limit. However, if Dick and Ellen become eligible for the regular flood program and do not increase their flood coverage to $80,000, they will receive *the larger* of the following amounts, subject to the $40,000 limit, in the event of a covered flood loss to their house:

1. The actual cash value of the loss
2. $40,000/$80,000 x the loss replacement cost

Suppose Dick and Ellen move to another home in the same community. Their new home has a replacement cost of $250,000. Under the regular flood program Dick and Ellen are required to purchase at least 80 percent of the total replacement cost to receive full replacement cost coverage for flood loss. However, 80 percent of the replacement cost is $200,000, which is greater than the $185,000 maximum limit on coverage available under the flood program. In this case, the replacement cost provision replaces the 80 percent requirement with the requirement to purchase the maximum amount of flood coverage—$185,000. Dick and Ellen purchase only $150,000 of flood insurance. In the event of a covered flood loss, they will receive *the larger* of the following amounts, subject to the $150,000 policy limit:

1. Actual cash value of the loss
2. $150,000/$185,000 x the loss replacement cost

Deductible Clauses
The dwelling and contents flood policy has two deductible clauses, which are

applied separately in the event of loss. One applies to the dwelling and other structures, and the other applies to insured contents. The standard deductible in each clause is $500. In a loss involving both the dwelling and its contents, the insured may retain $1,000—$500 on the building and $500 on the contents. For properties in coastal areas, a $3,000 deductible for each clause is available but not mandatory. Optional higher deductibles are also available.

Limitations

Covered flood damage to jewelry, precious metals, paintings, other works of art, and furs is limited to $250 worth of coverage in the aggregate for any one occurrence. Higher limits are available on a floater policy or endorsement to a homeowners policy. Recall that floater policies, such as the personal articles floater or the scheduled personal property endorsement, do not exclude flood.

Cancellation Clause

Under the cancellation clause, the policy will not be canceled by the insurer, except for nonpayment of premium with twenty days' notice. The insured can also cancel the policy, but the premium is not refunded if the insured retains an interest in the property.

Other Insurance

Other insurance on property is permitted and undoubtedly would be necessary to cover loss against other perils such as fire, windstorm, explosion, and vandalism or malicious mischief. However, if other applicable insurance exists for a flood loss, the dwelling building and contents flood policy pays only its proportionate share, based on the maximum available from NFIP.

Fair Access to Insurance Requirements (FAIR) Plans

The riots and civil disorders that took place in many other metropolitan areas during the years following the Los Angeles Watts section riot in 1965 resulted in property losses of catastrophic proportions. Those enormous losses increased the problem of insurance availability in some areas of the United States. As a result, many homeowners and business owners found it difficult or impossible to obtain insurance. To overcome this problem, Congress passed the Urban Property Protection and Reinsurance Act of 1968. It was designed to relieve the restricted market for property insurance in certain urban areas with riot potential. The act also made provision for increasing the availability of insurance through a combined effort of private insurers and state and federal governments.

The act consists of two major parts. The first part deals with the particulars of

Fair Access to Insurance Requirements (FAIR) plans comprising participating insurers and a state insurance authority. **FAIR plans** make standard lines of property insurance available for exposures located in areas underserved by the voluntary market. Each state enacted its own legislation in response to local market needs and the Urban Property Protection and Reinsurance Act of 1968. Thus, considerable variation exists in the coverages provided and the methods of operation among the thirty-two jurisdictions with plans.

The second part of the Urban Property Protection and Reinsurance Act provided federal riot reinsurance against excess losses resulting from riots and civil disorders sustained by insurers participating in the FAIR plan. The need for reinsurance was prompted by the exclusion of the riot peril in catastrophe reinsurance treaties following the riots of the 1960s. With no excess protection available against riot losses, insurers became increasingly reluctant to write property insurance in those areas especially vulnerable to large losses. In 1983, Congress enacted legislation to terminate the riot reinsurance program because only a very small number of insurers were buying reinsurance.

Operation

A property owner unable to obtain basic property insurance in the voluntary market may apply to the state's FAIR plan for protection through an authorized insurance agent or broker. The FAIR plan may operate as a policy-issuing syndicate in which the plan issues the policies and the plan's staff handles underwriting, processing, and possibly claim adjustment. Eight FAIR plans contract with one or more voluntary insurers to act as servicing carriers. These insurers, for a percentage of premium, perform underwriting, policyholder service, and claim adjustment functions. For example, in 1993 Florida created the Residential Property Joint Underwriting Association in which several insurers issue and service the policies. In nearly all plans, all licensed property insurers are required to participate in plan losses in proportion to their share of property insurance premiums in the state.

Eligibility

However the policies are serviced, if the property meets standards of insurability under the FAIR plan rules, the property owner will be issued a policy. Generally, insurance cannot be refused because of **environmental hazards**, defined as any hazardous condition beyond the control of the property owner that might give rise to loss under the insurance contract, such as the condition of neighboring properties. Property may be subject to inspection before acceptance. Furthermore, any recommendations by the inspector to make the property insurable must be completed before a policy is issued.

Under most plans, the following types of exposures are considered uninsurable:

- Property that is vacant or open to trespass
- Property in poor physical condition or that has unrepaired fire damage
- Property subject to poor housekeeping, including overcrowding and storage of both rubbish and flammable materials
- Property in violation of law or public policy
- In some states, property not built in accordance with building and safety codes

Coverages

FAIR plans commonly issue coverage for the perils of fire, lightning, windstorm or hail, explosion, riot or civil commotion, aircraft, vehicles, smoke, and vandalism or malicious mischief. In some states, crime, sprinkler leakage, and earthquake may also be covered. Homeowners policies are available under the plans in several states. The available limits of insurance coverage, as well as mandatory deductibles, vary considerably among plans.

Federal Crime Insurance

The Federal Crime Insurance Program was established by Congress under the Housing and Development Act of 1970 and became operational in 1971. This program was designed to provide property owners, tenants, and business owners with a means of meeting their crime insurance needs at an affordable cost. The program was administered by FEMA through the FIA and made available only in states having a critical problem with crime insurance availability. In 1992, the FIA discontinued the Federal Crime Insurance Program. If a state insurance regulator determined that an availability problem existed in his or her state, the state could extend the FAIR plan to cover crime. As of September 1993, only the Georgia FAIR plan had extended its plan coverage to include crime as a result of the discontinuation of the federal program.

Beach or Windstorm Plans

Properties located along the Atlantic and Gulf Coasts are especially vulnerable to windstorm loss. In addition to serious winter storms from the mid-Atlantic states northward (Northeasters), the southern Atlantic and Gulf Coast states are subject to damage from hurricanes. Many insurance companies withdrew from writing property insurance in the coastal areas during the 1960s, precipitating an availability crisis for homeowners, not only for windstorm and hail coverage, but for insurance against all perils. North Carolina responded to this availability crisis by creating the North Carolina Insurance Underwriting Association in 1969—the first beach plan. The states of Alabama, Florida, Louisiana, South Carolina, and Texas followed with their own plans in 1970 and 1971. Mississippi launched a windstorm and hail plan in 1987.

Hurricanes Andrew in Florida and Iniki in Hawaii in 1992 precipitated another availability crisis for insurance on coastal property. Insurers realized that had either storm made landfall a few miles away, insured damage would have been much greater and a greater number of insurers would have been threatened with insolvency. Insurers determined that their exposure to coastal losses should be reduced and began to withdraw from areas along the Atlantic and Gulf Coasts.

State insurance regulators and FAIR plan administrators examined the extent of the availability problems in the affected areas and the need to expand eligibility for FAIR plan coverage to coastal properties. Hawaii decided to extend its FAIR plan coverage. As of September 1993, Massachusetts, New Jersey, and New York FAIR plans were still considering how to address the availability of insurance for owners of coastal property.

Operation

Louisiana and Mississippi operate with a single servicing carrier providing the underwriting, policyholder services, and claim adjusting services. The remaining plans operate as policy-issuing syndicates with the plan issuing the policies and the plan staff providing the services. In all plans, property insurers are required to share in plan losses according to their share of state property insurance premiums.

Eligible Property

Each of the beach and windstorm plans offers coverage only in designated coastal areas. Virtually all real and personal property in beach areas is subject to coverage. Each plan requires buildings that are constructed or rebuilt after a certain date to conform to an applicable building code in order to be eligible for coverage. In addition to dwellings and other residential buildings, mobile homes may be eligible, subject to certain construction and tie-down requirements. Like the FAIR plans, beach and windstorm plans will not insure the following types of property:

- Property in poor physical condition or with unrepaired previous damage
- Property subject to poor housekeeping
- Property in violation of law or public policy

Coverages

The perils insured against in beach plan policies vary from state to state. Alabama, Louisiana, and North Carolina offer coverage for fire, lightning, windstorm or hail, explosion, riot or civil commotion, aircraft, vehicles, smoke, and vandalism or malicious mischief. North Carolina also offers a policy that covers only windstorm and hail damage. The remaining beach plans provide only windstorm and hail coverage.

The limits of insurance available through beach plans vary. Deductibles are generally mandatory but may vary in amount depending on the state as well as on the amount of insurance purchased.

Plans vary greatly as to when coverage can become effective. All plans safeguard against short-term adverse selection by refusing to accept applications when potential storm damage is imminent. Although property is subject to inspections, some state plans make routine inspections on new business, while others only inspect mobilehomes on a regular basis.

Cancellation of coverage is commonly subject to a thirty-day statutory notice with three exceptions: (1) nonpayment of premium, (2) material misrepresentation, and (3) evidence of arson at the direction of or by the owner or occupant.

Residual Market Auto Insurance

Auto insurance must be available to all drivers if the uninsured motorist problem is to be minimized. Insurance is not necessarily available to all drivers in the normal, voluntary insurance market, because some drivers with high loss potential are rejected by insurers applying normal underwriting standards. To some extent, this problem of insurance availability can be alleviated by increasing the cost of insurance for those drivers with the greater loss potential. However, this creates another problem—affordability. If insurance is "available" only at a price that the driver cannot afford, the problem has not been solved. Insurance regulators have imposed various types of rate restrictions on insurers in an attempt to keep insurance rates affordable. To compensate for such rate restrictions, insurers are sometimes forced to impose more stringent underwriting standards—making the availability problem worse in the process.

As a result, each state has some type of program intended to make insurance available and somewhat affordable to drivers who cannot obtain insurance in the voluntary market. In general, provisions are made whereby insurance companies, taxpayers, and other insureds collectively bear some of the costs of insuring the drivers with the high loss potential. These drivers are called the **residual market** or **shared market** because they may be viewed as those left over after the acceptable drivers have obtained insurance and their losses are shared in some way by a group of insurers.

Every automobile shared market program has a method of (1) providing services and (2) distributing applicants and losses to the insurers. The following paragraphs discuss the types of plans that have been developed to provide auto insurance to drivers that are unable to get standard auto insurance.

Automobile Insurance Plans

Automobile insurance plans, also known as **assigned risk plans**, are the oldest type of residual market plan and are still the type of plan most commonly in use. Each state's plan is administered by a governing board representing the insurance companies licensed in that state.

When a driver is turned down for insurance in the voluntary market, that driver can apply for coverage through the automobile insurance plan. The plan assigns the application to an insurance company. Each insurance company is obligated to accept a specified percentage of plan applicants determined by the total volume of business it does in the state. As Exhibit 6-6 illustrates, if All Car Insurance Company writes 5 percent of the auto insurance premium volume in the state, All Car Insurance Company will be assigned 5 percent of the residual market business. Limo Insurance Company, with 10 percent of the auto insurance volume in the state, will be assigned 10 percent of the state's residual market business.

Exhibit 6-6
Automobile Insurance Plan (Generalized)

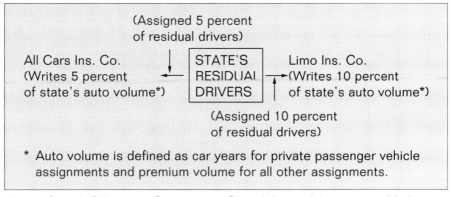

Adapted from J. Finley Lee, *Servicing the Shared Automobile Insurance Market*, Chapel Hill, NC, August 1977, p. 16.

Three types of plans are currently in use for handling an automobile insurance plan: Plan B, modified Plan B, and Plan C. (The first uniform method for handling the residual auto insurance market was referred to as Plan A, but it is no longer in use.)

- **Plan B.**   This plan requires that policy coverage and rates be uniform for all applicants regardless of the insurer to which they are assigned. However, Plan B is deficient in some ways with respect to other plans. Insureds are subject to the minimum limits specified by state law; they cannot increase their liability limits. Medical payments coverage is available subject to a certain limit (usually $1,000), but no physical damage coverage is available. And, in some states, Plan B does not permit the payment of insurance premiums on an installment basis.

- **Modified Plan B.**   Under modified Plan B, applicants are given the option to increase their liability limits up to a specified maximum, such as $100/300/50, and to add personal injury protection where available. Medical payments coverage is generally available in those states that have voluntary no-fault or add-on plans. Furthermore, both of the physical damage coverages are available on an optional basis, subject to a mandatory deductible of at least $100. Finally, rates are uniform for all insurers, and all insurers of auto liability insurance participate in the plan.

- **Plan C.**   Plan C is basically similar to the modified Plan B insofar as the availability of coverages and higher limits is concerned. The primary difference is that all auto insurance companies participate in Plan C; those that write only physical damage coverages in the voluntary market are assigned applications for physical damage coverages only.

When any insurer gets an application from the auto insurance plan, it issues a policy in its own name and performs all service work, including paying any claims. Any profit or loss on the account is treated as though the customer had been a voluntarily accepted driver. Since residual market drivers are usually more likely to generate losses, insurers generally need to make a profit on the voluntarily accepted drivers in order to pay for the losses caused by the drivers assigned by the plan. Thus subsidy is involved.

Reinsurance Facilities

Auto insurance plans have run into trouble because of excessive losses in some states coupled with substantial growth in these plans, which stem largely from general rate inadequacies. (To generate enough premium volume to pay for losses, insurers enforced strict underwriting standards that forced many drivers into the plans.) Alternative systems for handling the shared market are being sought and tried. Among these systems is the **reinsurance facility**. Its objectives are to achieve more equitable pricing, to improve service, and to avoid the stigma associated with being in the assigned risk plan.

A reinsurance facility is operational in four states (Massachusetts, New Hampshire, New Hampshire, North Carolina, and South Carolina). With a reinsurance facility, premiums and losses are ceded (transferred) to the facility, and the operating losses and expenses of the facility are shared by all insurers. The facility generally works in the following manner, as illustrated in Exhibit 6-7: The producer accepts the application for auto insurance and submits it to his or her own insurer. After issuing the policy and receiving the premium, the insurer can do one of two things: (1) it can handle the submission as part of its normal voluntary book of business or (2) it can cede the premium to the facility and just service the policy. (The amount of premium each insurer can cede is limited in order to prevent "dumping" of insureds into the facility.) When a claim occurs, the servicing insurer that issued the policy handles the entire claim process. If the claim is paid, the insurer is reimbursed by the facility for its claim and adjustment expenses. On a periodic basis, losses and operating expenses are apportioned among the insurers on a formula basis.

Typically, the *insurer* who receives the initial application decides whether to

Exhibit 6-7
Reinsurance Facility Operation

1. An insurance contract is issued to an insured and a premium is paid to the insurance company.
2. For an insured whom the insurance company does not want to retain, a portion of his or her premium is ceded to the reinsurance facility.
3. When an insured loss occurs, the insurer investigates and pays the claim to the insured.
4. The insurance company is reimbursed for losses it pays on policies it had ceded to the reinsurance facility.
5. Periodically, the underwriting experience of the reinsurance facility is allocated to the member companies.
6. Periodically, the operating costs and miscellaneous income are allocated to the member companies.

Adapted with permission from J. Finley Lee, *Servicing the Shared Automobile Insurance Market*, Chapel Hill, NC, August 1977, p. 52.

cede a given applicant. The insured cannot readily detect whether he or she is in the shared market. The producer also deals with the same insurer for voluntary and residual business and may not know that the applicant has been ceded.

Joint Underwriting Associations (JUAs)

Joint underwriting associations, or **JUAs**, currently used in four states (Hawaii, Florida, Mississippi, and Missouri), are another alternative to automobile insurance plans. A JUA, like a reinsurance facility, includes the pooling of experience among all insurers. However, the method of handling individual applicants differs between the two systems, as illustrated in Exhibit 6-8. Under a JUA, a limited number of servicing insurers are designated to handle all residual auto insurance business. The servicing insurers provide, for a fee, services for an industry pool to which all applicants are submitted. The results of the business handled by the pool are shared by all insurers based on each insurer's share of the voluntary auto insurance written.

If an applicant submitted to an insurer as regular business is found to be unacceptable, the application is forwarded to the JUA servicing insurer. Each producer may be assigned to a particular servicing insurer depending upon territory. (Generally, several servicing insurers are designated within the state. They are selected on the basis of their size and their capabilities in providing a wide range of services.) A servicing insurer issues the policy, handles the collection of premiums and claims, and provides whatever else is required to service the insured.

Servicing insurers have much greater control over the operations and results of the JUA than an insurer involved in an auto insurance plan or a reinsurance facility. Each submission to the JUA is carefully screened. Servicing insurers receive a percentage of the premiums written to cover costs of placing the business in the JUA and another percentage of the premiums earned to handle claims. Unlike the reinsurance facility, the JUA's rates are based on the experience of the pool and are uniform for all servicing insurers. Like auto insurance plans, the JUA's rates are higher in most states than those in the voluntary market.

Maryland Automobile Insurance Fund

Maryland has the only state fund program in the United States. Under this system, the residual market is handled by a state-owned insurance company referred to as the **Maryland Automobile Insurance Fund (MAIF)**. Before a motorist can be insured with the fund, he or she must provide (1) evidence of cancellation from one insurer and (2) evidence that his or her application has

Exhibit 6-8
Joint Underwriting Association

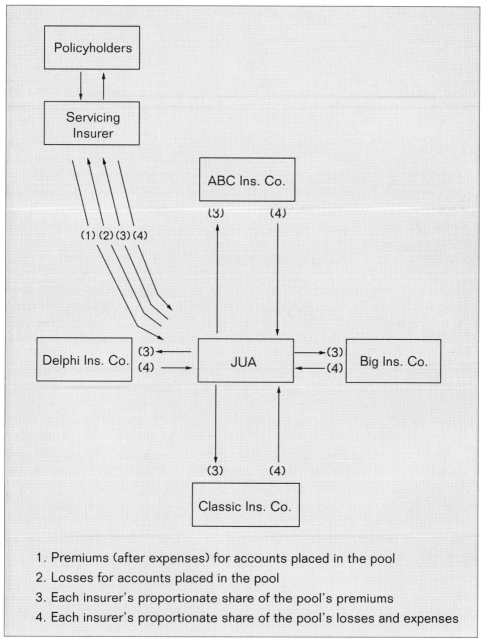

1. Premiums (after expenses) for accounts placed in the pool
2. Losses for accounts placed in the pool
3. Each insurer's proportionate share of the pool's premiums
4. Each insurer's proportionate share of the pool's losses and expenses

Adapted with permission from J. Finley Lee, *Servicing the Shared Automobile Insurance Market*, Chapel Hill, NC, August 1977, p. 40.

been rejected by another two private insurers. Although producers have binding authority, it is limited to coverage subject to statutory limits. Every applicant for private passenger and commercial vehicle insurance is guaranteed the minimum liability limits specified by that state's law. However, the fund may provide increased limits up to $100/300/100, as well as personal injury protection, uninsured motorists, and physical damage coverages. All services, including claims, are handled by personnel of that state-owned insurance company.

Summary

This chapter discussed property and liability coverages that an individual or family may purchase to supplement or provide an alternative to homeowners policies or personal auto policies. Some of these coverages are available from private insurers; other coverages are offered or guaranteed by federal and state governments.

Individuals and families that do not qualify for homeowners policies may find coverage for residential loss exposures through dwelling or mobilehome policies. Dwelling policies offer property insurance coverages similar to those available on homeowners policies to landlords and owner-occupants of dwellings that do not meet homeowners requirements. Mobilehome policies provide coverage based on homeowners coverages to owner-occupants of mobilehomes.

Individuals and families often have motor vehicle loss exposures that are not adequately insured by personal auto policies and homeowners policies. The loss exposures created by recreational vehicles and watercraft may be similar to those of autos, but are different in several significant ways. For example, less experienced or well-trained persons—including children and teenagers—are often allowed to operate trail bikes and motor boats. Recreational vehicles and watercraft may be insured through endorsements to homeowners policies or through separate, specific policies. Recreational vehicles may also be covered through endorsements to the personal auto policy, such as with the miscellaneous type vehicle endorsement.

Liability exposures can exceed the coverage available on homeowners and personal auto policies. Personal umbrella liability insurance policies are available to individuals and families to increase their liability coverage limits and broaden the perils covered by underlying policies.

As a last resort in many cases, residual market insurance is available to cover certain loss exposures that private insurers do not or cannot adequately cover.

The National Flood Insurance Program, FAIR plans, and windstorm or beach plans are the principal sources of residual market insurance for residential property exposures. High-risk drivers may find auto insurance available through various types of state programs, including assigned risk plans, reinsurance facilities, joint underwriting associations, or the Maryland Automobile Insurance Fund.

Chapter Notes

1. *Boating Statistics 1992* (United States Department of Transportation, June 1993), p. 23.
2. *Boating Statistics 1992*, p. 21.
3. *Boating Statistics 1992*, p. 17.
4. *Boating Statistics 1992*, p. 23.

Bibliography

Boating Statistics 1992. Washington, DC: United States Department of Transportation, June 1993, p. 23.

Chollet, Deborah. "Health Insurance." A presentation at Understanding Insurance: A Seminar for Legislators, sponsored by the Griffith Foundation for Insurance Education and the National Council of Insurance Legislators. Columbus, OH: February 6, 1993.

"Compulsory Auto Insurance." *Data Base Reports.* New York, NY: Insurance Information Institute, October 1987.

The Fact Book 1994: Property/Casualty Insurance Facts. New York, NY: Insurance Information Institute, 1994.

Leimburg, Stephan R.; Martin J. Satinsky; and Robert T. LeClair. *The Tools and Techniques of Financial Planning.* 2d ed. Cincinnati, OH: The National Underwriter Co., 1987.

Lorimer, James J.; Harry F. Perlet, Jr.; Frederick G. Kempin, Jr.; and Frederick R. Hodosh. *The Legal Environment of Insurance.* 4th ed., vol. 2. Malvern, PA: American Institute for Chartered Property Casualty Underwriters, 1993.

National Underwriter Co. "Development of No-Fault Automobile Insurance." *FC&S Bulletins: Personal Lines Volumes.* August 1991, pp. Noa-1.

1993 Life Insurance Fact Book. Washington, DC: American Council of Life Insurance, 1992.

"No-Fault Auto Insurance." *Data Base Reports.* New York, NY: Insurance Information Institute, July 1988.

Personal Inland Marine Manual. 5th ed. New York, NY: Insurance Services Office, Inc., November 1990.

Personal Vehicle Manual. 3d ed. New York, NY: Insurance Services Offices, Inc., September 1990.

Prahl, Robert J. "Underinsured Motorists Insurance." *CPCU Journal.* December 1993, pp. 219-222.

Uninsured and Underinsured Motorists Insurance: A Perspective. ISO Insurance Issues Series. New York, NY: Insurance Services Office, December 1992.

"Will Insurers Make the Right Choice?" *Emphasis.* 1990/4, pp. 6-9.

Index

F